Civil Partnership

Related titles by Law Society Publishing:

Child Contact: Law and Practice
Miranda Fisher and Sarah Whitten

Child Law Handbook: Guide to Good Practice
Liz Goldthorpe with Pat Monro

Resolution Family Law Handbook
General Editor: Andrew Greensmith

Family Law Protocol (2nd edition)
The Law Society

Pensions and Marriage Breakdown
David Davidson

Titles from Law Society Publishing can be ordered from all good legal bookshops or direct from our distributors, Marston Book Services (tel. 01235 465656 or email **law.society@marston.co.uk**). For further information or a catalogue, email our editorial and marketing office at **publishing@lawsociety.org.uk**.

CIVIL PARTNERSHIP

Law and Practice

Andrea Woelke

The Law Society

ISBN 10: 1-85328-973-6
ISBN-13: 978-1-85328-973-6

Published in 2006 by Law Society
113 Chancery Lane, London WC2A 1PL

Typeset by J&L Composition, Filey, North Yorkshire
Printed by TJ International, Padstow, Cornwall

Contents

To Professor Donald West for his courage to write on the subject over half a century ago and for his great friendship.

About the author and contributors

Andrea Woelke is an accredited expert in family law with particular expertise in international family law, child abduction and cohabitation. He is Chairman of the Lesbian and Gay Lawyers Association (LAGLA) and the Resolution International Committee. Andrea is originally from Germany and studied law and qualified in England. Many of his cases have an international aspect.

Andrea also chaired the LAGLA civil partnership working group. He followed the progress of the Bill and lobbied Parliament and Government on it. He has since extensively lectured on the subject.

Andrea regularly writes and lectures on family law in England as well as in Germany. He is co-author of *Model Letters for Family Lawyers*, in which he shows how legal concepts can be expressed in clear language that everyone can understand. Andrea is Principal of Alternative Family Law in London.

Bridget Garrood is a partner of Cartridges Solicitors in Exeter and Chair of Resolution Devon. One of the first solicitors to be accredited in 2001 by the Solicitors Family Law Association (now Resolution) as a specialist Family Lawyer in pensions on divorce. She joined the Lesbian and Gay Lawyers Association (LAGLA) as an articled clerk in 1994 and joined their civil partnership working party in 2003.

Bridget graduated with a sociology degree from the University of Exeter in 1984 and came late to the law after working as a researcher, including a spell at the Women's Studies Unit at North London Polytechnic. She has also worked as a debt counsellor and welfare rights officer for the Citizens Advice Bureaux and is a former trustee of the Exeter Rape Crisis Line.

Bridget and her partner Wendy believe they made legal history at midnight on 18 November 2004 by becoming the first couple formally to enter into an agreement under section 73(3) of the Civil Partnership Act 2004 as it received Royal Assent. They share grand-mothering for Victor aged 3.

Anne McMurdie is a solicitor at Public Law Solicitors in Birmingham. She specialises in public law, community care and housing cases. Anne worked in the field of housing advice from 1989 for SHAC and then the Terrence Higgins Trust, and then qualified as a solicitor at Anthony Gold solicitors, where she continued to specialise in housing cases, with particular emphasis on the right to housing and support for people subject to immigration control. Anne has been a member of the Housing Law Practitioner's Association (HLPA) for many years and was the Treasurer and member of the executive committee until December 2005. She co-organised the annual HLPA conference and was involved in the association's lobbying and law reform work. Anne trains regularly for Shelter and Legal Action Group on the housing rights of people from abroad and asylum seekers.

Barry O'Leary is a solicitor at Wesley Gryk Solicitors, one of the UK's leading personal immigration firms. He will be a partner of that firm from October 2006. He specialises in all areas of UK immigration law with particular emphasis on human rights, especially applications for same-sex partners and individuals who fear persecution on the basis of their sexual orientation. He is acknowledged by the Chambers Guide to the Legal Profession as a leading individual in the field of personal immigration and has lectured extensively on immigration matters for same-sex couples. He is a member of the executive committee of the UK Lesbian and Gay Immigration Group, an organisation for which he is also a volunteer lawyer. He was educated at Solihull School and Selwyn College, Cambridge University.

Keith Puttick is a Solicitor (and former Barrister), and is Principal Lecturer in Law at Staffordshire University where he teaches Public Law and Social Welfare Law subjects. He has worked in practice, and been a part-time Tribunal Chairman. His publications include *Welfare Benefits: Law & Practice* (EMIS, 2006 9th ed) and *Child Support Law: Parents, the CSA and the Courts* (EMIS). He is a co-author and editor of *Civil Appeals* (EMIS: Ed. Sir Michael Burton) with responsibility for the Social Security and Community Care Law sections and is General Editor of *Welfare Benefits & the Family: Law and Practice* (EMIS), now in its tenth year. He is a regular contributor to journals, including the *Family Law Journal* and has been a regular speaker and studio guest on Legal Network TV Social Welfare Law programmes.

Julian Washington is a partner of Forsters LLP in London where he practices in private client work and deals with a wide range of trust and estate, tax planning and charity law advice. He has developed a particular interest in the issues facing 'non-traditional families' (cohabitants, same-sex couples, second marriages and step-families) and has spoken and written widely about the advent of the Civil Partnership Act. Julian previously served on the Equal Opportunities committee of the Law Society and is a charity trustee. A graduate of Fitzwilliam College, Cambridge, Julian went on to qualify as a solicitor in 1993 and joined Forsters LLP in 2000.

Preface

My true love hath my heart, and I have his,
By just exchange one for another given:
I hold his dear, and mine he can not miss,
There never was a better bargain driven:

Philip Sydney 'The Bargain'

This book is a comprehensive companion to civil partnership, covering all the major areas of law. I recommend reading **Chapters 1** and **2** as an introduction and then those chapters that are of particular interest or relevance. The book is amply cross-referenced and it should therefore be easy to understand each chapter without having read the rest of the book. It is a practical book with flow-charts and diagrams and is intended to make a complicated area of law as easily accessible as possible for the English practitioner. While doing so, it should also be of interest to academics and those with an interest from outside England and Wales and, while it does not start from scratch to explain issues of English family law with which English practitioners will be familiar, it should be accessible enough for the overseas reader. Large areas of the law of course equally apply in Scotland and Northern Ireland.

I came to the topic as a family lawyer and a gay man and as the chairman of the Lesbian and Gay Lawyers Association (LAGLA). LAGLA looked at same-sex partnership rights in the mid-1990s at a time before anyone else in this country talked about it and when my own career was still in its infancy. Later the LAGLA working party replied comprehensively to the Government consultation on civil partnership and lobbied on various aspects of the Bill. I am grateful to all those who helped in that effort. This work gave me a perspective of the law that enabled me to write this book. It also put me in touch with some of the other contributors. With civil partnership in 2005 the UK is neither at the forefront of the development of same-sex partnership rights nor at the tail end. Other countries went there first and a number already have full same-sex marriage (see **1.2.2**).

The law is stated as of 1 May 2006. In the six months since the Civil Partnership Act came into force thousands of same-sex couples have registered their relationship; others have been holding out for better weather in the summer or want a larger celebration that involves longer planning. Others are still undecided whether to register their relationships which have endured for so long without the need for any formality.

There is no case law in the family law areas as yet, although the recent House of Lords decision *Miller* v. *Miller* and *McFarlane* v. *McFarlane* [2006] UKHL 24 has at least confirmed that conduct cannot be brought in by the back door under 'all the circumstances', a view expressed in **6.4.8**. For the reasons given in **Chapter 6** the principles set out in that case should also apply to financial applications on civil partnership dissolution. Capturing the law is of course like chasing a running target. There is constant change and there have been some significant developments in the weeks since we finished writing the book. If the Family Law (Property and Maintenance) Bill currently before Parliament becomes law, a new s.70A will be inserted into the Civil Partnership Act 2004 to reflect what is now s.1 of the Married Women's Property Act 1964. That section will be amended to be gender-neutral and the presumption of advancement and a husband's duty to maintain his wife in common law are abolished and the Act is renamed the Matrimonial Property Act 1964. This may be one of the many anachronisms that were noticed as a result of the trawl through matrimonial legislation in preparation for the Civil Partnership Act.

In the area of children law, we are still waiting for the government to announce how it is likely to reform the Human Fertilisation and Embryology Act 1990 (see **7.4**). Meanwhile society is becoming more aware of gay parenting. Indeed, there is a storyline on the issue is being introduced in 'The Archers' on BBC Radio 4 (see **7.1**).

On 26 May 2006 the Government published a White Paper on pension reform including automatic enrolment in a new earnings-related pension savings scheme, a higher basic state pension and an increase in the state pension age from 65 to 68. Part of the reforms would also be to abolish the Adult Dependency Increases altogether. These are currently available only to wives and widows and under the White Paper husbands, widowers and civil partners would not get them in 2010 as was planned and envisaged in this book after all (see **9.2**). Pensions are under constant review and therefore whether, and in what way, the delayed equality measures will in fact happen remains to be seen.

The problems arising for same-sex couples out of immigration control measures are still with us. Despite the initial decision in *Baiai & Ors, R (on the application of)* v. *Secretary of State for the Home Department* [2006] EWHC 823 the Home Office has not changed its policy as it is waiting for the final order that is expected to deal with those applicants who are unlawfully here, such as Mr Baiai (see **11.4**). While **Chapter 13** takes account of the provisions for the taxation of trusts in the 2006 Budget, the exact provisions will of course only become clear once the Finance Bill becomes law. These provisions will of course radically change the way that private client practitioners advise on estate and tax planning.

While writing this, I am sitting on a plane back from a weekend away in Spain. The incident I witnessed here is maybe significant for this country's attitude to gay men and lesbians at the moment:

A gay couple were smooching in the last but one row of the plane when all of a sudden one of the air stewards asked them to stop. They did not seem to be greatly disturbed and wondered who complained. There was nobody behind them and only a heterosexual couple in the same row across the aisle and a single middle-aged man in the last row behind the heterosexual couple. Then the man in the heterosexual couple talked to another member of the crew. The single man in the last row then pretended to sleep for the rest of the journey. Later the senior steward apologised to both the gay couple and the heterosexual couple for his colleague's interference: The man in the last row had complained. After the 'telling off' the man of the heterosexual couple had asked the crew if they would have been asked to stop if someone had complained about him kissing his girlfriend.

This shows quite poignantly where our society is at this moment in time: lesbians and gay men are more confident than they were; there is, however, still hostility towards lesbian and gay couples; some heterosexuals find this hostility so outrageous that they speak out against it; and those showing hostility at least know that they are no longer in a majority and perhaps even shut up.

The moment I realised society had changed was when I watched the debate on the Bill in the House of Lords on 17 November 2004. The House was packed as the Hunting Bill, which had raised a lot more publicity, also came back to the House that day. After a heated debate the result of the division was announced 136:251 (*Hansard* 17 Nov 2004: Column 1481). It took me about a minute or so for it to sink in that the Bill had passed by a majority of 115 rather than being defeated. I then realised that if this most ancient and conservative institution in the United Kingdom had endorsed same-sex relationships, society had truly changed.

Britain has come a long way in the last decade to get here. Yet, as Patrick Ness put it in *The Guardian* ("'We two boys together clinging'", *The Guardian*, 24 June 2006):

> The real changes are going to come when young homosexual couples begin their relationships with the prospect of marriage, just like straight couples do, and see it as a goal to reach for rather than as a confirmation of what they already know.

Andrea Woelke, London
30 June 2006

Acknowledgements

First of all I would like to thank the other contributing authors: Bridget Garrood, Keith Puttick, Barry O'Leary, Anne McMurdie and Julian Washington. They contributed with invaluable expertise in areas of law that I could not have covered. As a result this book will be a comprehensive guide to the law on civil partnership. They accepted my innumerable queries and together we reworked each chapter so it fitted into the style of the book to make it a unified work rather than a collection of essays. Enormous thanks go to Janet Noble at Law Society Publishing who was extremely patient but determined to see me through this project, and sustained me during a difficult time when I was setting up Alternative Family Law at the same time as writing this book. Thanks also go to Marie Gill and all the staff at Law Society Publishing.

I would like to thank in particular Dr Stephen Whittle, who gave invaluable input to Chapter 5, and Dr. Ian Curry-Sumner of the University of Utrecht, who clarified many issues surrounding overseas registered partnerships in my mind when I first looked at the issue.

A variety of civil servants have been extremely helpful in clarifying particular issues and answering my sometimes annoying questions. Amongst others, I would like to thank Collin Dingwall, formerly Team Leader of the Bill team at the Women and Equality Unit and Yuen Cheung there, Norman Cockett, Jimmy Murray and Irene Rafferty at the Department for Work and Pensions, Vicky Rayne at the Department for Constitutional Affairs and Selwyn Hughes at the General Register Office as well as many others.

Of course I also want to thank all those who have helped to bring about the Civil Partnership Act 2004, including of course Jane Griffith MP and Lord Lester who introduced the early Bills that led to the Government putting civil partnership on the agenda, Baroness Scotland of Asthal who managed to turn the defeat in the Lords in the summer of 2004 into such an overwhelming victory in November and Jacqui Smith MP, the government minister in charge of the Bill. Special thanks go to Stonewall and in particular the skilful lobbying of Ben Summerskill and Alan Wardle. Not only did this mean that the Bill passed in the end, it also led to many necessary improvements. I am also grateful to the many others in Stonewall, other organisations, in government and politics, who have helped. They are too numerous to mention. While many people helped me on this book all remaining errors are of course entirely my own.

Table of cases

Table of statutes

Table of statutory instruments

Table of European legislation

Abbreviations

ACA 2002	Adoption and Children Act 2002
AVCs	additional voluntary contributions
CA 1989	Children Act 1989
CGT	capital gains tax
CPA 2004	Civil Partnership Act 2004
CSA	Child Support Agency
CTB	Council Tax Benefit
CTC	Child Tax Credit
DMG	DWP's *Decision Maker's Guide*
DMPA 1973	Domicile and Matrimonial Proceedings Act 1973
DWP	Department for Work and Pensions
EEA	European Economic Area
EU	European Union
FLA 1996	Family Law Act 1996
FPR 1991	Family Proceedings Rules 1991, SI 1991/1247
GRA 2004	Gender Recognition Act 2004
HB	Housing Benefit
HFEA 1990	Human Fertilisation and Embryology Act 1990
HMRC	HM Revenue and Customs
HRA 1998	Human Rights Act 1998
IHT	inheritance tax
IND	Immigration and Nationality Directorate
IPFDA 1975	Inheritance (Provision for Family and Dependants) Act 1975
IS	Income Support
ISMI	Income Support Mortgage Interest Assistance
IUCs	interviews under caution
JSA (IB)	income-based Jobseeker's Allowance
LAGLA	Lesbian and Gay Lawyers Association

LTACP	'living together as civil partners'
LTHAW	'living together as husband and wife'
MCA 1973	Matrimonial Causes Act 1973
MCA 2005	Mental Capacity Act 2005
NI	national insurance
NIC	national insurance contribution
PC	Pension Credit
SDLT	stamp duty land tax
SERPS	State Earnings-Related Pension Scheme
SIG	Stonewall Immigration Group
SIPPS	self-invested personal pensions
SSAA 1992	Social Security Administration Act 1992
SSCBA 1992	Social Security Contributions and Benefits Act 1992
S2P	State Second Pension
TCA 2002	Tax Credits Act 2002
UKLGIG	United Kingdom Lesbian and Gay Immigration Group
WPA	Widowed Parent's Allowance
WTC	Working Tax Credit

CHAPTER 1

The new law

1.1 THE CONCEPT OF CIVIL PARTNERSHIP

Civil partnership is a regime of registered partnership for same-sex couples with most of the rights, responsibilities and other consequences of marriage. For the first time this enables same-sex couples not only to have their relationships recognised as such, but also to do what the majority of opposite-sex couples choose to do: publicly register their relationship and thus show their commitment to each other and gain a number of rights and acquire responsibility for each other. Lesbians and gay men are for the first time taken seriously by the law and their relationships are afforded the dignity they deserve. Similar regimes exist in other countries and more and more countries are following by providing recognition for same-sex couples (see **Chapter 8**).

The Civil Partnership Act 2004 (CPA 2004) received Royal Assent on 18 November 2004. Most of it came into force on 5 December 2005, and some parts in relation to children will come into force on 30 December 2006 (**Chapter 7**). The first regular registrations in England took place after a 15-day waiting period on 21 December 2005, although the first registration in England took place on 5 December 2005 ('Terminally ill gay man dies day after ceremony', *The Guardian*, 7 December 2005).

As we are still at an early stage in the life of the CPA 2004, this book intends to provide a guide for practitioners to the Act's implications for clients. Apart from explaining the concept of civil partnership in the various fields of law, it also looks at the overriding implications of this new regime. By way of introduction, this chapter considers the following issues:

- how civil partnership came about (**1.2**);
- what civil partnership is and what it is not (**1.3**) and where it differs from marriage;
- where same-sex partners continue to face discrimination (**1.4**);
- the language used in this book and best practice for language used by practitioners (**1.5**).

Where sections or Schedules are referred to with no reference to another Act, these will be references to provisions of the CPA 2004.

1.2 THE GENESIS OF THE ACT

1.2.1 Developments in recent years

Before the CPA 2004 there was little legal recognition of same-sex couples. Couples who had shared their lives for decades and taken on responsibilities for each other were simply invisible to the law. In the 1980s and early 1990s the issue became apparent in situations where, if a gay man was dying in hospital, maybe prematurely of HIV-related illness, his family could descend on the hospital and exclude his partner of many years, who would then not even be able to visit his dying partner, let alone go to the funeral. He might then find himself homeless a few weeks later when the deceased's property was sold by the family.

The injustice was maybe brought to the forefront of public consciousness after the nail bomb attack in a gay pub in Soho, the Admiral Duncan, on 30 April 1999. While the husband of a woman killed in the blast received a payment from the Criminal Injury Compensation Authority, and even if unmarried would have done so, the boyfriend of one of the gay men killed received nothing because the authority decided that he was not living as the 'husband or wife' of the deceased.

From 1 April 2001 the law in this area was at last changed, but only for deaths after that date: see Criminal Injuries Compensation Scheme 2001, paras.38 and 83 (**www.cica.gov.uk**). However it was litigation based on the Human Rights Act 1998 which gradually brought some limited recognition for same-sex couples. This culminated in the decision of the House of Lords in *Ghaidan* v. *Godin-Mendoza* [2004] 2 AC 557, in which reference to cohabitants ('living . . . as his or her wife or husband') in the Rent Act 1977 (Sched.1, para.2) was held to include same-sex cohabitants. However, in the most recent decision of the House of Lords in this area (*Secretary of State for Work and Pensions* v. *M* [2006] 2 WLR 637), it found with a majority of four to one (Baroness Hale of Richmond dissenting) that treating a non-resident mother who lived with her female partner for the purposes of a Child Support Act assessment as a single person (and therefore assessing her to pay £47 instead of £13 per week maintenance for her child) was not a breach of the Human Rights Act 1998. Unfortunately this overturned the decisions of the Court of Appeal and the tribunals below (see **10.8.2**).

1.2.2 Other countries

Even though same-sex couples had no recognition in the UK, other countries had started making provision. Over the years since 1989 all the Nordic countries followed Denmark, which introduced registered partnership in that year. These schemes typically excluded adoption and religious registration but otherwise simply cross-referred to marriage. The Netherlands, Belgium and

2

later Germany followed the example with similar regimes, although the statutes created new rules for same-sex registered partnerships rather than cross-refer to marriage. Whereas the German regime is a somewhat half-hearted measure that got stuck half-way in its federal constitution, Belgium and the Netherlands have since opened up marriage to same-sex couples.

Meanwhile France and some regions in Spain created regimes for same-sex and opposite-sex couples with limited rights and responsibilities. Litigation based on constitutions' non-discrimination articles in North America led to the introduction of similar regimes in Vermont and Canada and more recently to same-sex marriage in Massachusetts and Canada and registration regimes in various US states.

In Australia, Hungary and partly in some Spanish regions, amongst other countries, new laws introduced regimes of de facto recognition where couples living together for a certain period automatically had certain rights and also limited duties, e.g. to maintain each other after separation.

In the early years of the twenty-first century many more regimes have been introduced in countries as far apart as Andorra and New Zealand and Hawaii and Slovenia.

1.2.3 The political history leading up to the Bill

During the 2001/02 parliamentary session two separate bills were introduced to create a civil registration regime. Jane Griffith MP introduced the Relationships (Civil Registration) Bill on 24 October 2001 in the House of Commons under the 10-minute rule. Lord Lester of Herne Hill introduced the Civil Partnership Bill in the House of Lords on 9 January 2002. Both were private member's bills and had no real chance of becoming law. However, they found considerable support in Parliament and raised awareness that something ought to be done. The Commons bill ran out of time at second reading, while Lord Lester withdrew his bill on 11 February 2002 after the Government promised to review the law in this area. Both bills provided a regime for same-sex and opposite-sex couples who were already cohabiting but which entailed lesser rights and responsibilities than marriage.

The Women and Equality Unit in the Department of Trade and Industry, which was responsible for the Civil Partnership Bill, published its consultation paper *Civil Partnership: A framework for the legal recognition of same-sex couples* in June 2003. Responses were overwhelmingly supportive and the Civil Partnership Bill was introduced in the House of Lords on 30 March 2004. Since the Bill was a Lords Bill, it included no amendments to tax legislation. Instead the Finance Act 2005, s.103 gives power to the Treasury to amend tax law by statutory instrument to make provision to treat civil partners in the same way as spouses (see **13.4**).

Although the UK is not a federal state, in the area of family law the Westminster UK Parliament in general only legislates for England and Wales (usually referred to as 'English law'). Scots family law is quite different from English law and in Scotland family law is devolved to the Scottish Parliament. The Scottish Executive had consulted on proposals for a cohabitation rights for same-sex couples for several years. Since main areas of law that are affected by the introduction of civil partnership (e.g. tax and social security) are not devolved and because the Scottish Parliament did not have time to introduce its own regime of civil partnership in 2004, it decided to allow the Westminster Parliament to legislate for Scotland by a so-called Sewell Motion. The Scottish Executive was responsible for drafting and consulting on the Scottish part (Part 3 of the CPA 2004) and the CPA 2004 therefore extends to Scotland.

Although Northern Irish family law is in most parts the same as or very similar to English law, it is devolved to the Northern Irish Assembly. As a result of a political impasse the Assembly has, however, been suspended for several years and the legislating power therefore reverted to Westminster. Although it can be assumed that despite political disagreement on most things almost all political parties in Northern Ireland would have vehemently opposed any form of recognition of same-sex partnerships and therefore the Assembly (if not suspended) would not have passed any similar legislation, the fact that the Assembly was suspended created the ability to introduce the regime for the whole of the UK. If it had not extended to Northern Ireland, civil partners moving from England to Northern Ireland would have found themselves unrecognised in Northern Irish family law, but still recognised by UK law for welfare benefits and tax. Since the effect of the CPA 2004 is that all same-sex couples are now treated as a family unit for the assessment of social benefits (see **Chapter 10**), Northern Irish same-sex couples would have suffered the financial detriment on that basis for assessment without the benefit of the rights of civil partnership. Such discrimination was clearly not an option and the CPA 2004 therefore also extends to Northern Ireland (Part 4). This book, however, only deals with English law and the Parts of the CPA 2004 which apply to the whole of the UK.

1.2.4   The Government's intentions and the options for a new regime

Looking at the various regimes in other countries, a range of options were available:

- limited de facto recognition rights for same-sex and opposite-sex couples;
- a registration regime with limited rights and responsibilities;
- registered partnership with rights akin to marriage; or
- same-sex marriage.

The main driving force for the Government was the policy of equality for same-sex couples. The Consultation Paper stated that:

4

Civil partnership registration would be an important equality measure for same-sex couples in England and Wales who are unable to marry each other. It would provide for the legal recognition of same-sex partners and give legitimacy to those in, or wishing to enter into, interdependent, same-sex couple relationships that are intended to be permanent. [. . .] It is a matter of public record that the Government has no plans to introduce same-sex marriage.

(WEU *Civil Partnership: A framework for the legal recognition of same-sex couples* (June 2003), 1.2 and 1.3)

Equality would not have been met by any regime with limited rights, whether through de facto recognition or registration. Law reform for cohabitants (de facto recognition), in both same-sex and opposite-sex relationships, is still under review and this matter has been referred to the Law Commission, who issued a consultation paper on 4 May 2006, (*Cohabitation: The financial consequences of relationship breakdown*, Law Commission Consultation paper No. 179). The consultation ends on 30 September 2006. However, this could have given same-sex couples only limited rights in comparison to those of married couples and would therefore not have ended discrimination in fields like tax and dependants' pensions.

It seems that the other main underlying motivation was that the Government did not want to be seen to undermine marriage. The second option would have created a regime of registration for same-sex couples that would have given such couples some or all of the rights of married couples but without all the responsibilities. This would have provided strength to an argument that this discriminated against opposite-sex couples who did not want to be bound by the ties of marriage, but wanted a lesser and more informal regime for themselves. Whereas the two private member's bills in 2001/02 provided for a regime for both opposite-sex and same-sex couples, civil partnership is only open to same-sex couples. It is not an alternative for opposite-sex couples who do not wish to marry. The reason for this was that:

The Government believes that these situations are significantly different from that of same-sex couples who wish to formalise their relationships but currently are unable to do so.

(WEU *Civil Partnership: A framework for the legal recognition of same-sex couples* (June 2003), 1.4)

While several other countries have introduced regimes that were open to opposite-sex couples, the Government referred to civil marriage as the option for opposite-sex couples who did not want to have the religious connotations of 'holy matrimony'.

The political reason for not opening civil partnership up to opposite-sex couples is probably that such a regime would then have been in competition with marriage and this could have been open to the accusation of undermining the institution of marriage.

The obvious solution would have been to open up civil marriage to same-sex couples. However, from the numerous times that the different-but-equal message was reiterated in the various Consultation Documents and in Parliament it is plain that there was a clear policy decision not to do so for fear that this would result in a backlash from the religious right.

Therefore the UK regime of civil partnership mirrors marriage in almost all areas, with large parts of the CPA 2004 being the result of a copy-and-paste job from existing legislation. However, it differs in some limited but crucial areas set out in this chapter and throughout this book (particularly **1.4**). Now, at least on the face of it, there is no longer discrimination against same-sex couples as they can register as civil partners and acquire the rights that married couples already enjoy. Equally, opposite-sex couples cannot argue that they are discriminated against because they have the option to enter into a civil marriage with again (almost) the same rights.

1.3   WHAT IS CIVIL PARTNERSHIP?

1.3.1   The definition in the Civil Partnership Act 2004

Civil Partnership

(1)   A civil partnership is a relationship between two people of the same sex ('civil partners') –

   (a)   which is formed when they register as civil partners of each other –

      (i)   in England or Wales (under Part 2),
      (ii)   in Scotland (under Part 3),
      (iii) in Northern Ireland (under Part 4), or
      (iv)   outside the United Kingdom under an Order in Council made under Chapter 1 of Part 5 (registration at British consulates etc. or by armed forces personnel), or

   (b)   which they are treated under Chapter 2 of Part 5 as having formed (at the time determined under that Chapter) by virtue of having registered an overseas relationship.

(2)   Subsection (1) is subject to the provisions of this Act under or by virtue of which a civil partnership is void.
(3)   A civil partnership ends only on death, dissolution or annulment.
(4)   The references in subsection (3) to dissolution and annulment are to dissolution and annulment having effect under or recognised in accordance with this Act.
(5)   References in this Act to an overseas relationship are to be read in accordance with Chapter 2 of Part 5.

The main points therefore are that civil partnership:

- is for two people only;
- who are of the same sex;
- and who have to register.

Civil partnership:

- starts on registration;
- ends on death, dissolution or annulment.

In addition, there are provisions allowing:

- civil partnerships to be registered in Scotland and Northern Ireland;
- registration overseas; and
- recognition of overseas registered partnership regimes and same-sex marriage.

1.3.2   Why not gay marriage?

There is gay marriage in the Netherlands, Belgium, Spain, Canada and Massachusetts. The most striking is perhaps the Spanish law, which simply inserted a clause into the civil code stating that civil marriage is open to same-sex couples. The Spanish move was bold. Belgium and the Netherlands only introduced same-sex marriage after they had introduced registered partnership regimes; the law in Massachusetts and to some extent Canada was brought about by decisions of the supreme courts on constitutional and human rights principles (*Goodridge et al.* v. *Department of Public Health*, Supreme Judicial Court, Case No. SJC-08860, 18 November 2003 (US)). No doubt it was in order to avoid direct confrontation with the religious right and to avoid a debate on the religious connotations of the sacrament of holy matrimony that the Government in this country did not take that step.

The argument that creating civil partnership as opposed to allowing same-sex marriage avoids problems in international law is tenuous to say the least (see **Chapter 8**). The validity of same-sex marriage as marriage in a country that does not itself allow same-sex weddings has so far not been tested (see also **1.4** below). It may still be of an advantage for an individual couple in the UK to argue that, say, their Canadian marriage should be recognised as a marriage (see the discussion of pensions in **Chapter 9**).

Religious connotations

Although large parts of the CPA 2004 are copied and pasted from existing legislation on marriage, the draftsman has obviously tried to strip out all religious connotations. So instead of marriage, there is 'civil partnership' and instead of divorce there is 'dissolution'. There is no equivalent to the offence of bigamy and instead of engagements there are 'civil partnership agreements' (see also the glossary included at **2.2.1**).

1.3.3 Gay marriage in all but name?

Although civil partnership has been described as a line parallel to marriage that never meets it (Alan Duncan MP, *Hansard*, 12 October 2004, Column 184), commentators have said that:

> The truth of the matter from a legal perspective is that civil partnership to all intents and purposes is civil marriage in all but name.
>
> (Harper *et al. Civil Partnerships: The New Law*
> (Jordan Publishing, 2005), p.40)

It certainly appears that the similarities are so numerous and the differences so few that the latter pale into insignificance.

What is notable from s.1 is that there is no definition of the quality of the relationship between the parties; nor is there a hierarchy of the ways that the partnership may end.

Marriage is a concept in common law, defined by Lord Penzance in *Hyde* v. *Hyde* (1866) LR 1 P&D 130 at 133 as follows:

> I conceive that marriage, as understood in Christendom, may . . . be defined as the voluntary union for life of one man and one woman to the exclusion of all others.

Voluntary

Civil partnership is a voluntary union in the same way as marriage is. A civil partnership is voidable for lack of consent (s.50(1)(a)).

Monogamy

It may be significant that Lord Penzance qualified his definition by referring to Christendom. In other cultures polygamy is possible and indeed such marriages are recognised in England and Wales subject to certain precautions (Matrimonial Causes Act 1973 (MCA 1973), s.11(d)). Civil partnerships are similarly monogamous (CPA 2004, s.1(1)) and indeed if there was provision in another country for polygamous same-sex registered partnerships these would not be recognised (see **8.4**).

For life

Although there is provision for divorce, marriage is by default for life and divorce is the exception to the rule. Thus, a contract made at the time of marriage about what would happen on divorce is void for being against public policy because it goes against the whole concept of marriage (see **6.4.10**). Maybe this cannot be said for all jurisdictions and cultures when in some it is relatively easy to divorce and not even irretrievable breakdown needs to be shown (for example in Sweden).

In contrast to marriage in English law, there is no such presumption for civil partnership, which ends on 'death, dissolution or annulment' (CPA 2004, s.1(3)) without there being a hierarchy between the three. Although it is indefinite as opposed to being for a fixed period or ending on a certain event, there is nothing that prevents civil partners from agreeing to dissolve their civil partnership when, say, one of them forms a relationship with another person or simply when they fall out of love with each other. This is significant when one considers agreements between civil partners about finances: pre-registration (or indeed post-registration) agreements (see **6.4.10**).

Duty to maintain each other

This is similarly incorporated into civil partnership by the provisions of Chapter 3 of Part 1 of the CPA 2004, which makes provision for the courts to make maintenance orders in a variety of situations (see **Chapter 6**).

Duty to cohabit

It is doubtful if there is still a duty to cohabit in marriage. Although there is provision for judicial separation for married spouses (MCA 1973, s.17) and similar provision for civil partners (CPA 2004, s.56, see **4.4.1**), there is no way that cohabitation could be enforced. In contrast to marriage, there is no common law duty on civil partners to cohabit, nor is there an equivalent to MCA 1973, s.18(1), which relieves spouses from the duty to cohabit after a decree of judicial separation. It therefore seems that civil partners are under no such duty.

Sex

When asked for the difference between civil partnership and marriage by Lord Tebbit in the House of Lords on 17 November 2004, Baroness Scotland of Asthal, the Minister in the Home Office replied:

> My Lords, one of the major differences is, of course, consummation. For a marriage to be valid, it has to be consummated by one man and one woman and there is a great deal of jurisprudence which tells one exactly what consummation amounts to – partial or impartial, penetration or no penetration.
>
> (*Hansard*, Volume 666, Column 1479)

This is of course not entirely correct: non-consummation does not make a marriage void, but only voidable on the application of the other spouse. Indeed, there are no doubt marriages where sexual intercourse is never envisaged, for example because of age or disability. Although it is no longer the case that with the wedding vows spouses irrevocably agree to sexual intercourse (*R* v. *R* [1991] 2 All ER 257), a marriage remains voidable on the grounds of non-consummation or if the respondent suffered from a venereal disease (MCA 1973, s.12(a), (b) and (e)), which meant that the petitioner was unable to have safe unprotected sexual intercourse with the respondent. All these grounds have been omitted from civil partnership, presumably on the one hand to stress that one can have a fulfilled sex life while practising safer sex with protection, and on the other hand because these issues are linked to procreation being one of the traditional purposes of marriage, which is not reflected in civil partnership. Equally, therefore, adultery is not a fact for dissolution of civil partnership. Whereas of course a civil partner may be able to engage in sexual intercourse with a member of the opposite sex (and this may form part of an application for dissolution based on behaviour), 'adultery' implies a breach of a duty of sexual faithfulness, arising out of the husband's need to know that the male children of his wife are indeed his sons and heirs. There is no duty of sexual faithfulness in civil partnership and indeed civil partners may agree from the beginning to have no sex at all or that they will live in an open relationship which allows them to have other sexual partners (see **4.2**).

The significance of the differences

The possible implications for agreements between civil partners have already been mentioned and are dealt with in detail at **6.4.10**. There are also implications for applications for dissolution based on the behaviour of the respondent (see **4.2**). Finally, following the House of Lords decision in *Ghaidan* v. *Godin-Mendoza* (see **1.2.1** and **12.2.2**), the CPA 2004 provides in a number of places for certain rights and responsibilities for people who live 'as if they were civil partners'. Without a definition of how civil partners are supposed to be living their lives and with no restrictions on their freedom to live their relationship, this definition at the very least provides extreme difficulties, and at worst it is meaningless (see **1.4.8**).

Summary

In summary, therefore, civil partnership differs from marriage sufficiently to justify a different label. This may have been partially intended (in order to strip it of religious connotations), but in part unintended (the lack of substance behind the concept of 'living as if they were civil partners'). However, the position would have been clear and unambiguous without any unintended consequences if Parliament had simply opened up civil marriage to same-sex couples.

1.4 RESIDUAL DISCRIMINATION

There are a number of areas that have either deliberately or inadvertently not been covered by the CPA 2004 or were outside its immediate remit, but mean that there is continuing discrimination against same-sex couples.

1.4.1 Civil partnership

The most obvious point is that civil partnership is not same-sex marriage, but a separate regime. In practice this means that gay men and lesbians have to come out every time they fill in any form that requires them to tick their civil status. If there was same-sex marriage, this exercise would not reveal the gender of the partner, whereas civil partnership does. One would hope that official forms will be designed to have only one box each to tick for 'married or in a civil partnership', 'divorced or civil partnership dissolved' and 'widowed or surviving civil partner'. As a result of the policy of ending discrimination and the creation of equality between civil partners and spouses there is (with few exceptions) no reason for the relevant authority to know the gender of the spouse or civil partner even under the present provisions. Some exceptions will become apparent below.

A couple who want to register a civil partnership will have to give notice, which is then published. This and the public register of people in a civil partnership will enable anyone with a dislike or hate of gay men and lesbians to find them very easily. This may be significant outside the large cities in England and particularly in Northern Ireland where anti-gay violence is rife ('Gays and lesbians under siege as violence and harassment soar in Northern Ireland', *The Guardian*, 6 June 2005). As a result, it is likely that couples living in an intolerant area will go to another part of the UK or elsewhere to register, in order to avoid publicity which might make them vulnerable to violence, such as bricks being thrown through a window or worse.

1.4.2 Pensions

The Civil Partnership Act 2004 does not deal with pensions in any great detail, but enables secondary legislation to deal with pensions (s.255). It explicitly provides that provision in secondary legislation may be 'different to the provisions made with respect to widows, widowers or the dependants of persons who are not civil partners' (s.255(4)(a)). This is still the case in the Act as it was in the Bill. The explanatory notes to the Bill made it clear that any survivor's pensions in final salary schemes would only be backdated to

11

the date when the Act came into force. This means that if a man who had been a member of an occupational pension scheme since 1990 married a woman in 2006 and died a week later, she would receive a widow's pension based on 16 years of membership. By contrast if he registered a civil partnership with another man and died a week later, the surviving civil partner would receive almost nothing. At the end of the second reading of the Bill in the House of Commons the Parliamentary Under-Secretary of State for Scotland Anne McGuire MP announced that:

> for survivor pensions in public service schemes, registered same-sex couples will be treated in the same way as married couples. The change will be achieved by means of regulations, which will be introduced following Royal Assent. There is no need to amend the Bill. The regulations will provide equality, as they will allow registered same-sex partners to accrue survivor pensions in public service schemes from 1988.
>
> (Hansard, Volume 425, Columns 249–250, 12 October 2004)

In the Commons committee on 26 October 2004 Jacqui Smith referred to 'the final piece in the jigsaw of equality' and said that:

> the Secretary of State for Work and Pensions has further agreed that all members of contracted-out pension schemes will be able to build up rights for surviving civil partners on the basis of the contracted-out rights accrued from 1988.
>
> (Hansard, Standing Committee D, Column 182)

However, this does not apply to the part of the private sector occupational defined-benefits pension schemes (final or average salary) that is not contracted out. The Government takes the view that it cannot compel private employers to stop this discrimination. This means that there is continuing inequality and discrimination because these schemes will be able to calculate benefits for surviving civil partners by counting years from 5 December 2005 only (see **Chapter 9**).

1.4.3 Artificial insemination

The Human Fertilisation and Embryology Act 1990 (HFEA 1990) provides that where a woman gives birth to a child after treatment in a licensed clinic, her husband or boyfriend will be the father irrespective of whether or not he is the biological father. For a husband this does not apply if it can be shown that the husband did not consent to the treatment; for boyfriends it is necessary that the treatment was provided for the woman and the boyfriend together (HFEA 1990, s.28(2) and (3)). Since the new provisions under the Adoption and Children Act 2002 came into force and same-sex couples are able to adopt a child, some children will soon have two mothers or two fathers. It is not clear what the reason is for not extending the provisions for deemed paternity under the HFEA 1990 to two women, whether or not they are civil partners, who are treated as a couple and where one of them gives birth to a child. Under the provisions of the HFEA 1990 and the Adoption and Children Act 2002 such a couple would then have to go through the lengthy and cumbersome procedure of adoption with all that this involves, including the lacuna created if the birth mother dies before the adoption order (see also **Chapter 7**).

1.4.4 Immigration

It remains to be seen whether there will remain practical difficulties and de facto discrimination in the field of immigration. Any opposite-sex partner of a UK or EEA or Swiss citizen who wants to join his or her partner in the UK can marry overseas and make an application to enter the UK as a spouse. The provisions of the Asylum and Immigration (Treatment of Claimants, etc.) Act 2004 and Sched.23 to the CPA 2004 mean that certain foreign nationals will not be able to marry or register a civil partnership here (see **11.4**). This does not apply to weddings in the Church of England and discriminates not only against other religious groups such as Muslims, Jews, Hindus and Sikhs, but also against same-sex couples. However, opposite-sex couples who are not members of the Church of England are generally able to marry in the home country of the foreign partner and then apply from there for that partner to join their spouse in the UK. By contrast, civil partnership registration will not be universally available abroad.

In addition, in practice it may be impossible to apply to come to the UK on the grounds of a civil partnership from countries where this would make the applicant's sexual orientation public and could cause persecution by the authorities or harassment by the public (see also **8.3.1**). Many bi-national same-sex couples have lived in the UK together for some time without the ability to regularise the foreign partner's immigration status through registering their partnership. Through a combination of hurdles put up by:

- the need for permission to register as civil partners;
- rules against switching from certain immigration statuses to the status of civil partner; and
- the likelihood that the foreign partner may currently be an overstayer,

these couples will in most cases still not be able to regularise the foreign partners' immigration status easily (see **Chapter 11**).

1.4.5 International

Discrimination will remain in the international field for any civil partners who leave the UK on holiday or permanently and whose relationship is not recognised in the country they go to. This is largely inevitable and of course depends on the other country. Nevertheless, it is arguable that if Parliament had opened up marriage to same-sex couples instead of creating a new institution, these couples would at the very least have the possibility of arguing that their marriage should be recognised as a marriage in the other country. A test case along these lines is pending in Ireland at the time of writing. Two women who married in Canada are asking the Irish revenue to treat them as a married couple for income tax (*Zappone and Gilligan* v. *Inspector of Taxes and Attorney General* to be heard from 3 October 2006). In South Africa, for example, the Constitutional Court held that marriage could not be exclusive to opposite-sex couples and declared the relevant legislation unconstitutional. This declaration has been suspended for 12 months to give the South African Parliament time to remedy the defect. If it fails to do so, the legislation will be read in an inclusive way (see *Minister of Home Affairs and Another* v. *Fourie and Bonthuys*, 1 December 2005, Case No.60/04). There is also the (more theoretical) issue of the recognition of valid overseas polygamous same-sex marriages (see **Chapter 8**).

1.4.6   The possibility of future change

Nothing in the CPA 2004 prevents a future Government from eroding equality with marriage by either taking away from existing rights or by not extending new rights for spouses to civil partners. As so much of the regime is to be found in secondary legislation and there are wide enabling provisions, such discrimination would have very little Parliamentary scrutiny. If Parliament had opened up marriage to same-sex partners it would at least have been more difficult to discriminate and discrimination would be more obvious because it would have needed active new legislation to provide that those spouses that are of the same sex do not have the same rights as opposite-sex spouses.

1.4.7   General discrimination

There is as yet no general provision not to discriminate against same-sex couples or civil partners. The Human Rights Act 1998 jurisdiction only applies to agencies of the state. Therefore for example a hotel owner can continue to refuse to give a room to a same-sex couple or, if the hotel is approved for civil weddings, can refuse to allow civil partnership registrations; restaurants and pubs could ask apparently gay or lesbian people to leave; insurance companies can charge higher premiums for same-sex couples or not extend family discounts to civil partners.

In this area there may also be discrimination by private hospitals and care homes which are under no obligation to recognise a same-sex partner or civil partner as the 'next of kin' (see **14.1**).

This will only be brought to an end by legislation not to discriminate on grounds of sexual orientation, which is, of course, long overdue. It is hoped that the regulations under Equality Act 2006, s.81 will remedy this and outlaw discrimination throughout.

What even an anti-discrimination law would not end are private trust instruments and wills that included gifts to or a class of beneficiaries including, for instance, 'my children and their spouses' or similar wordings. Civil partners will continue to be excluded from benefiting from these. By contrast, provision has been made for the court to make provision in similar circumstances where trans people are affected (Gender Recognition Act 2004, s.18).

1.4.8   Unregistered partners

There are limited areas where unmarried couples have rights (such as the ability to make a claim under the Inheritance (Provision for Family and Dependants) Act 1975, succession to tenancies and protection from domestic violence). Most of these rights were probably effectively extended to same-sex couples by the House of Lords decision on the implications of the Human Rights Act 1998 in *Ghaidan* v. *Godin-Mendoza* [2004] 2 FLR 600 (see **12.2.2**), which were then confirmed by late amendments to the Civil Partnership Bill. If the Government's estimate that the ratio of same-sex couples who register their partnership is only 10 per cent of that for opposite-sex couples is correct, the majority of same-sex couples will be affected by the law relating to unregistered couples rather than by civil partnership.

'Living together as if they were civil partners'

In those places where the CPA 2004 has tried to make provision for same-sex cohabitants the draftsman has used the term 'living together as if they were civil partners' or similar and therefore tried to define cohabitation via civil partnership (e.g. in relation to the Rent Act 1977, see Sched.8, para.13; to the CPA 2004; see also **12.2.3**). The problem with this is that civil partnership is entirely defined via the registration process: 'A civil partnership is a relationship between two people of the same sex ... which is formed when they register as civil partners of each other' (s.1(1)). If two people are 'living as if they were civil partners' and this means anything other than actually being civil partners, it must refer to people who have not registered. However, if the registration is taken out, all that is left are 'two people of the same sex' without any qualification. This could refer to any two people living together, including landlord and lodger, or two friends or cousins. It may arguably exclude people who would lack capacity to register a civil partnership (two brothers or mother and daughter), but even this is not clear as a man and a woman could be cohabitants for certain purposes even if one of them is still married to someone else. Therefore the term 'living together as if they were civil partners' is entirely meaningless. The courts could not easily simply refer back to the definition of 'living as husband and wife' because civil

15

partnership is not marriage and Parliament went to great lengths (and the Government to great expense) to show exactly that. This error has probably been spotted in the area of social security law as here the term is defined further by reference back to the 'living as husband and wife' definition, which of course has a long history of case law available to define what this means (see **10.3.2**). There is a secondary question of whether the established test for opposite-sex couples is suitable for same-sex couples in the same way. It includes, for example, the question of whether the two people have presented themselves as a couple to their neighbours and society at large, something which same-sex couples may avoid doing for very good reasons. The proposed change of the definition for same-sex cohabitation in Part 4 of the Family Law Act 1996 to refer to civil partners was not put into force, possibly because the problem with the definition was recognised at the time (see **14.2.1**).

Disadvantages of legal change for same-sex cohabitants

The other side of the coin of the availability of new rights and civil partnership is that all cohabiting same-sex couples will be treated as a family unit for the assessment of social welfare benefits (see **Chapter 10**). In practice this means that same-sex couples who live together and where one or both partners receive benefits will lose out by up to £100 per week depending on the benefits. In addition anyone living with a same-sex partner will have to declare that to the benefits agency, job centre or HM Revenue and Customs (HMRC) when they claim benefits or tax credits. Since the decision-makers will specifically ask about the gender of the other people living in the same household, benefits claimants will in effect have to out themselves and declare their sexual orientation to strangers, something not everyone will feel comfortable doing. Whereas this may not be seen as a problem from the metrocentric viewpoint of a couple living in London, couples in other parts of the UK may well fear that this information could leak out and may fear discrimination and reprisals from the surrounding community as a result. Such discrimination is, of course, at the time of writing not illegal and could easily continue. For example, a landlord may indirectly find out that two men are a gay couple by the level of housing benefit that they are awarded and could then decide not to renew their assured shorthold tenancy. It is regrettable therefore that at this time there is still no general anti-discrimination law on the statute book in this country, although the measures to be taken under the Equality Act 2006, s.81 should provide an end to most discrimination.

1.5 LANGUAGE

Since people who are married may very well be gay, lesbian or bisexual (a notorious example being Oscar Wilde) it is wrong to talk about 'gay relationships' and 'straight relationships'. Indeed, people in a same-sex relationship may be heterosexual. There is no requirement for civil partners to have a sexual relationship and if two friends chose to register, they are able to do so in the same way that two friends of the opposite sex are able to marry each other if they so wish and if they are prepared to take on the far-reaching responsibilities that this entails. Even if there is a sexual relationship between civil partners, one or both of the partners may define themselves as heterosexual. Throughout this book we will refer to same-sex and opposite-sex relationships. Some people use the term 'different-sex' relationships, but this sounds odd as it implies that there are more than two sexes and, legally at least, there are only two.

Although marriage is open to same-sex couples in some other countries and these will be recognised here as civil partnerships (see **8.4**), for the sake of clarity, in this book opposite-sex couples who are not married are referred to as 'unmarried couples' and same-sex couples who are not in a civil partnership (or married to each other) are referred to as 'unregistered couples'.

The practitioner will find that a number of terms from marriage have been changed for civil partnership. Nevertheless clients in a civil partnership may talk about 'divorce' and 'my husband' and so on. However, while some lesbians and gay men may want to stress the equality of their relationship to marriage or use the same terms for ease of language, others may want to stress that their relationship is different (but equal) to marriage. Therefore it is probably best to be safe and use the terms from the CPA 2004 unless and until the client's preference is clear.

Practitioners who want to advise in this field and have no personal insight may be well advised to take the trouble to familiarise themselves with the language and lifestyles of modern gay men and lesbians. Having said that, the lifestyles of gay men and lesbians differ from one person or couple to another at least as much as in the heterosexual population, and it is important not to jump to conclusions from the example shown by one gay or lesbian friend or client. Nevertheless, familiarisation with gay men and lesbians will help to avoid major *faux pas*, such as referring to a lesbian client as 'lady' or even 'my lady', something few lesbian women will appreciate. Although of course civil partnership will equally affect bisexual people, heterosexual people (if they so chose) and transsexuals who are at a stage where they cannot (yet) marry their partner, this book will refer to gay men and lesbians as these will be the largest group of people affected by this law, but without wishing to exclude anyone else. On this point, it is probably best to refer to homosexual men as gay men and homosexual woman as lesbians. Some women object to being called 'gay' while 'homosexual' almost always sounds like a medical diagnosis and should be avoided.

CHAPTER 2

The Civil Partnership Act 2004

2.1 STRUCTURE OF THE ACT

Most of the law described in this book is contained in the Civil Partnership Act 2004 and it is therefore helpful for practitioners to have some guidance to help them find their way around the Act, not least because it is very long with 264 sections and 30 Schedules. Other law can be found in statutory instruments made by power conferred by the CPA 2004 or other legislation, and yet other law can be found in legislation that has been amended by the CPA 2004 or by statutory instruments (see **CD-ROM**).

2.1.1 The layout of the Civil Partnership Act 2004

'Civil partnership' is defined in Part 1 of the Act, which consists solely of s.1 (see **1.3.1**). Part 2 sets out the law relating to England and Wales, with registration covered in Chapter 1, dissolution in Chapter 2, financial and property issues in Chapter 3 (although the financial consequences on dissolution are in Scheds.5–7), 'civil partnership agreements' (same-sex engagements) in Chapter 4, children in Chapter 5, and miscellaneous matters in Chapter 6. Part 5 deals with all international issues ranging from UK registrations abroad (Chapter 1) and recognition of overseas relationships (Chapter 2) through to jurisdiction for and recognition of dissolutions (Chapter 3).

Several crucial rules are set out in Schedules (e.g. Scheds.5–7 for financial consequences of dissolution). Other Schedules amend existing law (e.g. wills, etc. in Sched.4, housing in Sched.8, domestic violence in Sched.9 and social security laws in Sched.24).

The complete list is set out in the box below. Note that only those elements of the CPA 2004 relevant to England and Wales are included here, with section numbers given in brackets.

19

SCHEDULES

> **Schedule 24: Social security, child support and tax credits**
>
> **Schedule 25: Amendment of certain enactments relating to pensions**
>
> **Schedule 26: Amendment of certain enactments relating to the armed forces**
>
> **Schedule 27: Minor and consequential amendments: general**
> (Schedules 28–29 relate to Scotland and Northern Ireland)
>
> **Schedule 30: Repeals and revocations**

2.1.2 Other sources of law

The Civil Partnership Act 2004 amends a vast number of existing statutes, ranging from the Declinature Act 1681 (CPA 2004, Sched.21, para.1) to the Gender Recognition Act 2004, which at the time when the CPA 2004 received Royal Assent was not even in force. Generally the practitioner can presume that where existing legislation uses wording such as 'spouse', 'husband or wife', 'widow or widower' etc. this will have been amended to include civil partners. However, there are some differences and it should always be checked whether this is in fact the case.

The Civil Partnership Act 2004 also confers wide-ranging powers on ministers to amend the Act itself, or other legislation, by statutory instrument. By way of example, statutory instruments have:

- amended the registration procedure (Civil Partnership (Amendments to Registration Provisions) Order 2005, SI 2005/2000, which makes significant changes to the registration procedure); and
- made other amendments to existing legislation, including an expedited civil marriage regime for couples where one civil partner changes gender (Civil Partnership Act 2004 (Overseas Relationships and Consequential, etc. Amendments) Order 2005, SI 2005/3129).

Vital parts of the law relating to civil partnership are not in the CPA 2004 and will be found in statutory instruments. Therefore, even if the law relating to a specific point cannot be found in the Act itself, a trawl through statutory instruments is vital to ascertain the position. This is made easier by the fact that all new legislation is available online (albeit always only in its original form) at the website of the Office of Public Sector Information (**www.opsi.gov.uk**). All material available as at May 2006 can be found on the CD-ROM accompanying this book.

2.2 TERMINOLOGY

For civil partnerships, the Government has generally tried to follow the law on marriage, but with departures in certain significant areas. The pattern seems to be that any rule for or concept around marriage that has connotations with religious marriage (the sacrament of 'holy matrimony') has been omitted or changed slightly. There is therefore of course no 'wedding', but a 'civil partnership registration' without vows (see **Chapter 3**). To end a civil partnership, the equivalent to 'divorce' is 'dissolution'. In the Matrimonial Causes Act 1973 the term 'dissolution' is used interchangeably for divorce in some sections, for example in s.5 and in s.25(2)(h) where the court needs to consider 'the value to each of the parties to the marriage of any benefit which, by reason of the dissolution or annulment of the marriage, that party will lose the chance of acquiring'. In other sections it seems to be further reaching (for example, s.19: presumption of death and dissolution of marriage). Although the CPA 2004 talks about 'applications' for dissolution and 'applicants', the amended Family Proceedings Rules 1991, SI 1991/1247 (FPR 1991) will talk about 'petitions' for dissolution, apparently to make it easier to amend them. However, there are plans to overhaul FPR 1991 and abandon the terms 'petition' and 'petitioner' altogether, and finally practitioners will no longer be asked by shocked clients whether they will have to collect signatures outside the supermarket to get a divorce. Nevertheless the CPA 2004 and the amended FPR 1991 will refer to conditional and final orders instead of decrees nisi and decrees absolute. A term to be wary of is 'civil partnership agreement' (Part 2, Chapter 4, ss.73–74), which is the equivalent of an engagement rather than an agreement between (prospective) civil partners about financial or other arrangements, which in this book are referred to as pre-registration agreements (the equivalent of pre-nuptial agreements).

2.2.1 Glossary

See below for a quick guide to terminology in the CPA 2004 in relation to existing terminology in relation to spouses.

CPA 2004	Existing terminology for spouses
application for dissolution	petition for divorce: *under the FPR, as amended, applications for dissolutions are also referred to as 'petitions'*
civil partner	spouse
civil partnership agreement	engagement: *not to be confused with a pre-registration agreement on financial or other issues*
conditional order	decree nisi
dissolution	divorce
final order	decree absolute

former civil partner	divorced (*when ticking the box for one's 'civil status'*)
having your civil partnership dissolved	getting divorced
home rights	*formerly* matrimonial home rights
living as if they were civil partners	living as husband and wife (see **1.4.8**)
objection	caveat
officiate at the signing of a civil partnership schedule	solemnise a marriage
order	decree
overseas relationship	a registered same-sex partnership or registered marriage in another country that is recognised under CPA 2004, Part 5 (see **8.4.1**)
proposed civil partners	fiancé(e)s (see **11.2.2**)
registered	married
registered partnership	marriage
registration	wedding
sale of property order	order for the sale of property
same-sex couple	unmarried couple (see **11.5**)
separation order	judicial separation (decree of)

CHAPTER 3

Registration of a civil partnership

3.1 OVERVIEW

3.1.1 Modelled on civil marriage

Civil partnership registration in England and Wales is modelled on civil marriage and most provisions are very similar or the same. There are rules for eligibility and consent (s.3; see **3.3**), notice needs to be given at a registry office (s.8), there is a waiting period and both civil partners have to attend the registration to sign a register, which also needs to be signed by a registrar and two witnesses (s.2; see **3.4.2**). There is also a prohibition against registration on religious premises (s.6) and against religious services during the registration (s.2(5); see **3.3.4**).

However, there are also some significant differences. These seem to stem from a policy decision to ensure that there is a clear distinction from marriage, to prevent an attack by the religious right against civil partnership on the basis that it was 'gay marriage' (see also **1.3**). The main difference here is that there is no provision for the exchange of vows and instead the signing of the civil partnership document makes the couple civil partners (see **3.3.3**).

At the time the Bill was drafted the Government intended to simplify the procedure for civil marriage as set out in its White Paper *Civil Registration: Vital Change* in 2002 and a subsequent Consultation Document in July 2003. This was going to be achieved by amending marriage legislation by order (secondary legislation) under the Regulatory Reform Act 2001. However, the committees of both Houses of Parliament rejected this in December 2004, and on 1 March 2005 the Financial Secretary to the Treasury, the Government minister responsible for the reform, Stephen Timms, announced that reform would no longer be pursued in this way and marriage law therefore remains unreformed. Therefore and in order to bring civil partnership registration into line with the (old) civil marriage regime, Chapter 1 of Part 2 of the CPA 2004 and some consequential provisions were amended by the Civil Partnership (Amendments to Registration Provisions) Order 2005, SI 2005/2000. The law as set out in this book reflects those changes, and the text of the Act on the CD-ROM accompanying this book has been updated accordingly.

Much of the procedure and administrative detail is set out in regulations. In practice it is unlikely that practitioners will be consulted to advise on the details of the formalities because information can simply be obtained from the local register office. There is also information for the public available on the General Register Office website (**www.gro.gov.uk**). More important are the general principles and options available and those aspects of registration that link with other areas which practitioners may be consulted on, such as:

- immigration (see **Chapter 11**);
- nullity (see **Chapter 4**);
- offences (see **3.5**); or
- discrimination issues (see **3.2**).

3.1.2 Ways to register

There are at least 11 ways to become civil partners under English law.

1. The standard procedure in England and Wales in a registry office or approved premises (ss.8–17).
2. The special procedure for terminally ill people with a Registrar General's licence (ss.21–27).
3. The amended standard procedure for house-bound people (s.18).
4. The amended standard procedure for people detained in prison or a mental hospital (s.19).
5. The amended standard procedure where one partner is resident in Scotland (ss.20(2) and 97).
6. The amended standard procedure where one partner is a sailor (ss.20(4) and 239, and the Civil Partnership (Armed Forces) Order 2005, SI 2005/3188, art.14).
7. Registration in Northern Ireland (Chapter 1 of Part 4).
8. Registration in Scotland (Chapters 1 and 2 of Part 3).
9. Registration overseas in one of the regimes that are recognised in the UK under s.212; certificates of non-impediment are possible for UK nationals and other British subjects under s.240 and the Civil Partnership (Registration Abroad and Certificates) Order 2005, SI 2005/2761, art.17, but only if their partner is not a UK national or British subject (as defined in art.2 of that Order) (see also **8.4**).
10. Registration in a British overseas mission under s.210 (see **8.3.1**).
11. Registration by armed forces personnel abroad under s.211 (see **8.3.2**).

Registration in Northern Ireland is similar to the provisions for England and Wales (although there is no special procedure), while registration in Scotland is in many ways simpler as it follows Scots law on civil marriage. In Scotland there is no residence requirement and no need for parental consent for 16- and 17-year-olds.

3.2 PROBLEMS FOR SAME-SEX COUPLES

There are a number of issues that may be faced by same-sex couples who wish to register a civil partnership, but which may not present a problem to couples who wish to marry. These include:

- publicity;
- foreign partners;
- religion;
- discrimination by registration authorities or managers of approved premises.

3.2.1 Publicity

As part of the registration process for the standard and amended standard procedures, the names of the proposed civil partners and other prescribed details will have to be on public display at the register offices where each civil partner lives (s.10). This is the same as for civil marriage. Once a couple has registered their civil partnership in England or Wales, anyone searching the public register can obtain a copy of the registration certificate.

As long as discrimination, harassment and anti-gay violence remain a problem, publicity may cause difficulty because it automatically reveals the parties' sexual orientation. A secret register would of course defeat the purpose of the entire regime as it would be impossible to determine whether a couple are civil partners and therefore have certain rights and responsibilities. However, it is another question whether publicity should single out gay men and lesbians in the way it does. If the Government had opened up marriage to same-sex couples, there would have been no obvious difficulty relating to publicity because (provided initials or gender neutral first names could be used) the parties' sexual orientation would not be revealed. In the same way, a public notice that John Smith and Tracy Taylor are getting married will not alert those people who object to marriage between people of different racial origin, with the accompanying threat of possible violence. (The brutal murder of the black teenager Anthony Walker on 29 July 2005 in Liverpool when he was with his white girlfriend illustrates that this example is not far fetched: see 'Racists axe black teenager to death', *The Observer*, 31 July 2005.) By contrast, the notice of future civil partnership will automatically label the parties as gay or lesbian. While this may not be such an issue in big cities, it may discourage couples in small towns and rural areas from registration. Of particular concern are small council areas, such as small counties and unitary authorities where prospective civil partners live in close proximity to the town hall and people generally know each other. The first notice of civil partnership on the town hall notice board may well trigger an article in the local paper, and a prospective civil partner who is running a local business may fear loss of custom if outed.

Another issue is of course that while there is legislation against racial discrimination, there is currently no legislation against discrimination on grounds of sexual orientation (except that limited to employment matters). Therefore, landlords who find out about their tenants' sexual orientation may refuse to renew a tenancy after the assured shorthold period of 6 or 12 months has expired (the usual tenancy in England and Wales for private landlords these days); a self-employed civil partner may lose custom and other businesses may refuse to deliver supplies or services to that person. None of this would be illegal, but could potentially make a couple homeless or ruin an individual's business.

Bizarrely, therefore, copying the provisions for marriage in this particular area is to the detriment of civil partners. There is no discernible benefit, particularly since in Scotland there is no requirement to publicise marriage or civil partnership in the register office where each partner lives.

If clients are concerned about these issues, one solution is for them to arrange to register in Scotland. No public notice will be displayed at their home in England and the chances of the Scottish publication being noticed by neighbours of the couple from their English or Welsh home is not high. There are no residence requirements for Scotland and any couple can choose to register their civil partnership there. It is therefore likely that Scotland, and probably particularly Edinburgh and Glasgow, will see a fair amount of civil partnership tourism from elsewhere in the UK.

There seems to be no residence requirement for Northern Ireland, but whether the Province would prove to be a suitable place for English or Welsh couples who wish to avoid anti-gay attitudes is highly questionable.

3.2.2   Foreign partners

If one partner is resident in Scotland or is a sailor in the Navy or Royal Marines, registration in England is possible under special provision (see **3.4.2**, **figure 3.3**). No such provision seems to be available if one partner is resident in Northern Ireland. The original provisions in ss.20(3) and 150 have been deleted by the Civil Partnership (Amendments to Registration Provisions) Order 2005, SI 2005/2000 to bring registration in line with the rules for civil marriage (see also **3.1.1**). Although such a couple could register in Northern Ireland, they may be reluctant to do so given the hostile attitudes to homosexuality there.

If one partner is not a UK, EEA or Swiss citizen, depending on his or her immigration status, permission from the Home Secretary will be required for a registration in the UK. This may not always be available (see **Chapter 11**). Although the same provision applies for marriage (albeit not for marriages in the Church of England), this provision affects same-sex couples disproportionately for the following reasons.

1. Bi-national opposite-sex couples have always had the ability to marry and, if the relationship is long-standing, they could have done so before the immigration control provisions came into effect in early 2005.
2. An opposite-sex couple will almost always be able to go to the country of origin of the foreign partner and marry there. By contrast same-sex registered partnership is not widely available overseas, with some exceptions, mostly within Europe (see **Chapter 8**).
3. Even if a couple manage to arrange to register here or in a third country, the foreign partner may not be able to switch to a civil partner visa and will have to return to his or her home country to apply, where identification of his or her sexual orientation may cause problems.

3.2.3   Religion

There is no provision for a religious registration and no religious service can take place during the registration (s.2(5), see also **3.3.4**). Some churches and non-Christian religious groups will provide blessing ceremonies, but for believers this means that their religion is not an integral part of the union created by the civil partnership registration. While this may not be significant to many prospective civil partners, there is, no doubt, a significant number of couples for whom this is a serious issue. It is also likely that same-sex couples with a strong religious belief are proportionately more likely to wish to register their partnership than non-religious couples, because most religions put a high value on stable relationships. Although it seems justified to exclude religion from all civil marriages as an alternative religious service is always available, the same logic does not apply to civil partnership.

3.2.4   Direct discrimination by registration authorities or managers of approved premises

The place of registration was not defined at all in the original version of the Act. With the amendments now made (see **3.1.1**), the registration authority must at least make the register office (as defined by the Registration Service Act 1953, s.10) available for registration of civil partnerships. However this does not mean that the usual rooms in the town halls (council chamber, historic wedding rooms, etc.) must be made available; nor does it mean that the registration authority must allow civil partners to have any kind of ceremony or exchange of words. The provisions in the CPA 2004 will have been complied with if the partners can register in the registrar's office even if there is no opportunity to have guests there nor any ability to have any form of ceremony. Some councils, such as the London Borough of Bromley, announced in June 2005 that this is what they were likely to do ('Mayor to challenge gay ceremony ban', *The Guardian*, 25 June 2005), although Bromley later retracted this intention. Whether the council would fall foul of the

Human Rights Act 1998 is questionable as the non-discrimination provision under Art.14 must fall within the ambit of a protected right.

The provisions for licensing approved premises under the new s.6A are supposed to be the same as for marriage and the list of premises is supposed to be the same. This does not mean that a venue that is licensed for weddings is compelled to apply to be licensed for civil partnerships, nor to allow civil partnership registrations to be conducted there if it already has an automatic joint licence for weddings and civil partnership registrations. Even if the local staff of a particular hotel, for example, would welcome and accommodate a civil partnership registration, head office policy may be that they should not apply for a licence. This may be particularly so if the hotel chain is owned by a foreign-based group whose religious convictions allegedly justify discrimination against gay men and lesbians. Unless regulations to be made under the Equality Act 2006, s.81 prohibit discrimination in this area, there are likely to be fewer venues available to same-sex couples. This may exclude civil partnership registrations from taking place at historic landmarks, football grounds and the like. By contrast, some gay venues which are currently not licensed for weddings may apply, as may church halls (see **3.3.4**).

3.3 CONDITIONS

3.3.1 Eligibility

The criteria for eligibility are copied over from those for marriage. They are that (s.3(1)):

- the proposed civil partners are of the same sex;
- neither of them is married nor a civil partner;
- neither is under 16; and
- neither is within the prohibited degrees of relationship.

If these conditions are not fulfilled, the civil partnership is void (s.49(a)).

Same-sex

This of course mirrors the opposite-sex requirement in marriage and on the face of it is the only difference between the two regimes.

Single

This includes overseas partnerships that are recognised in the UK under s.212. If there is any possibility that one partner has undergone any sort of registration or ceremony with someone abroad, they should carefully check that this is not recognised under s.212 and if the overseas partnership has been dissolved, that the dissolution is recognised here. This will be particularly difficult for regimes not listed in Sched.20, such as the regional regimes in Spain, or if the overseas partnership was dissolved other than by an order of a court (see also **8.4**).

It is unclear on the face of it whether a registration between two people who are already civil partners is possible or not and what the effect of it would be. As there are question marks over some overseas regimes (see **8.4.2**), the cautious approach for a couple who have moved to the UK from abroad would be to register again in the UK. It may also be that the UK regime is recognised in more countries than the original registered partnership. For example if Philippe (French) and Paul (New Zealander) entered into a Pacs in France when they lived there (which is not recognised in New Zealand) and move to England later on (a regime which is likely to be added to the list of regimes New Zealand recognises), they may want to register here to have recognition in New Zealand, for example to provide for the situation where Paul died domiciled there. A similar situation arose in the case of Mr and Mrs Marks who had married in a polygamous marriage in Nigeria (recognised in England) before undergoing a civil ceremony in this country. Thorpe LJ simply remarked that the civil ceremony in England 'was a nullity' (*Marks* v. *Marks* [2004] 1 FLR 1069 at para.7). This is a risk that a cautious couple may take. However, if s.3(1) is interpreted strictly, they would be committing an offence under s.80 by stating to the registry office that they were single.

Over 16

Parental consent is necessary for 16- and 17-year-olds to enter into a civil partnership. The provisions mirror those for marriage. Although it is relatively rare that marriages take place in these circumstances, it is conceivable that young gay men and lesbians may be inclined to enter into a civil partnership partly in order to escape from parents who do not accept their sexual orientation and therefore the percentage of young people wishing to enter civil partnerships may be higher. In England, they would in that case need the consent of the court under Sched.2, para.10. The more straightforward route would, however, be a trip to Scotland where no parental consent is necessary for anyone over 16 and where there are no residence requirements.

A civil partnership registered in England is not void for lack of parental consent (s.52(1)(a) but the registrar would have had to make a mistake), but if the parent, etc. explicitly forbids the civil partnership, it is void (s.49(c)).

Relatives

The list of relatives who are not allowed to enter into a civil partnership with each other mirrors the list for marriage. While other countries have left it at a prohibition against marriage between direct descendants and siblings and possibly have added adoptive children (e.g. Germany, see §§1307 and 1308 BGB), English law includes qualified prohibitions (Sched.1, para.2). The Marriage Act 1949 also forbids marriages between a man and his son's former wife, etc. and Sched.1, para.3 makes similar provision for civil partnership registration. However, before the Act came into force just such a couple successfully challenged this law in the European Court of Human Rights (*B and L* v. *UK* (Application No.36536/02) 19 September 2005; see **www.echr.coe.int**) and Sched.1, para.3 was therefore not put into force. The prohibition against marriage between relatives has its origins in the prohibition of incest, which again probably originates from the problem that inbreeding can trigger certain inheritable diseases. This is of course not the case for same-sex partners, who cannot procreate with one another (with the potential exception of those who have changed gender, see **5.4.4**). Nevertheless, it is probably an unexpressed revulsion against the thought of sexual relations between close relatives that has led the Government to mirror these provisions for civil partnership.

Domicile

Since civil partnership is a regime not known in any other country, a requirement that prospective partners must have capacity to enter into civil partnership under the law of the country where they are domiciled (as is the general rule for marriage), would mean that only English, Scottish or Northern Irish domiciled people could ever enter into a civil partnership. This would deny this human right to a large number of gay men and lesbians living in the UK and make the immigration provisions meaningless. There is therefore no reference to domicile in the CPA 2004 (see also **8.3**). Therefore all that is required is that the individual has capacity under English law to register in England and Wales. The same applies to the other parts of the UK, and this is why an English 16-year-old can register a civil partnership in Scotland.

3.3.2 Consent

Mirroring English law on marriage, lack of consent does not make a civil partnership void, but merely voidable, as does severe mental illness that prevents the partner from giving valid consent (s.50(1)(a) and (b)). The only situation where consent or mental capacity may be a prerequisite to registration is in the case of registration under a Registrar General's licence, where a medical practitioner has to certify that the terminally ill partner 'understands the nature and purport of signing a Registrar General's licence' (s.22(2)(c)).

3.3.3 Formalities

The formalities for the registration of a civil partnership are almost identical to civil marriage. The main difference is that the partners become married the moment they have exchanged their vows and the signing of the document is then evidence of what has just taken place (see Marriage Act 1949, s.44(3)–(3A) and compare with CPA 2004, s.55(2). By contrast, there are no vows in a civil partnership registration and, indeed, there need not necessarily be a ceremony. The couple may want to exchange some words of their choice but they become civil partners only from the moment that they have signed the civil partnership document (s.2(1)). In the extreme situation where an unlucky fiancé dies of a heart attack immediately after vows have been exchanged but before signing the document, the surviving woman will become a widow, and will inherit under the intestacy rules (if there is no will), receive any widow's pension and so on. However, in similar circumstances where one of the couple dies after exchanging vows in a civil partnership ceremony but before the document is signed, the survivor would not be a surviving civil partner and would be in the same situation as an unregistered partner.

Certain formalities are vital and their lack will make a purported civil partnership registered in England and Wales void, while others will not. The civil partnership is void if:

- the appropriate notice has not been given (s.49(b)(i));
- the civil partnership document was not duly issued, i.e. the civil partnership schedule under s.14 or the Registrar General's licence for registration under the special procedure under s.25 (s.49(b)(ii));
- the registration took place once the civil partnership document had expired (s.49(b)(iii));
- the registration took place elsewhere than the place that was in the notice and the civil partnership document (s.49(b)(iv));
- the registrar was not present (s.49(b)(v)); or
- the place of registration was not approved although it was purported to be approved premises (s.49(b)(vi)).

Arguably these are all issues which will be difficult to ascertain maybe years later and a couple may be unduly penalised for something which may have been an administrative fault by the registration authority. Issues which cannot be clearly established one way or another may cast a doubt over a civil partnership.

Lack of other formalities which do not make the civil partnership void are:

- that there was no parental consent for a 16- or 17-year-old (s.52(1)(a)) unless the parent specifically forbade it (s.49(c)); or
- that the civil partners did not reside in the area where they said they resided (s.52(1)(aa));

- that the registrar did not have the particular designation by the registration authority (s.52(1)(b)).

The distinction seems entirely arbitrary. Furthermore, nothing is said about registration outside the prescribed hours of the day. Nevertheless, a couple should not be complacent about these formalities, because a false statement on the notice about residence may attract a hefty penalty under s.80 (see **3.5**).

3.3.4 Religion

The registration cannot take place in religious premises (s.6(1)(b)) and no religious service can be used during the registration (s.2(5)). The definition of religious premises (s.6(2)) was changed during the course of the Bill in Parliament to allow deconsecrated churches now used as community centres or gay night clubs (on the suggestion of Alan Duncan, MP) to apply for a licence. A venue is 'religious premises' if it is used 'solely or mainly for religious purposes' or even if it used to be so used and it has not been used 'solely or mainly for other purposes'. This would, for instance, not exclude the church hall of a Methodist church and the couple could register there (if the hall has a licence under regulations under s.6A) and then with their guests walk across to the church and have a blessing service there (see also 'Methodists will bless gays', *The Times*, 30 June 2005). By contrast, Church of England clergy are allowed to bless battleships, but not perform a blessing service after a civil partnership registration (' "Marriages" but no sex for gay clergy', *The Daily Telegraph*, 26 July 2005; see also The Rev. Dr Giles Fraser 'Love is the answer', *The Guardian*, 29 July 2005).

The interpretation of the equivalent provision against religious services during the marriage ceremony (Marriage Act 1949, s.45(2)) has been interpreted extremely restrictively. In 2005 the Registrar General consulted on changing this to allow readings from E.M. Forster's *Howards End* and similar works (*Content of Civil Marriage Ceremonies – A consultation document on proposed changes to regulation and guidance to registration officers*, General Register Office, June 2005). It was proposed to define 'religious service' as 'a ceremony containing recognised religious rites, rituals or singing or hymns' and allow 'readings, songs or music that contain an incidental reference to a god or deity in an essentially non-religious context' (Consultation Document, p.6). The outcome of the consultation was published in November 2005 and accordingly guidance to registrars on registrations in register offices will be the same as the amendment to what were the Marriages (Approved Premises) Regulations 1995, SI 1995/510, and have now been replaced for both marriage and civil partnership by the Marriages and Civil Partnerships (Approved Premises) Regulations 2005, SI 2005/3168. This reads in Sched.2, para.11:

33

(1) Any proceedings conducted on approved premises shall not be religious in nature.

(2) In particular, the proceedings shall not –

(a) include extracts from an authorised religious marriage service or from sacred religious texts;

(b) be led by a minister of religion or other religious leader;

(c) involve a religious ritual or series of rituals;

(d) include hymns or other religious chants; or,

(e) include any form of worship.

(3) But the proceedings may include readings, songs, or music that contain an incidental reference to a god or deity in an essentially non-religious context.

(4) For this purpose any material used by way of introduction to, in any interval between parts of, or by way of conclusion to the proceedings shall be treated as forming part of the proceedings.

The intention is that this will not allow readings from the Bible, the Koran, the Thora or similar books, but may include playing music such as *Zadok the Priest* or a contemporary song such as 'Angels' by Robbie Williams, or reading from a work of fiction such as E.M. Forster's *Howard's End*. This will of course not end the problem for religious same-sex couples who would prefer to have a religious service.

3.4 TYPES OF REGISTRATION IN ENGLAND AND WALES

3.4.1 When to use a different procedure

There are essentially two procedures for registration: the standard and the special procedure. Then there are variations on the standard procedure for various cases. This is illustrated in **figure 3.1**.

3.4.2 Time-lines

As practitioners are unlikely to advise directly on the mechanics of the various registration procedures, these will not be set out in detail here. Instead, **figures 3.2–3.5** illustrate the procedures and refer to the relevant sections of the CPA 2004.

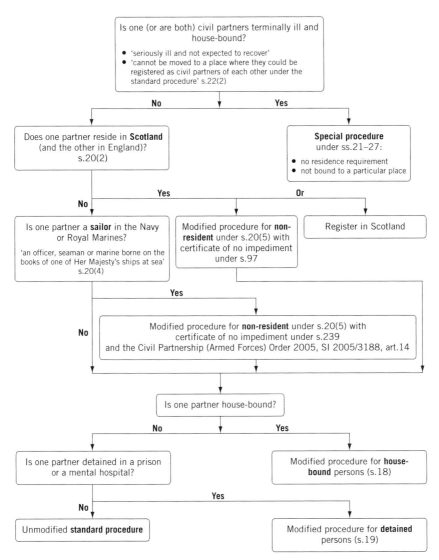

Figure 3.1 Choice of procedure for civil partnership registration in England and Wales

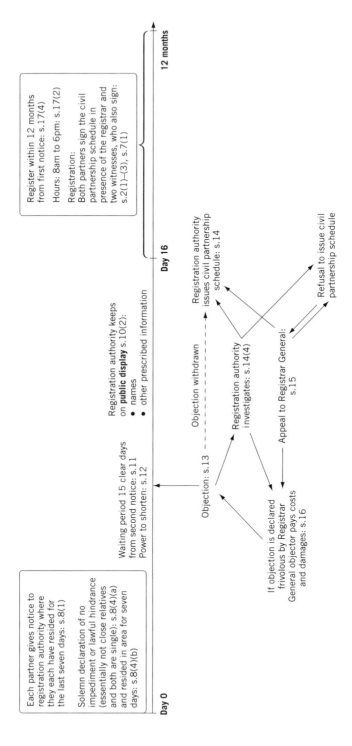

Figure 3.2 Standard procedure

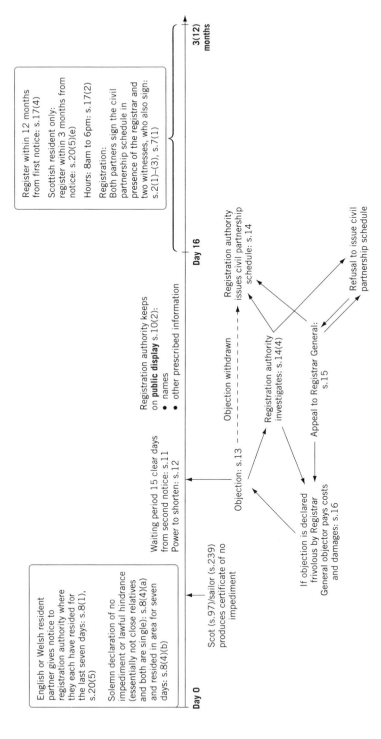

Figure 3.3 Scots and sailors (one partner is resident in Scotland or is a sailor in the Navy or Royal Marines)

37

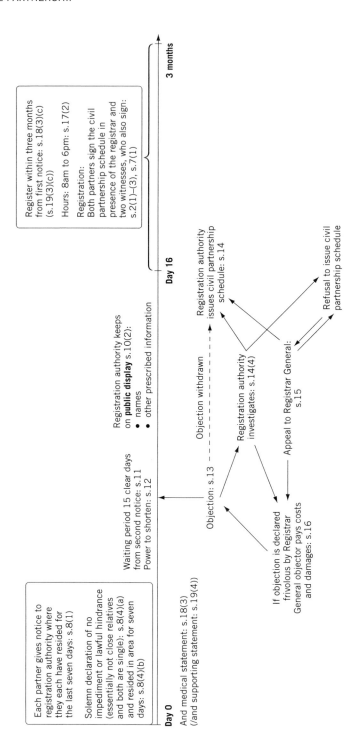

Figure 3.4 House-bound (detained) persons

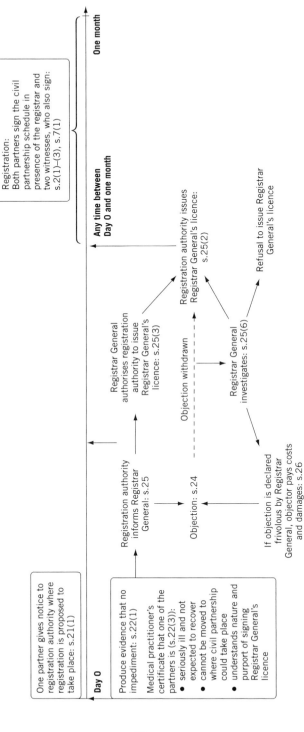

Figure 3.5 Special procedure by Registrar General's licence

39

3.4.3 Fees

Fees for registering a civil partnership in England and Wales are the same as the fees for civil marriage (Registration of Civil Partnerships (Fees) Order 2005, SI 2005/1996). At the time of writing they are as follows:

1. Registry office registration: £107 plus fee for certificates (£30 each for giving notice and £47 for the registration).
2. Shorten waiting period: £28 extra.
3. House-bound or detained people: £124 plus fee for certificates (£30 for the notice given at the registry office, £47 for the notice given at home or at the place of detention and £47 for the registration).
4. Registration in approved premises: these depend on the registration authority. They should be the same as those for a marriage or the fees would be discriminatory.
5. Special procedure: £20 (£3 for the notice, £15 for the licence and £2 for the registration). The reason why these fees are so much lower is that the fees for the equivalent procedure on marriage are in the Marriage (Registrar General's Licence) Act 1970 and can only be increased by primary legislation, whereas the fees for registry office weddings are in secondary legislation and are periodically increased (most recently by the Registration of Births, Deaths and Marriages (Fees) Order 2002, SI 2002/3076, as amended by the Registration of Births, Deaths and Marriages (Fees) (Amendment) Order 2005, SI 2005/1997).

3.5 OFFENCES

We will not set out the details of every single offence here, as these can easily be found in the Act, but a list of the various types of behaviour which are an offence in plain English is provided below.

Offences relating to registration

Who may commit the offence	The offence	Civil Partnership Act 2004	Penalty: indictment	Penalty: summary	Limitation period
General					
Any person	Pretending to be a parent, etc. and forbidding the civil partnership of a 16- or 17-year-old.	s.80(1)(c)	7 years or fine or both	fine (statutory maximum)	
	In a case where a civil partnership may be prohibited between step-relatives and the proposed civil partners have made a declaration that the younger was not a child of the family in relation to the other: falsely making a written statement that this declaration is false.	s.80(1)(d)	7 years or fine or both	fine (statutory maximum)	
Prospective civil partners	Making a false declaration or giving a notice or certificate required for registering a civil partnership in England and Wales or for the recognition of an overseas relationship.	s.80(1)(a)	7 years or fine or both	fine (statutory maximum)	

Who may commit the offence	The offence	Civil Partnership Act 2004	Penalty: indictment	Penalty: summary	Limitation period
General					
Prospective civil partners	Making a false statement or causing someone to do so about any information required for the registration in England and Wales or recognition of an overseas relationship.	s.80(1)(b)	7 years or fine or both	fine (statutory maximum)	
	Giving false information for the conditions for the special procedure: i.e. no lawful impediment, sufficient reason for special procedure, seriously ill and not expected to recover, and understanding of 'nature and purport of signing the Registrar General's licence'.	s.32(1)(a)	3 years or fine or both	fine (statutory maximum)	3 years
Special procedure					
Medical practitioners	Making a false certificate about the conditions for the special procedure: i.e. seriously ill and not expected to recover, and understanding of 'nature and purport of signing the Registrar General's licence'.	s.32(1)(b)	3 years or fine or both	fine (statutory maximum)	3 years

Rogue registrar	Officiating at special procedure registration.	s.32(2)(b)	3 years or fine or both	fine (statutory maximum)	3 years
Registrar	Officiating at special procedure registration: • where due notice of the civil partnership was not given; • where the civil partnership document was not duly issued; • where the time for registration had expired; • where the place of registration is not the one specified in the notice and Registrar General's licence; or • where a parent, etc. has forbidden the registration in case of a 16- or 17-year-old.	s.32(2)	3 years or fine or both	fine (statutory maximum)	3 years

Who may commit the offence	The offence	Civil Partnership Act 2004	Penalty: indictment	Penalty: summary	Limitation period
Standard procedure					
Official	Issuing a civil partnership schedule in the standard procedure although: • waiting period has not expired; • time for registration has expired; or • parent, etc. has forbidden the registration in case of a 16- or 17-year-old.	s.31(1)	5 years or fine or both	–	3 years
Rogue registrar	Officiating at standard procedure registration.	s.31(2)	5 years or fine or both	–	3 years
Registrar	Officiating at standard procedure registration: • before the waiting period for the standard procedure has expired; • where due notice of the civil partnership was not given;	s.31(2)	5 years or fine or both	–	3 years

					3 years

- where the civil partnership document was not duly issued;
- where the time for registration had expired;
- where the place of registration is not the one specified in the notice(s) and civil partnership schedule;
- where the place of registration is not approved when it is purported to be approved; or
- where a parent etc. has forbidden the registration in case of a 16- or 17-year-old.

Registrar	Officiating at a standard procedure registration other than between 8am and 6pm	s.31(2)(ab)	14 years or a fine or both	–

Who may commit the offence	The offence	Civil Partnership Act 2004	Penalty: indictment	Penalty: summary	Limitation period
Generally by officials					
Registrar	Refusal or failure to comply with provisions: this means that a registrar cannot, for instance, refuse to register a couple for religious reasons – such a person would need to change jobs.	s.33(1)	loss of job and 2 years or a fine or both	fine (statutory maximum) and loss of job	
Official	Refusal or failure to record registration of civil partnership as soon as practicable.	s.33(3)	–	fine (level 3)	
Official	Recording information in the register in the knowledge that the civil partnership is void under s.49(b) or (c) (standard procedure).	s.33(5)	5 years or a fine or both	–	3 years
Official	Recording information in the register in the knowledge that the civil partnership is void under s.49(b) or (c) (special procedure).	s.33(7)	3 years or a fine or both	fine (statutory maximum)	3 years

3.6   WHAT IS THE SAME – WHAT IS DIFFERENT?

Same as marriage

- exclusivity
- various procedures
- eligibility: prohibited degrees of relationship
- parental consent for 16- and 17-year-olds
- as for civil marriage, not in religious premises and no religious services during registration
- notices
- publication
- waiting period
- special procedure

Different from marriage

- same-sex
- no alternative religious registration procedure
- no vows
- partners are registered on signing of the civil partnership documents
- no bigamy (but false declarations are an offence)
- no reference to domicile on capacity

CHAPTER 4

Ending a civil partnership

4.1 INTRODUCTION

According to s.1(3) 'a civil partnership ends only on death, dissolution or annulment'. This chapter will deal with all three ways a civil partnership ends, which is dealt with in Chapter 2 of Part 2 of the CPA 2004. Almost all the law in this Chapter of the Act has been copied and pasted from Part 1 of the Matrimonial Causes Act 1973 (MCA 1973), with a few additions from other statutes. Some of the terminology was changed and the order of the sections was modernised. Instead of starting with the facts for divorce as in MCA 1973, s.1, the Chapter starts with some general points applying to dissolution, nullity and separation orders and then goes on to deal with each type of application in turn. A comparative list of sections is provided at **4.5**.

The most significant difference from divorce and nullity law is that Chapter 2 lacks the references made in the MCA 1973 to heterosexual intercourse. Thus there is no fact of adultery for divorce (see **4.2**) (and no ground of adultery for a separation order) and no grounds to annul a marriage based on non-consummation and venereal disease (see **4.3**). When asked by Lord Tebbit in the final debate in the House of Lords on 17 November 2005 what the difference between marriage and civil partnership was, the minister, Baroness Scotland of Asthal, said:

> My Lords, one of the major differences is, of course, consummation. For a marriage to be valid it has to be consummated by one man and one woman and there is a great deal of jurisprudence which tells one exactly what consummation amounts to – partial or impartial, penetration or no penetration.

This is of course not strictly correct: a marriage is voidable, not void, on the ground of non-consummation and no third party can apply for nullity on the ground of non-consummation or enquire into whether a marriage was consummated. Therefore a marriage is valid even if the couple (for whatever reason) never consummate it. It is perhaps a significant point in the concept of civil partnership that homosexual sexual intercourse, which has so long plagued parliamentarians, has been entirely left outside. For the first time gay men were seen as stable couples that needed protection rather than people engaging in buggery. This may have contributed to the large majority the Bill received in the House of Lords – in contrast to legislation to equalise the age of consent only a few years previously.

Divorce has been relabelled 'dissolution'. As mentioned elsewhere (**2.2**), it is not clear in the MCA 1973 whether 'dissolution' is just another word for divorce or encompasses all forms of ending a marriage. Other terms have been updated. Thus there are no 'decrees' but 'orders' and the two stages of a dissolution or annulment are 'conditional' and 'final orders'. Although the Act talks about 'applications' and 'applicants' the amendments to the Family Proceedings Rules 1991, SI 1991/1247 (FPR 1991) ignore this and refer to 'petitions' and 'petitioners' instead (as amended by the Family Proceedings (Amendment) (No.5) Rules 2005, SI 2005/2922). Since this is seen as a stop-gap measure to save drafting work pending the wholesale overhaul of the FPR 1991, this book generally adopts the terminology of the Act rather than the Rules. In the amended FPR 1991 orders to end a civil partnership are labelled 'civil partnership orders' and the proceedings 'civil partnership proceedings', which is unfortunate as these orders end rather than start a civil partnership, as the words might imply.

This chapter deals with:

- the facts for dissolution (**4.2**);
- the grounds on which a civil partnership is void (**4.3.1**);
- the grounds on which a civil partnership is voidable (**4.3.2**);
- other applications, such as separation orders, presumption-of-death orders and declarations of validity (**4.4**); and
- procedural issues, including a list comparing the provisions for dissolution etc. of marriage and civil partnership (**4.5**).

4.2 DISSOLUTION

As with divorce, the only ground for a dissolution of a civil partnership is that the relationship has broken down irretrievably (s.44(4)), which has to be shown by one of four facts (s.44(5)). These are identical to those on divorce except that the fact of adultery is missing. Of course sexual relations of what-ever form outside the civil partnership may be a reason for the breakdown of the relationship and these can form the basis of an application for dissolution based on behaviour, in the same way that sexual relations not amounting to adultery can form the basis of a behaviour petition for divorce. A third party could even be named with the permission of the court (see s.64 and FPR 1991, r.2.7(3), which applies equally to civil partnership dissolutions). However, as in divorce, this should be rare. Adultery is defined as:

consensual sexual intercourse between a married person and a person of the opposite sex, not the other spouse, during the subsistence of the marriage. There must be at least partial penetration of the female by the male for the act of adultery to be proved. The attempt to commit adultery must not be confused with the act itself, and if there is no such penetration, some lesser act of sexual gratification does not amount to adultery.

(*Rayden and Jackson on Divorce and Family Matters*,
17th Edn (Butterworths, 1997), Chapter 8, Section 1, para.8.2)

Whether vaginal penetration is the highest form of sexual gratification shall be left a moot point, but it is clear that the act is required. Although sexual behaviour outside the relationship of two civil partners may well amount to penetrative vaginal heterosexual intercourse, this is not adultery because the very term 'adultery' implies the betrayal of marital sexual faithfulness, which no doubt has its roots in a husband's need to have certainty of parentage of his son and heir (although this may be considered redundant since the advent of DNA testing). Therefore copying the fact of adultery into the CPA 2004 was not an option. There was no need to replace it with some other definition as any sexual unfaithfulness could, if appropriate, be part of an application based on behaviour.

The fact of behaviour is often referred to as 'unreasonable behaviour' when it fact that is not the test. Rather the test is behaviour 'in such a way that the applicant cannot reasonably be expected to live with the respondent' (s.44(5)(a)). The reasonableness or otherwise therefore relates to the subsequent cohabitation, not the behaviour itself and behaviour which may be perfectly reasonable (at least in a certain context) may still suffice. The test therefore is semi-objective. The court has to look at the situation from the subjective point of view of the respondent and make an objective decision as to whether continuing cohabitation can reasonably be expected. No doubt in divorce cases district judges use their own preconceptions of what marital life entails and anecdotal evidence shows that mild behaviour petitions are rejected in some courts by some judges, while similar particulars of behaviour are routinely accepted by others. In the context of civil partnership, many judges will find themselves faced with the difficulty of being entirely ignorant of what life in a same-sex partnership involves. In marriage, there is at least a common law definition of marriage that can be used as a yardstick (see **1.3.3**). Civil partnership is a statutory creation with a total lack of definition of the nature of the relationship. It therefore sits uneasily with a semi-fault-based dissolution system. Will, for instance, sexual behaviour with a third party suffice for a behaviour petition if the respondent says that the relationship has been an open relationship from the outset and even before registration? Does it depend on the type of sexual act? In practice, the prohibitive costs of defending a dissolution application and the prospect of a trial in open court should make parties reluctant to litigate these points. However, if they are to be contested, judges will find themselves with nothing to go by.

Practitioners acting for applicants therefore have even more reason to advise their clients to instruct them to follow the Resolution Code of Practice and send a draft of the application to the respondent before issuing, with a view to agreeing the particulars and avoiding contested proceedings.

As in divorce, a respondent to an application based on five years' separation can apply to the court for the order not to be made final for reasons of financial hardship. This is unlikely now because pension sharing orders filled the last part of the jigsaw of financial orders available to the court, so that the respondent can be protected adequately in financial terms. Some cases are possible where assets are contingent or where the petitioner has an overseas pension scheme that cannot be the subject of a sharing order.

In applications based on two or five years' separation the respondent can apply for the finances to be considered before the order is made final. In practice this means that the same financial procedure is started as in any financial application (s.48(2) and FPR 1991, r.2.51A(1)(c)). Therefore, apart from delaying the final order, there is no practical implication of this provision.

4.3 NULLITY

4.3.1 Void civil partnerships

When a civil partnership is void there is no need for a court to make any order as there will never have been any civil partnership. Nevertheless one or both non-civil partners may want to apply to the court for a nullity order confirming that the civil partnership never existed in order to:

- prove this to third parties, e.g. for a future registration with a new partner; or
- apply for financial provision under Sched.5.

Although financial applications by fraudsters will be ill-fated (*Whiston* v. *Whiston* [1995] 2 FLR 268, CA), they are not excluded and in certain circumstances they will have merit either because there was a true relationship of cohabitation and the applicant or both parties were innocent (or both guilty, see *Rampal* v. *Rampal* (No.2) [2001] 2 FLR 1179, CA) or to restore property transferred in the belief that the civil partnership would be valid (see also **6.2.2**).

A civil partnership registration that took place in England or Wales will be void for the reasons set out in s.49 as well as for lack of the essential conditions for registration (see also **3.3**). The full list is:

- the partners are not of the same sex (ss.1(1), 3(1)(a) and 49(a));
- one of the partners was already married or a civil partner (ss.3(1)(b) and 49(a));
- one partner was under 16 at the time of registration (ss.3(1)(c) and 49(a));

- the partners are within the prohibited degrees of relationship (s.3(1)(d), Sched.1 and s.49(a));
- the appropriate notice had not been given (s.49(b)(i));
- the civil partnership document was not duly issued, i.e. the civil partnership schedule under s.14 or the Registrar General's licence for registration under the special procedure under s.25 (s.49(b)(ii));
- the registration took place once the civil partnership document had expired (s.49(b)(iii));
- the registration took place elsewhere than the place that was specified in the notice and the civil partnership document (s.49(b)(iv));
- the registrar was not present (s.49(b)(v)); if someone who is present acts as a registrar, the civil partnership is not void if that person was not designated as a civil partnership registrar by the registration authority (s.52(1)(b)) (it is not clear whether this person still needs to be a registrar, simply an employee of the local authority or could be any impostor and how this could be ascertained in retrospect);
- that the place of registration was not approved premises although it was purported to be approved premises (s.49(b)(vi));
- although a civil partnership is not void if there was no parental consent for a 16- or 17-year-old (s.52(1)(a)), it is void if the parent, etc. expressly forbade the civil partnership under Sched.2, para.6(5) (s.49(c)).

Civil partnership registrations that took place elsewhere than in England and Wales are void if they are void under the law of the country or territory where they are purported to have been registered. For overseas relationships they are also void if they are not an overseas relationship under Part 5, Chapter 2 (see **8.4**).

If a civil partnership would be void for reasons of formality under s.49(b) the Lord Chancellor may validate the civil partnership by order under s.53. This reflects a little-used law on marriage (Provisional Order (Marriages) Act 1905 and Marriages Validity (Provisional Orders) Act 1924).

4.3.2 Voidable civil partnerships

The grounds for declaring a civil partnership voidable are the same as for the annulment of a marriage, save that the grounds based on heterosexual intercourse have been left out; i.e. the grounds based on:

- non-consummation (MCA 1973, s.12(a) and (b); see also **4.1**); and
- venereal disease (MCA 1973, s.12(e)).

The latter is also a reflection of the fact that the partners can have a fulfilled sex life while practising safe sex, e.g. if one partner is HIV positive.

The grounds that are left from the MCA 1973, therefore, are:

- lack of consent (s.50(1)(a));
- mental disorder making a party 'unfitted for civil partnership' (s.50(1)(b));
- the respondent's pregnancy by someone else (s.50(1)(c); see also **5.4.4**).

In addition, as for annulment of marriage, there are the two new grounds linked to gender recognition (see also **5.4**):

- an interim gender recognition certificate has been issued (s.50(1)(d));
- the respondent changed gender and the applicant did not know this (s.50(1)(e) and s.51(6)).

There are rules in s.51 relating to the time of the application and the knowledge of the applicant in each case. If the civil partnership registration took place outside England and Wales, any application for annulment will be under the law governing the registration. However, in any case an application for annulment can be made if an interim gender recognition certificate has been issued.

In practice there is little difference between an annulment of a voidable civil partnership and divorce save that there will have to be a hearing in open court, except if there is an interim gender recognition certificate, when the nullity application can be dealt with under the special procedure (see FPR 1991, r.2.24(3), see also **5.4**). The civil partnership will be treated to have existed up to the final nullity order (s.37(3)) and all forms of financial relief are available.

4.4   OTHER APPLICATIONS

4.4.1   Separation orders

At first it seems odd that there should be provision for separation orders. Applications for judicial separation used to be made where there were significant widow's pensions that would be lost on divorce, and this has largely been superseded by pension sharing. People objecting to divorce (or to divorce on grounds other than certain ones that may not apply) may still prefer judicial separation to divorce. However, it is unlikely that this motivation would play a significant role for civil partners as there is no religious basis to civil partnership. In any event, while there is a common law duty on spouses to cohabit (albeit not enforceable) there is no such duty on civil partners (see **1.3.3**). There is no equivalent to the MCA 1973, s.18(1), which provides that a decree of judicial separation relieves the spouses from such a duty.

Nevertheless, judicial separation may still be necessary:

- if the relationship breaks down within the first year after the registration and the applicant wants to apply for a capital order rather than just ongoing maintenance; neither party can apply for dissolution within the first year (s.41); or

- for certain immigration reasons: it seems that despite a decree of judicial separation or a separation order a foreign national can still apply for naturalisation after only three years in the country instead of five years, making use of the shorter period for spouses and civil partners (see also **11.7**).

The procedure is the same as for dissolution applications save that the facts for dissolution become grounds for a separation order and there is only one order (rather than a conditional and final order).

4.4.2 Presumption-of-death orders

As in marriage (MCA 1973, s.19) a civil partner can apply for an order that the other civil partner is presumed dead if he or she has been absent for seven years and there is no reason to believe that he or she is still alive (CPA 2004, s.55).

4.4.3 Declarations of validity

Under s.58 a civil partner or purported civil partner can apply for a range of declarations about the validity of the civil partnership. This may be of particular importance if there is doubt about whether a foreign registered partnership is an overseas relationship under Part 5, Chapter 2. As the court cannot make an order declaring a civil partnership void on an application for a declaration of its validity (s.59(5)), the applicant needs to consider carefully which applications to make in the alternative in order to avoid later further applications (such as an application for nullity) in order to regularise the situation.

4.5 COMPARISON WITH THE LAW ON ENDING MARRIAGES

4.5.1 Procedural steps

Almost all the procedural steps necessary to bring a civil partnership to an end are identical to those for divorce, etc. These include the following.

1. Certificates about reconciliation for applications for dissolution and separation orders (CPA 2004, s.42 and FPR 1991, r.2.6(3)).
2. Statements of arrangements for children and the obligation on the court to consider whether it should make orders under the Children Act 1989 (CPA 2004, s.63 and FPR 1991, r.2.2(2), following MCA 1973, s.41). Note that the court has no jurisdiction to make any order in relation to the children if they are habitually resident elsewhere in the EU (other than Denmark) under EU Regulation 2201/2003 ('Brussels II').

3. The drafting of the petition (as an application for dissolution, etc. is called under the amended FPR 1991) is almost identical as for divorce (see FPR 1991, Appendix 2, as amended).

4. Curiously, where in a petition for divorce the petitioner must state whether the wife has had any children from another man, but no such information is required for the husband (for no apparent reason), for similarly no apparent reason FPR 1991 require this to be stated for both the applicant and the respondent in an application to end a civil partnership. This cannot be connected to the statement of arrangements and the duties of the court under the MCA 1973, s.41 and the CPA 2004, s.63 as all children of the family are listed separately. If the existence of a child is relevant for the wife's or civil partner's financial application, this can be stated elsewhere (on the Form E for example). This provision that nobody has thought to remove seems a leftover from sexist days or days when the legitimacy of a child was an issue.

5. The jurisdiction clause in para.3 of the petition is of course slightly different, reflecting the fact that Brussels II does not apply (see **8.5.1**).

6. There is a two-stage process of conditional and final orders corresponding to decrees nisi and decrees absolute with the same time limits for application, etc. (other than for separation orders).

7. No application for a dissolution can be made in the first year after the formation of the civil partnership. Overseas relationships that were registered before 5 December 2005 can be dissolved one year after they were registered overseas (ss.41 and art.3(1) of the Civil Partnership (Treatment of Overseas Relationships) Order 2005, SI 2005/3042; see also **8.4.3**)

8. As for marriage, only the parties to the civil partnership may apply for dissolution or annulment of a voidable civil partnership. One consequence of this is that after a civil partner has died the relatives cannot set aside the civil partnership for lack of consent, as this is a ground that makes a civil partnership voidable (s.50(1)(a)), not void. This means that the surviving civil partner may inherit free of inheritance tax under the intestacy rules if there is no new will. By contrast, if the civil partnership is void, relatives with a sufficient interest may apply for an appropriate order (see *Ray v. Sherwood and Ray* (1835) 1 Curt 193).

4.5.2 Courts

Not all family courts are designated 'civil partnership proceedings county courts' (FPR 1991, r.1.2 as amended). So far only the following courts have been so designated: Birmingham, Brighton, Bristol, Cardiff, Chester, Exeter, Leeds, Manchester and Newcastle (Civil Courts (Amendment) Order 2005,

SI 2005/2923) as well as the Principal Registry. This is of course a very short list, but at least in the first year of the life of the CPA 2004 few applications will be necessary. It is expected that the list will be extended in due course hand-in-hand with relevant judicial and staff training.

4.5.3 List of corresponding sections

Civil Partnership Act 2004	Existing legislation	Content
s.37		Orders that the court can make
s.37(1)		
s.37(2)	MCA 1973, s.1(5)	
s.37(3)	MCA 1973, s.16	
s.38	MCA 1973, s.1(5)	Period before applying for final orders orders
s.39	MCA 1973, s.8	Intervention of Queen's Proctor
s.40	MCA 1973, s.9	Respondent's application for final order
s.41	MCA 1973, s.3	One-year rule
s.42	MCA 1973, s.6	Reconciliation attempts
s.43	MCA 1973, s.7	Consideration of agreements
s.44	MCA 1973, s.1	Ground and facts for dissolution
s.45	MCA 1973, s.2	Reconciliation times for behaviour, etc.
s.46	MCA 1973, s.4	Dissolution application after separation order
s.47	MCA 1973, s.5	Hardship defence to five years' separation petition
s.48	MCA 1973, s.10	Financial considerations in separation cases
s.49	MCA 1973, s.11	Void civil partnerships
s.50	MCA 1973, s.12	Voidable civil partnerships
s.51	MCA 1973, s.13	Conditions on nullity applications
s.52	Marriage Act 1949, s.48(1)(b)	Exceptions to void marriages
s.53	Provision Order (Marriages) Act 1905 and Marriages Validity (Provisional Orders) Act 1924	Lord Chancellor can validate marriages by order

Civil Partnership Act 2004	Existing legislation	Content
s.54		Clarification of validity of civil partnerships registered outside England and Wales
s.55	MCA 1973, s.19	Presumption of death orders
s.56	MCA 1973, s.17	Separation orders
s.57	MCA 1973, s.18(2)	Consequences of separation order
s.58	Family Law Act 1986, s.55	Declarations of validity
s.59	Family Law Act 1986, s.58	Provisions about declarations
s.60	Family Law Act 1986, s.59	Attorney General's rule in declaration proceedings
s.61	Family Law Act 1986, s.60	More provisions about declarations
s.62	MCA 1973, s.20	Power to grant the respondent relief
s.63	MCA 1973, s.41	Orders affecting children (leading to Statements of Arrangement)
s.64	MCA 1973, s.49(4)–(5)	Joinder of parties

CHAPTER 5

Gender recognition

5.1 OVERVIEW

The previous two chapters have set out how people can get into and out of a civil partnership. There are special rules and special issues that arise if one of the partners is a trans person. Therefore this chapter gives a brief overview of the regime for gender recognition established by the Gender Recognition Act 2004 (GRA 2004) and how it interlinks with civil partnership.

Under the GRA 2004 regime, trans people can apply for a gender recognition certificate, which will make them legally a member of their acquired gender. If the birth was registered in the UK, the trans person will then be provided with a new birth certificate in that gender (GRA 2004, s.21).

Once the trans person has a gender recognition certificate, discrimination on grounds of acquired gender is sex discrimination. If a person does not have a gender recognition certificate, but 'intends to undergo, is undergoing or has undergone gender reassignment' discrimination against that individual because of this is sex discrimination only in the field of employment or vocational training. Discrimination in other areas on the grounds of transsexualism is not sex discrimination.

There are exemptions to the full recognition of the acquired gender in areas like the succession to peerages and competitive sports (GRA 2004, ss.16–20).

In particular, this chapter will:

- look at transsexualism and the terminology used (**5.2**);
- give an outline of the procedure to obtain a gender recognition certificate (**5.3**);
- set out the procedure where a trans person applying for gender recognition is in a civil partnership or married (**5.4**);
- briefly set out consequences for parentage (**5.4.4**); and
- provide points to note for practitioners (**5.5**).

It is important to look at the issue of gender recognition in the context of civil partnership (see **Bibliography**) because the Government has continued the strict line of not allowing same-sex marriage and therefore any trans person who is married and wants to have the acquired gender recognised must first end the marriage. The same applies for someone in a similar situation who is in a civil partnership, because otherwise by default there would be either opposite-sex civil partners or a same-sex marriage (see **5.4**).

Although some marriages and relationships will come to an end when one partner comes out as transsexual, others may not. Since one condition for acquiring a gender recognition certificate is that the applicant has lived in the acquired gender for two years, it is indeed possible and not uncommon that an individual may form a relationship in the acquired gender. In order to provide security for their partner or for themselves before the new gender can be legally recognised, individuals may decide to marry or form a civil partnership based on their original gender, depending on the situation.

Example 5.1

George and Jane have been married for 15 years. George eventually realises that he has gender dysphoria and tells Jane. They support each other through the process and decide that they want to stay together.

Example 5.2

Jack (a trans man, born Elizabeth) has lived in his acquired gender for one year when he meets Bill and they start a relationship. Jack is a high-level civil servant with a public sector pension scheme and wants to ensure that Bill would receive a dependant's pension should anything happen to Jack even before he is able to obtain his gender recognition certificate. They will be able to marry (as Jack is still legally a woman), but the marriage has to end before Jack can obtain a gender recognition certificate. They can subsequently register as civil partners.

The various permutations of these scenarios are fairly complicated, and ultimately they serve to highlight the problems that have resulted from the creation of civil partnership as a separate regime from marriage, as opposed to opening up marriage to same-sex couples.

5.2 TRANSSEXUALISM

5.2.1 Introduction

Most people are born with a gender identity that correlates to that normally attributed to a member of their birth sex. Whether or not they are attracted to their own or the opposite sex, or both, is another question. However, there are a small number of people who are born physically as one sex but identify as the other gender. This is called transsexualism or gender dysphoria and is a recognised medical condition. Treatment is often gender reassignment treatment, which in most cases includes hormone treatment, which will bring about some characteristics of the acquired gender. In many cases it also includes gender reassignment surgery. Although throughout this book we talk about 'same-sex' and 'opposite-sex' couples, in socio-psychological terms, the word 'sex' defines physical characteristics whereas 'gender' defines identity. Whether the two match, or whether they match with what is shown on the birth certificate, is an entirely different question.

Most transsexuals (or trans people) will have had hormone treatment and some degree of surgery. However, hormonal treatments carry some medical risks, and surgery is always extremely invasive and risky, so some trans people will not have had any or all of the available surgery. They may therefore still have the physical genitals of their former gender. The GRA 2004 recognises this and it is not a prerequisite of application for a gender recognition certificate for an applicant to have had hormone therapies or gender reassignment surgery (see **5.3.3**) although if the applicant has had some surgery to alter secondary sexual characteristics it will make the fast-track procedure more straightforward (see **5.3.4**).

Therefore it is possible for a trans woman to retain the sexual organs of a man. Although hormone treatment is likely to result in sterility, even hormone treatment is not legally necessary for a trans woman to acquire a gender recognition certificate. It is therefore possible for two women (one of them a trans woman) to procreate, and this does of course similarly apply to a trans man. Genital reconstruction for trans men is still very problematic and, even if undergone, rarely involves removal of the vagina. See also the grounds on which a civil partnership is voidable (**4.3.2**).

5.2.2 Glossary of terms

ftm	Female-to-male trans person.
gender	Masculine or feminine identity.
intersex	People who are born with a wide range of conditions that result in a variety of mixed male and female physical characteristics. As children, such individuals are often forced into one sex, determined by the doctors at birth, followed by 'corrective' surgery, which can lead to extreme problems in later life including gender dysphoria.
mtf	Male-to-female trans person.
sex	The physical characteristic of being male or female.
trans man	A female-to-male transsexual, also sometimes referred to as 'ftm'.
trans people	People who consistently feel that they want to live in the opposite gender.
trans woman	A male-to-female transsexual, also sometimes referred to as 'mtf'.

transgender	People living as the opposite sex.
transitioning	The process of acquiring a new gender. Apart from the psychological stress of having to adapt to an entirely new life, hormone treatment usually results in emotional upheaval similar to that experienced by teenagers in puberty, but condensed into a period of one to two years.
transsexual people	Trans people who have surgery, also the medical term for trans people.
transvestite or cross-dresser	Someone, whether lesbian, gay or heterosexual, who chooses to dress in clothes of the opposite sex, although usually with no desire to live permanently as the opposite sex.

5.3   PROCEDURE UNDER THE GENDER RECOGNITION ACT 2004

5.3.1   The three ways to apply

There are three procedures:

- standard applications (available since 4 October 2005);
- fast-track applications for applicants who have lived in their acquired gender for at least six years (only available from 4 April 2005 to 3 April 2007);
- overseas applications for applicants who have had their acquired gender legally recognised in prescribed foreign countries (available since 4 April 2005).

The dates when the GRA 2004 comes into force have been staggered in order to enable those applicants who have waited longest to apply first, while others can apply six months later. The fast-track procedure can also be somewhat simpler if the applicant has had surgery (see below **5.3.4**).

5.3.2   Which procedure?

For a flow chart depicting which procedure to choose see **figure 5.1**.

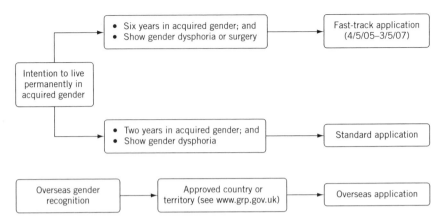

Figure 5.1   Different types of application

5.3.3   Standard application procedure

For further detail on the standard application procedure see **figure 5.2**.

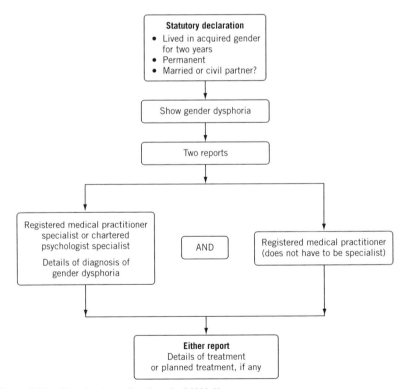

Figure 5.2   Standard application (s.1(1)(a))

5.3.4　Fast-track application procedure

For further detail on the fast-track application procedure see **figure 5.3**.

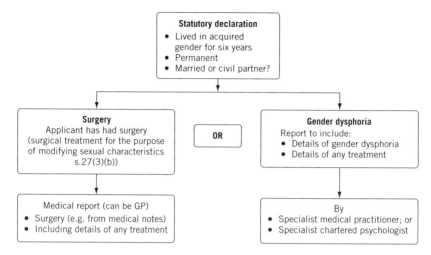

Figure 5.3　Fast-track application (s.27)

5.3.5　Overseas applications

Overseas gender changes are not recognised in UK law at all (GRA 2004, s.21(1)), nor are marriages or civil partnerships which trans people have entered into in their new gender (GRA 2004, s.21(2); CPA 2004, s.216(1)). This is questionable because issues in relation to status are generally governed by the law of the person's domicile under English conflict of law rules, for instance in relation to the question of whether a marriage is void for polygamy or lack of capacity, questions of paternity and so on. Therefore if a foreign domiciliary enters the UK with a birth certificate saying that she is a woman, English law should accept that and not apply substantive English law. So a trans woman recognised as such under the law of her domicile who has an accident while in England on holiday and is hospitalised should be treated by the hospital as a woman and her husband should be treated as her next-of-kin. The provisions in the GRA 2004 do not sit well with the general rules on private international law. In addition, EU citizens may have rights in relation to freedom of movement, bringing their spouse with them when they move to the UK and non-discrimination on grounds of nationality, which may make these rules inapplicable for EU citizens. The Gender Recognition Panel itself acknowledges in its guidance that 'the law in this area is unclear and complex' (Gender Recognition Panel *Guidance for Married People or those in Civil Partnerships*, updated May 2005, p.5).

If someone has married or registered an overseas relationship (see **Chapter 8**) abroad in their new gender, the marriage or overseas relationship will subsequently and retrospectively be recognised in the UK if that person obtains a gender recognition certificate in the UK and neither party has married or entered into a civil partnership with someone else in the meantime (CPA 2004, s.216; GRA 2004, s.21). This leaves those who come from countries where marriage is only available to opposite-sex couples in a legal limbo.

Example 5.3

Alexandre and Janine married in France. Alexandre is a trans man whose new gender was legally recognised in France before the marriage. When they come to the UK their marriage is not recognised because Alexandre is regarded as a woman and same-sex marriage is not an option in France. If and when Alexandre obtains a gender recognition certificate under the GRA 2004 the marriage will retrospectively be recognised.

Example 5.4

Alex (formerly Alexandra), a Belgian trans man whose new gender is recognised in Belgium, and James enter into a registered partnership ('legal cohabitation') in Belgium. Later they move to England. Their partnership is not recognised in England because Alex is still legally a woman under English law and English law does not recognise Belgian opposite-sex domestic partnership. When Alex applies for gender recognition in the UK, he will be treated as a single applicant and the domestic partnership will not need to be annulled or dissolved. With the granting of the gender recognition certificate, the Belgian domestic partnership is automatically recognised as a civil partnership in the UK retrospectively. If, however, either James or Alex had entered into a civil partnership, overseas relationship or marriage with a third person in the meantime, it would not be recognised (see also **8.4**). If Alex and James had simply married in Belgium, that marriage would not have been labelled 'opposite-sex' or 'same-sex' and so it would be recognised in England, but as an opposite-sex marriage. In that case, the marriage would need to be annulled for Alex to be granted a full gender recognition certificate.

The same principles apply to same-sex and opposite-sex couples coming from overseas where one partner is a trans person. Opposite-sex registered partnerships are of course not recognised in the UK. In some countries a marriage may survive one spouse's gender recognition and detailed advice on the relevant local law will be necessary.

The overseas application is the simplest. The applicant only needs to complete the application form and provide evidence of the change of gender overseas and a statutory declaration as to whether the applicant is married or in a civil partnership and any other prescribed information or evidence (GRA

2004, s.1(1)(b) and s.3(5) and (6)). The list of approved countries and territories is available on the Gender Recognition Panel's website (**www.grp.gov.uk**) and at the time of writing includes all EU countries except the Czech Republic, Hungary, Ireland and Lithuania. In addition it includes the following European countries that are not part of the EU: Bulgaria, Iceland, Moldova, Norway, the Russian Federation, Serbia and Montenegro, Switzerland, Turkey and the Ukraine. Outside Europe only Japan, New Zealand, South Africa and certain parts of Australia, Canada and the US are included.

5.4 GENDER RECOGNITION APPLICANTS WHO ARE MARRIED OR IN A CIVIL PARTNERSHIP

5.4.1 The conceptual problem

Marriage in English law is and remains an institution for two people of the opposite sex. Civil partnership is a statutory regime for two people of the same sex only. In order to prevent same-sex marriage or opposite-sex civil partnership an existing marriage or civil partnership is not allowed to survive the gender recognition. One solution would have been to convert the marriage to a civil partnership or the civil partnership into a marriage automatically on gender recognition. However, the Government decided against creating a way for a marriage to come into existence by operation of law.

5.4.2 The legal solution

Any applicant may be married or in a civil partnership at the time of the application. Of course the relationship may have broken down for any unrelated reason or for reasons to do with the gender dysphoria of one partner and the parties may decide to formalise the breakdown of the relationship. They are of course free to divorce or dissolve their civil partnership before the trans person lodges an application for gender recognition. However, it may not be possible in all cases to base a divorce on one of the five facts in the Matrimonial Causes Act 1973 (MCA 1973), s.1(2) or a dissolution on one of the four facts in CPA 2004, s.44(5), and it would be inequitable to force the trans person to postpone application for gender recognition for several years so that the couple could use the facts of two or five years' separation.

On the other hand, an applicant could be married or in a civil partnership at the time of the application and both partners might want the relationship to continue (see **5.1**). Divorce or dissolution is of course only possible if the relationship has irretrievably broken down. For this reason there is provision for the marriage or civil partnership to be voidable and terminated by nullity. There are also fast-track procedures for the couple subsequently to marry or register their civil partnership (see **figure 5.4** below). The new ground for nullity is that one partner (the applicant/petitioner or the respondent) has been granted an interim gender recognition certificate. Applicants for a gender recognition certificate who are married or in a civil partnership will in the first instance only be granted an interim gender recognition certificate. This then triggers the new ground for nullity (MCA 1973, s.12(g) and CPA 2004, s.50(1)(d) respectively; see also **4.3.2**). Of course nullity is also an option for couples who want to end their relationship and who either do not want to wait for two years' separation or wish to avoid the antagonistic option of a behaviour petition. Although nullity petitions generally require a full hearing in open court, there is provision for nullity petitions based on this ground to be dealt with under the special procedure (if the respondent does not defend the petition) and therefore no attendance at court is required (see FPR 1991, r.2.24(3)). Since there is no such thing as a voidable marriage or civil partnership in Scottish law, there is a separate fact for divorce or dissolution along similar lines (Divorce (Scotland) Act 1976, s.1(1)(b) and CPA 2004, s.117(2)(b)).

The system is designed to make the gap between the previous marriage and the subsequent civil partnership (or vice versa) as short as possible, and theoretically this could be less than a day. Of course if one partner died during that time, the other partner would not receive any dependant's pension linked to marriage or civil partnership, inheritance tax might be payable and the intestacy rules would not leave anything to the surviving partner. It is therefore advisable for such couples to make at least some basic provision by making wills immediately on granting of the full gender recognition certificate and nominating each other as dependants to their pension trustees, if possible. Such wills should be made with the express intent to survive the new marriage or registration of the new civil partnership (see **Chapter 13**).

The procedure provides that the court makes the gender recognition certificate final when it makes the decree of nullity of marriage absolute (or when it makes the order of nullity of civil partnership final) and the fast-track procedure for marriage or civil partnership registration means that this could all be done on the same day. On a practical level, this could potentially cause problems as in many courts it is not possible to predict exactly when the court staff will deal with an application for decree absolute, as this is done on paper. Although there is a target to deal with an application for decree absolute within five working days, many courts take longer and they may then take even longer to send the decree out. It is therefore advisable to talk to the court manager and request an appointment for the decree to be made absolute or the order to be made final so that the parties can collect the decree or order there and then. The appointment should preferably be early in the morning so that the couple can then re-register their relationship or marry on the same day.

Equally, the partners should make arrangements with the registrar so that any checks can be carried out in advance (although there is no provision for this) and an appointment should be made for the same day that the decree is made absolute or the order is made final. The parties can then give notice of their marriage or civil partnership and the registrar must then issue the superintendent registrar's certificate or civil partnership schedule. The registrar is, of course, under a duty to ensure that all the criteria for eligibility are met and it is not guaranteed that the parties to a previous marriage will be able to register as civil partners, for example if they married abroad and are too closely related to enter into a civil partnership under English law.

Example 5.5

Susanne (a trans woman) and Kristine married in Germany before Susanne's new gender was recognised and without applying for gender recognition in Germany subsequently. Kristine is Susanne's niece, a degree of relationship which does not exclude marriage in German law. They would not be able to register as civil partners after UK gender recognition as they fall within the prohibited degrees of relationship (Sched.1, para.1). If possible, Susanne should have her gender recognised in Germany, register there with Kristine as life partners (recognised as an overseas relationship under s.212 and Sched.20), then apply for gender recognition in the UK. The overseas relationship would then retrospectively be recognised as a civil partnership in accordance with s.216 (see **5.3.5** above).

A similar situation would arise if a foreign marriage was polygamous and recognised here. If a country had provision to convert an opposite-sex marriage into a same-sex marriage, any pre-recognition marriage that was so converted would not be recognised here. It is likely that in countries where no distinction is made between same-sex and opposite-sex marriage, no formal annulment or conversion would be required (see also **5.3.5** above).

There is no publicity or waiting period and the registration or marriage can follow immediately (see CPA 2004, Sched.3 and Marriage Act 1949, s.39A as inserted by the Civil Partnership Act 2004 (Overseas Relationships and Consequential, etc. Amendments) Order 2005, SI 2005/3129).

There are fairly short time limits between the various steps and if they are left to lapse, the partners will need to marry or register in the usual way.

If two trans people have married or registered a civil partnership in their previous gender, and then apply for gender recognition at the same time, they will still have to go through the procedure to end their marriage or civil partnership despite the fact that the conceptual issues described above in **5.4.1** would not arise.

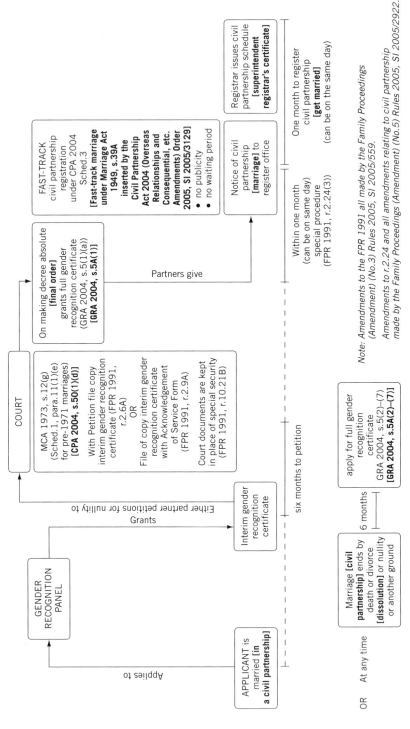

Figure 5.4 Procedure for married applicants [procedure for applicants in civil partnership]

5.4.3 Finances

Although those couples who want their relationship to continue and who take advantage of the fast-track marriage or registration procedure are unlikely to want to make claims for financial provision, all types of financial provision are available on nullity as they are on divorce. There is therefore no disadvantage to any couple if they formalise the end of their relationship in such a situation through nullity rather than divorce. Equally, for the question of substituting one's own contribution records of national insurance contributions with those of a former spouse or civil partner, there is no difference between the two. Thus, for instance, a wife who did not pay full national insurance contributions throughout her working life can be treated for her claim to a basic state pension as if she had her former husband's contribution record.

As far as the trans person is concerned any state pension (or other benefit) entitlement will be recalculated on the basis of the new gender. Since at the present time women can retire earlier than men (at the age of 60 rather than 65, although this will be phased out until 2010, see **9.2**) a trans man whose new gender is recognised between the age of 60 and 65 may lose his pension on gender recognition and it will only resume when he reaches 65. Conversely a trans woman aged between 60 and 65 will immediately be entitled to a pension (although this will not be backdated to age 60).

Wealthy couples where one partner has a large pension fund coming close to the £1.5m lifetime limit applicable since April 2006 may consider sharing this pension on nullity even if their relationship is to continue because this will then allow the partner with the large pension to start making further contributions into the scheme.

Example 5.6

Graham has various pension schemes with nominal values of £1.4m. He is 55 years old and plans to work for another 5 to 10 years and would like to contribute further into his pension schemes. He is in a relationship with Sandra, a trans woman, who has pension values totalling £60,000. They registered as civil partners before Sandra obtained her gender recognition certificate because Graham wants Sandra to inherit without having to pay inheritance tax and he also wants her to receive any death-in-service benefits from his pensions. Sandra is granted an interim gender recognition certificate and applies for nullity. She can include in her nullity petition a claim for pension sharing and Graham and Sandra could file a consent order providing for £500,000 to be transferred out of Graham's and into Sandra's pension. This will allow Graham to make further contributions of £600,000 into his pensions and claim this against tax. There should be no objection from the court or HMRC as it is a legitimate aim to equalise pension schemes and also it would provide protection for Sandra in the gap between the final order of nullity and the marriage.

69

5.4.4 Children

Paternity and maternity are not affected by gender recognition (GRA 2004, s.12). It is of course possible for a trans person to obtain a gender recognition certificate without having surgery or even hormone treatment. As such, it is possible for a trans man to bear children and for a trans woman to father children before or after gender recognition.

Maybe more likely, someone who is embarking on treatment may have sperm or eggs frozen for future use. If that person is then in a relationship with someone of the same (new) gender, this same-sex couple could have children together which are biologically theirs. A surrogate mother may be needed in the case of a trans man who had become sterile due to hormonal or surgical treatment.

This is why the words 'by some person other than the applicant' are in the ground for declaring a civil partnership voidable because at the time of formation the respondent was pregnant (s.50(1)(c)) (see **4.3.2**).

In the case of two women (one of whom is a trans woman) who use the trans partner's sperm for the other woman to conceive it should not be necessary to take any further legal steps to ensure that both partners are the legal parents of the child. However, some explanation may be required when the birth is registered. The status provisions under the Human Fertilisation and Embryology Act 1990 (HFEA 1990), ss.27–29 would not assist such a couple as they are of no assistance to any same-sex couple. At the time of writing the Department of Health has consulted on a revision of these provisions (see **7.4.1**). A similar situation would arise in the case of two men, one of whom is a trans man who is legally recognised and bears their child, who should appear on the birth certificate as the child's mother.

For an opposite-sex couple the HFEA 1990 would provide that after conception following treatment in a recognised clinic the female partner is the mother and the male partner is the father, wherever the gametes (egg or sperm) come from. Indeed, the consequence of s.27 would be that in a case where a wife or female partner of a trans man gives birth to a child conceived with donor sperm and the egg taken from the trans man before transition, the child would only have one mother, namely the woman. Her husband or male partner would be the father under HFEA 1990, s.28 provided that the treatment was carried out in a licensed clinic and all the other conditions of s.28 are met.

5.5 POINTS TO NOTE FOR PRACTITIONERS

The Gender Recognition Act 2004 tries to provide for maximum confidentiality regarding the gender change. This is in contrast to the total lack of confidentiality in connection with the registration of civil partnerships (see

3.2.1). It is therefore an offence for certain people to disclose this information and this includes legal practitioners because they have acquired the information 'in the course of, or otherwise in connection with, ... the supply of professional services' (GRA 2004, s.22(3)(c)). There are exemptions listed in GRA 2004, s.22(4) including disclosure pursuant to a court order or an application to the court and further exemptions may be added by statutory instrument. The maximum penalty is a fine of level 5 on the standard scale (GRA 2004, s.22(8), currently £5,000). This confidentiality duty may go beyond that of solicitors' duty of confidentiality to their own clients as it can relate to non-clients. In any case where a solicitor considers disclosure, the solicitor should check carefully that it falls within the exemptions or that the express consent of the transsexual person has been obtained.

Court documents on a petition for nullity on the basis of an interim gender recognition certificate are similarly kept in a place of special security (FPR 1991, r.10.21B). In contrast to these provisions a trans person must tell any prospective civil partner or fiancé(e) about the gender recognition or risk having the marriage or civil partnership annulled (MCA 1973, s.12(h); CPA 2004, s.50(1)(e)).

As with all areas of advice of a personal and intimate nature, and especially if a practitioner has no personal knowledge of the subject, it is advisable to obtain information about transsexualism and gender recognition before taking on any client who seeks advice in this area. Language can be offensive if used wrongly and practitioners should also be careful here (see **5.2**). It is better to listen and ask than to make assumptions.

CHAPTER 6

Financial provision between civil partners

6.1 INTRODUCTION

The law that governs financial claims between civil partners is essentially the same as that for spouses. Everything has been conveniently pulled together in one Act of Parliament. However, the structure and arrangement of the sections and paragraphs is not the same and it may be difficult to find the corresponding provisions. The law on financial claims between spouses is almost exclusively statutory. Where a statute says one thing for spouses and there are mirror provisions saying the same for civil partners, this should, on the face of it, have exactly the same effect. However, the main provisions for financial relief between spouses are of course discretionary and judges hearing a case have wide powers concerning the orders they can make. Only in limited circumstances can an order be appealed.

> . . . any appeal from a decision of a district judge in ancillary relief shall only be allowed by the circuit judge if it is demonstrated that there has been some procedural irregularity or that in conducting the necessary balancing exercise the district judge has taken into account matters which were irrelevant, or ignored matters which were relevant, or has otherwise arrived at a conclusion that is plainly wrong.
>
> (*Cordle* v. *Cordle* [2002] 1 FLR 207, CA at [32])

Therefore, although reported cases on, say, the application of the discretion under the Matrimonial Causes Act 1973 (MCA 1973), s.25 will give guidance, they are not strict precedent and each case must be decided on its individual facts and circumstances. Underlying the statutory provisions is a common law concept of marriage (see **1.3.3**) and the perceptions, traditions and statistics we have about marriage in twenty-first century Britain. There is, of course, neither such common law concept of civil partnership, nor any history of civil partnership that could provide guidance about the nature of the relationship of the parties.

This chapter will discuss the following areas.

- Claims akin to the Matrimonial Proceedings and Property Act 1970, s.37 and the Married Women's Property Act 1882, s.17 and related provisions

(**6.2**). These are mainly based on declaratory relief, but also include the powers to make orders for sale and give one partner an interest in a property as a result of contributions (even if there is no equitable interest under trust law).

- Discretionary claims in the High Court and county courts under Sched.5, in magistrates' courts under Sched.6 and after overseas dissolution under Sched.7 (**6.3**).
- The circumstances a court must take into account and how they may apply to civil partners (**6.4**). This looks in detail into the factors listed in the statute as well as various other factors and circumstances that are not listed.
- Finally there is brief mention of applications under the Inheritance (Provision for Family and Dependants) Act 1975 (**6.5**) and considerations for financial applications on divorce (**6.6**).

6.2 DECLARATORY RELIEF

The provisions for declaratory relief are all found in the body of the CPA 2004 itself, namely ss.65–70 (in Chapter 3 of Part 2) and 73–74 (Chapter 4 of Part 2: Civil Partnership Agreements). These mirror the provisions for spouses.

CPA 2004	Equivalent provision for marriage
s.65	Matrimonial Proceedings and Property Act 1970, s.37
s.66	Married Women's Property Act 1882, s.17
s.67	Matrimonial Causes (Property and Maintenance) Act 1958, s.7
s.68	Matrimonial Proceedings and Property Act 1970, s.39
s.69	Law Reform (Husband and Wife) Act 1962, s.1(2)
s.70	Married Women's Property Act 1882, s.11
s.73	Law Reform (Miscellaneous Provisions Act) 1970, s.1
s.74	Law Reform (Miscellaneous Provisions Act) 1970, ss.2–3

6.2.1 Civil partners and former civil partners

Section 65 provides that a civil partner who contributes money or money's worth to the property of the other civil partner will acquire an interest in that property. This goes beyond the ability to acquire a beneficial interest under trust law and under the doctrine of proprietory estoppel because no express or implied agreement or understanding by the owner or reliance on a mistake or similar is necessary.

Under s.66 the court has power to make declarations as to ownership of property and shares in property and make orders for sale or to postpone a sale or for a transfer of the property. Section 67 extends this to property that the other civil partner no longer has in his or her possession or under his or her control, and a lump-sum order can be made instead. Section 68 allows former civil partners to make applications under s.66 for three years after dissolution or annulment, and s.69 allows the court to stay tort proceedings between civil partners in certain circumstances.

Since the court's powers under Sched.5 are wider, there will in most cases be no point in making applications under these sections, and the corresponding provisions for spouses are also rarely used. There are, however, a number of situations where they may prove to be useful or essential, including the following.

1. The partners do not want the civil partnership to be dissolved for whatever reasons (an alternative here may be a separation order with financial provision ancillary to it).
2. None of the facts apply to prove irretrievable breakdown and a financial order is necessary before five years' separation; the facts are the same for separation orders so that this is not an alternative.
3. After a dissolution and without making an application for financial provision a civil partner has entered into a new civil partnership or has married and is therefore unable to make an application for financial provision under Sched.5.
4. There is a risk of bankruptcy or a third party creditor is trying to enforce a court order or similar against one civil partner's property; it can then help to have an order declaring the other partner's interest in such property to protect it from the bankruptcy or enforcement proceedings.
5. An order for sale is required before the end of the financial proceedings under Sched.5.
6. There are or have been dissolution proceedings abroad and therefore an application under Sched.5 is not possible. In contrast to an application under Sched.7, permission from the court is not necessary for an application under s.66.

Section 70 is drafted entirely at odds with the rest of the Chapter in that it refers to and incorporates the provisions of the Married Women's Property Act 1882, s.11, to provide for life assurance policies in favour of the other civil partner or any of the civil partners' children to pay to the beneficiaries rather than into the deceased's estate.

6.2.2 Prospective civil partners

Chapter 4 is headed 'civil partnership agreements', which are defined in s.73(3) and correspond to engagements to marry. The term chosen is misleading and in particular it should not be confused with the equivalent of pre-nuptial agreements or other agreements about finances (see **6.4.10** below). There is no provision in the definition in s.73(3) that the partner had to have capacity to enter into a civil partnership. This follows case law on engagements, which can be entered into even if one party was still married at the time (*Shaw* v. *Fitzgerald* [1992] 1 FLR 357). There could of course be an issue about whether an agreement to enter into a registered relationship overseas met the criteria of an overseas relationship under s.73(3)(b) and ss.212 and 214 (see **8.4**) and some local regimes may cause particular difficulty. On the domestic side, an informal blessing ceremony, for example, by Manchester City Council, or a religious institution, would not be enough, unless it was part of an agreement to enter into a civil partnership or overseas relationship. Agreements before the CPA 2004 came into force are covered (s.73(4)). An interesting point would be a case where a couple agreed to enter into a UK civil partnership many years before the Act came into force in 2005. Certainly since 18 November 2004, when the Act received Royal Assent, a couple should have been able to enter into an agreement to register as civil partners when the CPA 2004 eventually came into force (even if that day was as yet uncertain). However, the situation would be more uncertain if such an agreement had been made during the time when the Bill was before Parliament, or even earlier, during the period after the Government had announced that it intended to introduce civil partnership but before the legislation was drafted. If the agreement to enter into a civil partnership survived until after Royal Assent, however, this should suffice because no action or point is necessary and an enduring intention which was perhaps uncertain beforehand then became certain. Thus a real issue would only arise if parties had agreed to register when the planned new law came into force but then broke off the agreement, both before 18 November 2004. There is a three-year limitation period, however, so any such claim would need to be brought by 17 November 2007 at the latest (s.74(4)).

Discretionary relief under Scheds.5, 6 or 7 is of course not available to those who have not registered as civil partners. However, there should be the option for those who went through some sort of ceremony that did in the end not turn out to be a civil partnership or overseas relationship to make an application for nullity on the ground that the civil partnership is void (s.49), which would then allow them to apply under Sched.5. Provided that neither party was deceptive or in any other way blameworthy, there is no reason in principle why the financial relief should be different from that available on a dissolution (see *Rampal* v. *Rampal (No.2)* [2001] 1 FLR 1179, CA, see **4.3.1** for void civil partnerships). In that case a man of Indian origin who had

75

married while on a stay in India subsequently went through a marriage ceremony with another woman, his partner, in England. The court found that both parties had known that the man had been married at the time of the English marriage ceremony. The Court of Appeal held that statute provided that the court would need to take into account all the circumstances of the case and that the man's bigamy was no bar to financial relief, which was expressly provided for under the MCA 1973. In the case of a registration where both parties innocently believed or maybe even hoped that it would be valid, the case for financial provision must be even stronger. In practice this means that even if two partners went through, say, a wedding ceremony in San Francisco at the time when the local mayor allowed this (a decision which was subsequently overturned by the courts), financial relief should be possible – provided of course they are able to come within the ambit of the English court's jurisdiction.

The provisions for prospective civil partners and those who break off a civil partnership agreement are almost the same as for fiancé(e)s and those who break off engagements. Section 73 provides that such agreements are not enforceable as contracts in English law. Section 74 allows those who had agreed to a civil partnership to use ss.65–67 if the agreement breaks down. The reference to s.65 allows the extra option of claiming an interest in the other's property to which the civil partners contributed money or money's worth without having to show an implied, constructive or resulting trust or a claim under proprietory estoppel. This may make a claim much cheaper and easier, and is not something available to cohabitants in general. It is therefore important to ask clients who only cohabited whether they had previously agreed to register as civil partners. Section 74(5) provides that even the party who ends the agreement can ask for the return of any gifts made expressly or impliedly on condition that they be returned if the agreement is broken off. The corresponding provision for engagements in the Law Reform (Miscellaneous Provisions Act) 1970, s.3(2) reads on to create a rebuttable presumption that the gift of an engagement ring is an absolute gift. There is no corresponding provision for prospective civil partners. No doubt this has been omitted from the CPA 2004 because a ring is a religious symbol (see **1.3.2**) and not because of any cruelty or heartlessness. If any gift was made, the question of whether it was conditional or not is therefore a question of fact and needs to be proved on a balance of probabilities without any presumptions.

6.3　DISCRETIONARY CLAIMS

6.3.1　Financial provision arising from the end of the civil partnership

Each Schedule (5, 6 and 7) to the CPA 2004 follows the relevant legislation for marriage. While s.72 expressly states that Scheds.5 and 6 correspond to Part 2 of the MCA 1973 and the Domestic Proceedings and Magistrates' Court Act 1978 respectively, it is unclear why it does not also state that Sched.7 corresponds to Part 3 of the Matrimonial and Family Proceedings Act 1984. The main difference from matrimonial statutes in all three Schedules is the order of the sections or paragraphs. In particular, Sched.5 is quite different from Part 2 of the MCA 1973, on which it is based. Some terminology is slightly different, but this is probably merely due to the style of the individual drafter. Thus do not expect that 'sale of property orders' (heading of Part 3 of Sched.5) means that the court fee will be discounted. Such an order has been cleverly defined as 'a sale of property order under this Part' (para.10(2)), but is probably the same as an order for sale of property under MCA 1973, s.24A.

In the same way as the corresponding statutory provisions for marriage and divorce, Scheds.5 (paras.20–22), 6 (paras.4–6) and 7 (para.10) provide that the court must take into account all the circumstances of the case and then go on to list a number of factors, which are familiar from MCA 1973, s.25. This is in contrast to most other jurisdictions, certainly in the civil law countries, where statute prescribes a formula of capital division, usually based on an equal division, but with varying rules on which assets form part of the matrimonial assets that are to be divided equally. By going down this route in the MCA 1973, Parliament has left an enormous discretion to each individual judge. It has also left both parties and practitioners with a great deal of uncertainly as to what exactly the court will do at a final hearing. Even the factors themselves are very broad, and essentially all that the statute says is that the court takes everything into account and makes a fair order. How a judge weighs each of the factors is largely dependent on the individual judge's understanding of what marriage is about in twenty-first century Britain including:

- the common law definition of marriage (see **1.3.3**);
- the concept of marriage in modern British society;
- the recent addition to domestic law of the Human Rights Act 1998;
- the recent case law of the House of Lords, in particular in the case of *White* v. *White* [2000] 2 FLR 981 reminding the courts of the need not to discriminate on grounds of sex and indirectly on the issue of whether contributions were made to the family by way of homemaking or breadwinning and Lord Nicholls's yardstick of equality; and
- each judge's own experiences and perceptions of marriage.

No doubt if a copy of the MCA 1973, a copy of the resolution consent order precedents and a copy of the submissions often prepared by advocates for a financial dispute resolution hearing for an individual case were sent to judges in other countries with a request to draft an order, the results would differ widely. This leaves those who need to advise civil partners with a problem, because out of the points listed above, only the third and perhaps the fourth points will apply to civil partnership because:

- there is no common law concept of civil partnership and no substantive definition in the statute (see **1.3.3**); civil partnership is defined only via the registration procedure and not as to the quality of the relationship;
- there is (at least as yet) no general concept of civil partnership in British society; and
- finally, one would hope that judges' own experiences and perceptions about same-sex relationships or perhaps even any personal prejudices against them will not be determinative in the decision making.

If it is right that all these sources fall away, the courts and advisers will be left only with the words of the statute, the Human Rights Act 1998 and concepts of equality and fairness. Deciding how the factors should be weighed must therefore be a question of looking closely at the circumstances of each individual case, perhaps more so than is currently done for marriage.

In dealing with financial cases on divorce, judges as well as lawyers frequently cling to the factors listed in MCA 1973, s.25. However, as Coleridge J in *CO* v. *CO (Ancillary Relief: Pre-Marriage Cohabitation)* [2004] 1 FLR 1095 reminds us in the context of the question of how to weigh a lengthy period of cohabitation before the wedding:

> [41] Section 25 was and is intended to be all-inclusive. But the specific factors set out in the subsections (drafted over three decades and more than a generation ago) are not an exhaustive list nor ever intended to be so. They are no more than an aide memoire or checklist of the more obvious factors to be found in every case. Sometimes there is a factor or factors, a circumstance of the case, which does not fall within the list but which is every bit as important as any that does. . . .

> [46] Section 25 is concerned with taking into account the reality of a couple's circumstances and situation during their relationship. It is concerned with establishing fact not fiction in all areas including the financial. To ignore such a factor as cohabitation would lead the court to be considering the case on an untrue basis and almost inevitably lead to unfairness.

Although the checklist for civil partnership (in Sched.5, para.21) is the same as for marriage (in MCA 1973, s.25), it is possible and indeed likely that a number of factors that are not usually relevant for spouses will be found to be highly relevant for civil partners. If these were not thought of by Parliament in 1973 they therefore would not have been included in the MCA 1973. Therefore other factors can and must be taken into account.

Some district judges are said to have expressed the view that *White* equality yardsticks do not apply to civil partnership because when both parties are of the same sex, sex discrimination does not come into it. This would only be relevant if one started from a point of favouring the breadwinner over the homemaker. In *White* v. *White* [2000] 2 FLR 981, Lord Nicholls of Birkenhead said (at 989):

But there is one principle of universal application which can be stated with confidence. In seeking to achieve a fair outcome, there is no place for discrimination between husband and wife and their respective roles. Typically, a husband and wife share the activities of earning money, running their home and caring for their children. Traditionally, the husband earned the money, and the wife looked after the home and the children. This traditional division of labour is no longer the order of the day. Frequently both parents work. Sometimes it is the wife who is the money-earner, and the husband runs the home and cares for the children during the day. But whatever the division of labour chosen by the husband and wife, or forced upon them by circumstances, fairness requires that this should not prejudice or advantage either party when considering para (f), relating to the parties' contributions. This is implicit in the very language of para (f): '. . . the contribution which each has made or is likely . . . to make to the welfare of the family, including any contribution by looking after the home or caring for the family'. If, in their different spheres, each contributed equally to the family, then in principle it matters not which of them earned the money and built up the assets. There should be no bias in favour of the money-earner and against the home-maker and the child-carer.

It is clearly wrong to assume that this only applies to opposite-sex couples because:

- it would introduce new discrimination, namely on the ground of sexual orientation, which the courts are almost certainly prohibited from exercising under the Human Rights Act 1998 (and Art.14 of the European Convention on Human Rights, see *Ghaidan* v. *Godin-Mendoza* [2004] 2 AC 557; **1.2.1** and **10.8.2**); and
- the statute itself says that 'contributions by looking after the home or caring for the family' are to be taken into account as a contribution towards the welfare of the family.

Being bound by the Human Rights Act 1998 and principles of equality and non-discrimination, a judge cannot, for example, say that the fact that the relationship was a gay relationship means that provision made to the financially weaker party should be less than it would be in a marriage context. In particular, the fact that a civil partnership will probably not have been contracted in a church does not mean that it can be looked at in a different way – in the same way that a Muslim or Atheist wife should not receive less provision than a Christian wife. Nevertheless, different cultural backgrounds in, say, the Muslim marriage as well as different lifestyles by civil partners must be taken into account without, however, any element of discrimination. Judges and lawyers may find this a hard exercise to undertake.

While no doubt many same-sex couples lead their relationship and their lives in exactly the same way as their heterosexual neighbours, a significant number do not. Instead, they may for a variety of reasons lead their lives in unconventional ways, both in the way that they view their relationship as well as in the choices they make in their life. This may be because their relationship has been or is to remain private and to some degree secret, or because they have made a conscious decision not to lead their lives in the same way that a heterosexual couple might be expected to do.

In the international context there are a large number of, mainly statutory, same-sex partnership regimes around the world. While marriage is a fairly universal concept, however, the partnership regimes differ widely (see **8.4.1**). Some regimes may for example not have any rules on sharing capital on dissolution of the partnership and the parties would simply walk away with whatever happened to be in their name at that time; others have very limited ways of claiming maintenance. In such situations the only way for provision may be an application under Sched.7 for financial provision after overseas dissolution and advisers must consider whether this is an option in the individual case. It is therefore likely that, in relative terms, there will be more applications made under Sched.7 than there are under Part 3 of the Matrimonial and Family Proceedings Act 1984.

6.3.2   Financial provision for children

As in financial applications ancillary to divorce, in financial applications ancillary to dissolution of a civil partnership under Scheds.5 (para.20), 6 (para.4) and 7 (para.10(2)) the court must give first consideration to the welfare of any minor child of the family. At first glance, it may not appear to be obvious that children are a significant factor in civil partnerships, but more and more same-sex couples are bringing up children (see **7.1**). Where there are children, they will play a significant part in the court's decision making. If children are jointly adopted (or are joint biological children, see **5.4.4**), child maintenance is of course governed by the Child Support Act 1991. All other children can be 'children of the family' in the same way as they are in the context of marriage (Sched.5, para.80(2), Sched.6, para.48 and Sched.7, para.1(4)). This includes stepchildren from a previous relationship, children naturally born into the relationship after donor insemination where there is no other parent, and children born after a private co-parenting or donor arrangement (see **7.1**).

The definition of 'parent' in the Children Act 1989 (CA 1989), Sched.1, para.16(2) has been amended by CPA 2004, s.78(4) to include civil partners in relation to whom the child concerned is a child of the family. Therefore financial applications under CA 1989, Sched.1 are possible against a same-sex step-parent, but only if he or she was the civil partner of one of the parents. This does not only allow periodical payments for a child's maintenance, but also lump-sum payments, settlements of property or transfers of property during the child's minority (para.1(2)). So, for example, the other parent may be ordered to pay a lump sum to cover one-off expenses for furniture, white goods or a car, or to finance the purchase of a home, or to transfer a home on trust for the child until the child has reached majority, when the property (or the parent's share) will revert to the parent from whom it came. The options to apply for financial provision for children are therefore:

- child is child of both same-sex partners (natural or adopted): CA 1989, Sched.1;
- same-sex partners are civil partners: CPA 2004, Scheds.5, 6 or 7 and CA 1989, Sched.1;
- same-sex partners are cohabitants and not civil partners and child is not the child of the other parent: none, unless the child is living with the non-biological parent under a residence order, in which case CA 1989, Sched.1 applies.

At first glance CA 1989, Sched.1 seems superfluous in the case of civil partners. However, as with spouses it can be useful in a number of scenarios, such as:

1. A final financial order ancillary to dissolution with a (capital) clean break was made on the basis that the child should live with one parent but the child then lives with the other parent, for example because the child 'votes with their feet'.
2. Circumstances change and financial provision is needed after a capital clean break, for example if the child has an accident and becomes disabled or if the circumstances of the parent with whom the child lives changes.
3. A final order was made abroad without adequate provision. The CA 1989, Sched.1 does not require permission to bring the application, in contrast to CPA 2004, Sched.7
4. Proceedings for dissolution are pending in another jurisdiction and for some reason there is no interim maintenance order.
5. No dissolution or separation proceedings are contemplated or appropriate.

Therefore an application under CA 1989, Sched.1 can be a useful alternative and sometimes the only way to ensure adequate financial provision.

6.4 FACTORS THAT THE COURT TAKES INTO ACCOUNT

6.4.1 Resources

As under MCA 1973, s.25, the parties' financial resources are one of the factors listed in CPA 2004, Sched.5, para.21:

21(2)(a) the income, earning capacity, property and other financial resources which each civil partner

(i) has, or
(ii) is likely to have in the foreseeable future,

including, in the case of earning capacity, any increase in that capacity which it would in the opinion of the court be reasonable to expect a civil partner in the civil partnership to take steps to acquire; . . .

This is probably one of the most straightforward points as this is mainly a question of disclosure. The uncertain part is the addendum of 'any increase in [the earning] capacity which it would in the opinion of the court be reasonable to expect a civil partner in the civil partnership to take steps to acquire'. Apart from the painful tautology, this raises the issue of when a partner who may have not worked for years can be expected to go back to work. After long marriages in which, say, the wife has never worked, her earning capacity is often set at nil with the argument that she has been out of the labour market for so long that it would not be reasonable to expect her to work, especially when the husband is a high earner. There is no reason why the same principle should not apply after a long civil partnership (or a long relationship followed by civil partnership, see **6.4.5** below) where one has been the breadwinner and the other the homemaker. However, especially in cases where there are no children, this situation is not always perceived as having been brought about by agreement. The working partner may say that the other partner was lazy and refused to work and that the only alternative would have been to break the relationship at a much earlier stage or go along with it. This is therefore likely to be a cause of contention.

A further issue under this heading is likely where one partner brings capital into the relationship. That partner may, for example, have children from a previous relationship, and may wish them to inherit the capital in due course. If the relationship breaks down, the partner may fight very hard to preserve the capital earmarked for the children. This is different from the situation found in most marriages, where the children are joint children of the divorcing couple.

6.4.2 Needs

21(2)(b) the financial needs, obligations and responsibilities which each civil partner has or is likely to have in the foreseeable future;

The parties' needs are in most cases of course highly dependent on the couples' standard of living. While it may be reasonable for a wife (or husband) of a high earner to spend £200 per week on cut flowers or £275 a day on hairdressing, for many people, this may be sufficient for them to feed themselves for a month. Often the length of a marriage will determine whether a spouse is 'fully entitled', including that the spouse will be allowed to maintain their standard of living without being required to change their life and start working. In the civil partnership context, this again may depend on what is considered as the length of the civil partnership (see **6.4.5**).

While it is almost universal that spouses cohabit, and indeed there is a common law duty (if not in reality then at least in theory, see **1.3.3** and MCA 1973, s.18(2)), this may not be the case in all civil partnerships, especially where partners may have met later in life and have different lifestyles. Therefore, while on divorce housing needs are in many cases the main or a very important consideration, this may not be the same for civil partnership.

Example 6.1

Geoffrey and Robert have been in a relationship for 20 years and civil partners for four years. Geoffrey works in the City of London and lives in a loft apartment near Tower Bridge worth £750,000. Robert is a deputy head teacher of a secondary school and lives in Hastings in a three bedroom semi-detached house with garden and sea views in a good area worth £250,000. They spend the weekends either at the seaside or in London (if they visit friends or have guests or see a show). This is the way that they have always lived their relationship, as Geoffrey did not want to commute for two hours every day and Robert would not think of teaching in London. The court would need to ask whether an adjustment in the capital to provide each man with the same fund for housing is appropriate when Robert does not really need extra funds.

Other couples may not have lived together because they wanted to keep their relationship secret from society at large for fear of discrimination or persecution. It is to be hoped that this will be a less frequent occurrence now and in the future than it has been in the past.

6.4.3 Standard of living

The standard of living of the family is addressed in para.21:

> 21(2)(c) the standard of living enjoyed by the family before the breakdown of the civil partnership;

While some couples, especially those with no children, may have a high disposable income and a high standard of living, others may not. There is likely to be a world of difference in the standard of living between, say, two gay men who are both working full-time in professional jobs and have no children, and two lesbians who each have children from previous relationships and where only one is working in a semi-skilled job after many years of looking after children and the other is a full-time mother. Of course the gender example may be reversed.

A further complication may be that spending priorities are different from what one would maybe expect in the population in general. So although there may be high income, this may all have been spent on holidays or a hobby or entertainment. Especially in cases where there are no children, the parties have much more freedom to choose what their income should be spent on.

6.4.4 Age

> 21(2)(d) the age of each civil partner . . .

From anecdotal evidence, at least, there seem to be a higher number of same-sex couples, particularly gay men, with a large age difference between them. A 'biological clock' that may make heterosexuals choose a partner of a similar age in order to procreate is of course not a consideration for most same-sex couples, and of course there may also be other reasons. In such cases, issues like provision for old age, pension sharing, career development and so on will need to be looked at in detail and the particular circumstances will need careful consideration. Importantly, most pension schemes provide a less generous survivor's pension if the age difference is greater than a prescribed number of years.

6.4.5 Duration

> 21(2)(d) . . . and the duration of the civil partnership;

The duration of a civil partnership should be something that is easily ascertainable. In cases of an overseas relationship under s.212 that was registered before 5 December 2005, art.3(3)–(4) of the Civil Partnership (Treatment of Overseas Relationships) Order 2005, SI 3042/2005, provides that the duration for the purposes of Scheds.5, 6 and 7 is the duration of the overseas relationship (see also **8.4.3**).

Until 5 December 2005 there was, of course, no form of registration for same-sex partners available in the UK. Nevertheless civil partners may have been a couple for many years or decades before registration, especially if this was before 2005. The question is then how the court should weigh this factor. Following *CO* v. *CO (Ancillary Relief: Pre-Marriage Cohabitation)* [2004] 1 FLR 1095 (see **6.3.1** above) the court must take into account the reality of the relationship and should consider the period of pre-registration cohabitation as a major factor. There may be other reasons for a long pre-registration cohabitation in the case of same-sex partners, including reluctance to make the relationship public for fear of adverse reaction from others (see **3.2.1**), or the lack of the pressure to marry often found when an opposite-sex couple decides to have children. Some couples may not live together at all, or not for a long time into their relationship, maybe to keep their relationship secret in order to avoid prejudice and for fear of persecution. Nevertheless, a long stable relationship is a significant factor that the court should take into account.

Even when the length of the relationship is ascertained, this is of course only the first step in weighing this factor. The second step is often to categorise the marriage as a long, medium and short marriage, although there are no guidelines in statute on how that is to be done. Arguably, a medium marriage will have lasted a similar length of time as the average marriage, a long marriage is one that is significantly longer, and a short marriage one that is significantly shorter. The average length of marriages ending in divorce is published from time to time by the Office for National Statistics and has been between 9 and 12 years ever since statistics have been available since 1963 (*Divorces: 1957–2002, (Numbers) Duration of Marriage at Divorce by Age of Wife at Marriage*, Office for National Statistics, published on **www.statistics.gov.uk**). However, civil partnerships are, of course, an entirely new concept and no equivalent statistics currently exist, nor are they likely to exist (for want of a large enough sample, no doubt) for some time to come. It seems likely that in the meantime courts will simply use the yardstick of marriage. Whether that is the correct approach is, at the very least, doubtful. It will only become apparent in years to come whether the average length of civil partnerships before ending in dissolution is the same as that for marriage.

6.4.6 Disability

21(2)(e)   any physical or mental disability of either of the civil partners;

Although disability seems an obvious factor, an important and difficult consideration in the case of gay men will be how to regard HIV. A large number of people, including gay men, live with HIV, often on combination therapy, without developing AIDS-related disease. There is therefore the question of whether HIV infection of one partner should make any difference at all. While combination therapy has been widely available for about the last decade, there is no information by the very nature of it about the long-term success or effects of it. The drugs are strong drugs and have short-term and long-term side-effects. The latter include fat loss or accumulation, high blood lipids, liver problems, diabetes and insulin resistance and peripheral neuropathy (nerve damage). These alone may therefore lead to a person with HIV becoming unable to work, or needing extra care, or having additional financial needs, including for private medical treatment. In addition, HIV strains that are drug-resistant can develop and so the long-term stability of the HIV status cannot be taken for granted. Researchers found that 14 per cent of newly infected patients were resistant to at least one drug class (*HIV Drug Resistance High in the UK*, Medical Research Council, 20 February 2006, available on the Medical Research Council's website, **www.mrc.ac.uk**).

In cases where one partner lives with HIV, the situation and the future development of the infection must therefore be carefully considered and it must be kept in mind that a situation that appears to be stable may not in fact be so. At the same time, HIV is still a delicate subject that some people who live with HIV may not want to discuss. Advisers and judges should therefore tread with extreme caution and understanding. Although HIV is mentioned in this context, it must be born in mind that HIV is no longer a 'gay disease'. While HIV diagnoses are on the rise and have doubled from 2000 to 2004, less than a third of new diagnoses in 2004 were amongst men who have sex with men, and 59 per cent of the newly infected persons were infected through heterosexual sex. Nearly half of new infections were in people of African origin (source: **www.tht.org.uk/informationresources/factsandstatistics/uk/**, 20 February 2006).

6.4.7 Contributions

21(2)(f)   the contributions which each civil partner has made or is likely in the foreseeable future to make to the welfare of the family, including any contribution by looking after the home or caring for the family;

In same-sex relationships, as in all relationships including marriage, at any stage each partner may perform the same tasks and roles within the relationship, or each partner's role may be different, while at other times changes in circumstances may mean that these roles may change. If both partners are working, even if their income is different because of different pay levels in their respective professions, these contributions are valued in the same way. This was made clear by Hale LJ (as she then was) in *Foster* v. *Foster* [2003] 2 FLR 299 at [18]:

[18] . . . The Matrimonial Causes Act 1973 was designed to move away from the application of strict property law principles, with their dependence upon evaluating contributions in money or money's worth, towards the recognition of marriage as a relationship to which each spouse contributes what they can in their different ways. There can be no justification for treating differences in income any differently from differences between breadwinning and homemaking. These days things are rarely as simple as one breadwinner and one homemaker. Both may work equally hard but in jobs which are unequally remunerated. They may agree that one should work part-time, or take a career break, in order to enable the other to move or take promotion. They may agree that one should work full-time at the outset to enable the other to gain qualifications which will then enable the first to concentrate on domestic responsibilities. As it happens, differences in income and career progression are also frequently the result of inequalities in earning power between the sexes, although not always, as this case shows. If both go out to work

and pool their incomes or spend a comparable proportion of their incomes for the benefit of the family, it would be a surprising proposition indeed if they were not to be regarded as having made an equal contribution to the family home or other family assets.

In this case a couple in their early 30s divorced after four years of marriage during which they had made significant money from investing in various properties. The wife had contended that her higher income should be reflected in a higher share in the assets. This was rejected by the district judge, allowed on appeal to the circuit judge and reversed on a further appeal to the Court of Appeal. The question of whether *White* v. *White* principles should apply in same-sex cases has already been addressed (**6.3.1**).

It is also clear from a string of cases that if one spouse (traditionally the wife) did not earn because she was looking after the household to bring up children, this still entitles her to have her contributions counted in the same way as those of the breadwinner (*Lambert* v. *Lambert* [2003] 1 FLR 139). The situation is less clear when it comes to a case where one partner did not earn because she was looking after the household but where there are no children. This situation is found more frequently for same-sex couples (at least for now and particularly for men) than for opposite-sex couples.

Example 6.2

Richard, a banker in the City, is 37 when he meets Marcio, 24, who is an arts student from Brazil. They start a relationship and register a civil partnership the following year as Marcio's student visa would otherwise have run out. Richard pursues his career earning in excess of £150,000 with bonuses of several hundred thousand pounds a year. They decide to buy a house as a home for themselves, entirely financed by the equity from Richard's flat and a high mortgage, which Richard later pays off from bonuses received over the years. They decide that Marcio with his artistic talent and practical skill should oversee the redecoration and modifications on the house. Once this is done, Marcio pursues his art and organises performances and exhibitions of his own work and the works of other artists, none of which makes any money. Later he enrols on a further part-time doctorate course, which lasts six years. Marcio is a good cook and runs the household. They travel a lot when Richard has time off and on weekends when Richard can get away and Marcio always organises all the travel. The civil partnership lasts 22 years and by this time there are considerable investments, a large pension in Richard's name and a house in Sitges, Spain of considerable value. At the time of separation Richard is 60 and Marcio is 47.

There is nothing in principle in the CPA 2004 that requires the presence of children in order to ensure that the homemaker's contribution is valued in the same way as the breadwinner's. The wording of para.21(2)(f) expressly states 'looking after the home' and 'caring for the family' as alternative methods of contributing. In many marriages the wife will have done both, but this is not a prerequisite to value the contributions in the same way. Therefore there is no reason why Marcio's contribution as a homemaker should in any way be regarded as different from Richard's contribution by way of his considerable remunerations package.

Of course there are, no doubt, cases where these roles are in no way part of an agreed lifestyle, but instead the behaviour of one partner (who will no doubt allege that this was as part of an agreement between the partners), which, however, is interpreted as laziness by the other. It is difficult to see how far the court would, and indeed could, investigate whose version is true. In most cases the court will no doubt refuse to make that value analysis and simply make assumptions. In divorces after long marriages with children, case law and experience indicate that wives who claim to be homemakers are readily believed, even if the husband claims that he did most of the childcare on top of his full-time job while the wife went out to enjoy herself. This no doubt has its roots in the traditional gender roles. Whether this possible presumption in favour of the alleged homemaker will be the same in civil partnership dissolutions remains to be seen. In any event a pre-registration agreement setting out that the partners do not choose for one to be a home-maker only and instead both plan to work full-time may go some way to persuade the court later that these assumptions should not readily be made (see **6.4.10**).

6.4.8 Conduct

> 21(2)(g)   the conduct of each civil partner, if that conduct is such that it would in the opinion of the court be inequitable to disregard it;

The wording of the statute regarding conduct is probably one of the least clear of all the factors. Courts have over the years tried to grapple with the issue of conduct. At times they have tried to restrict arguments and allegations of conduct (*Wachtel* v. *Wachtel* [1973] Fam 72 where conduct had to be 'both obvious and gross', per Ormrod J at 80); and indeed the financial disclosure form, Form E, states that 'bad behaviour or conduct by the other party will only be taken into account in very exceptional circumstances when deciding how assets should be shared after divorce/dissolution'. In the recent case of *Miller* v. *Miller* [2005] EWCA Civ 984 the husband's counsel contended that allegations of behaviour can only be brought before the court as conduct and not otherwise. As such, they have to satisfy the test of it being inequitable to disregard them. Thorpe LJ rejected this and endorsed that behaviour allegations can be brought before the court as part of 'all the circumstances of the case':

[29] . . . In my judgment the language of s25(2)(g) is intended to discourage allegations of conduct unless it is such that it would be inequitable to disregard. In other words it is pointless, and in terms of costs, risky, to assert misconduct that does not measure high on the scale of gravity. But conduct that would not merit advancing under s25(2)(g) is not therefore irrelevant or inadmissible. Often the court's assessment of the worth of the comparable contributions will require consideration of motives, attitudes, commitments and responsibilities.

While the last sentence is no doubt correct, this does not necessarily make the conduct point much clearer. At the time of writing *Miller* is awaiting the outcome of a petition to the House of Lords, which may clarify the law in this area.

While it is of course correct that para.21 and MCA 1973, s.25 require the court to consider all the circumstances of the case and the list of factors are simply examples (see **6.3.1** above), conduct has a particular status because Parliament in qualifying the conduct that is allowed to be taken into account deliberately restricted the scope of allegations of behaviour or conduct. If all conduct could indeed be taken into account either under the conduct heading or under the general duty to consider all the circumstances, the qualification deliberately inserted into the MCA 1973 would be meaningless. For these reasons the husband's counsel's analysis in *Miller* must be preferable to the Court of Appeal's judgment. It is hoped the House of Lords will throw light on the issue. Even then it is not clear what is meant by the qualification of conduct by their disregard being 'inequitable'. This will need further clarification.

What then could be conduct in the case of a civil partnership? If sexual relationships outside the marriage can in certain circumstances be conduct (*Miller*), either under the heading of conduct or as part of all the circumstances, is sexual promiscuity conduct? Sexual fidelity is not part of the definition of civil partnership (see **1.3.3**). While in a particular relationship it may have been agreed that sexual relations should only happen between the partners and a breach of that agreement may form the basis of a behaviour application for dissolution (**4.2**), it is not clear whether this could be conduct for financial proceedings. Suppose for argument's sake that in future years statistics show that the vast majority of female civil partners are committed to a sexually exclusive relationship and a large number of male civil partners agree some form of open relationship. Could the courts then say that in civil partnerships sexual infidelity is conduct only for women but not for men? What if the civil partners never agree to have sexual relations with each other (either because they are old or infirm or because their relationship simply is not sexual)? It is clear that courts would be faced with impossible decisions to make that could mean that they easily slip down a route where the judgment is discriminatory and offensive whichever way the court decides the case. The preference therefore must be to keep conduct out of the arguments as far as possible, which was no doubt Parliament's intention when it inserted the qualification to the conduct heading.

6.4.9 Pensions

21(2)(h) in the case of proceedings for a dissolution or nullity order, the value to each civil partner of any benefit which, because of the dissolution or annulment of the civil partnership, that civil partner will lose the chance of acquiring.

In practice this refers to the loss of a dependant's pension and similar rights (see generally **Chapter 9**). Of course dependants' pensions for civil partners are unlikely to be the same as widows' or widowers' pensions from the same pension scheme. Section D of the new Pension Information Form, Form P, asks simply 'What proportion of the member's pension would be payable as of right to the spouse or civil partner of the member if the member were to die . . .?' as if there were no difference. Instead, public sector final salary schemes only count years of service from 1988 towards civil partners' dependants' pensions, and private sector defined benefit schemes are only required to count service after 5 December 2005 (see **9.4** and **9.5**). Where there is a large age difference between the partners, the dependant's pension may be reduced (see **6.4.4**). The fact that a civil partner would not have received a dependant's pension as a result of ongoing discrimination should probably not mean that there should be added disadvantage in not sharing a pension on dissolution.

On a practical level, it is likely that pension providers will simply complete Form P with the details of widows' or widowers' pensions and not with details of the dependants' pensions for civil partners because many computer systems are unlikely to supply this information automatically and it may have to be calculated manually at great expense. As this is information which the court may need, pension providers will need to be specifically reminded to supply it. This in turn may indicate to them that the client is lesbian or gay, and as the pension provider may be part of the client's employer, the employer may thus also become aware of the client's sexual orientation. It may be that clients do not want their employers to be aware of their sexual orientation, and so this possibility must be explained to clients in advance. On a first attempt the letter should be worded as generally as possible without indicating that the case in question is a civil partnership dissolution.

6.4.10 Pre-registration agreements

Many couples contemplating civil partnership enquire about the possibility of making a binding agreement between them before (or shortly after) registration of a civil partnership. As with pre-nuptial agreements there is no statutory footing for such agreements and, of course, no case law on them as yet. In relative terms, it may be found that there is a larger number of instructions for pre-registration agreements than for pre-nuptial agreements, because many couples may have lived together for a long time already and made financial arrangements in a way that they want to continue and which they do not want to be disturbed by the courts. The term 'pre-registration agreement' is the writer's own coinage. These agreements should not be confused with 'civil partnership agreements', which are equivalent to engagements (see **6.2.2**). The question is whether pre-registration agreements are enforceable and what status they have in law.

Pre-nuptial agreements face two hurdles.

1. English law allows parties a wide freedom to make contracts. This is only restricted in specific circumstances, such as for illegality (e.g. contract killing), or for being against public policy (e.g. prostitution). An agreement about what should happened on a divorce made before or during a subsisting marriage is not enforceable in contract law. Marriage is for life and therefore any contract intended to regulate for the event that the marriage ends prematurely, goes against the whole concept of marriage and is thus unenforceable for being against public policy. This was most recently reiterated by Wall J in *N* v. *N (Jurisdiction: Pre-nuptial Agreement)* [1999] 2 FLR 745 where he said that '. . . an agreement made prior to marriage which contemplates the steps the parties will take in the event of divorce or separation is perceived as being contrary to public policy because it undermines the concept of marriage as a life-long union'.

2. The court has an overall discretion under the MCA 1973 and a duty to take into account all the circumstances of the case. It is not bound by agreements made between the parties (*Hyman* v. *Hyman* [1929] AC 601). This applies to pre- and post-nuptial agreements as well as separation agreements. However, separation agreements do not fall foul of the public policy issue because they are made at a time when the marriage has already irretrievably broken down.

Looking at case law, it seems that pre-nuptial agreements and separation agreements (which include agreements concluded at the doors of the court, in correspondence between solicitors and Minutes of Agreement and Consent Order) are treated differently from pre-nuptial agreements for this reason. There is a line of cases starting with *Edgar* v. *Edgar* (1981) FLR 19 that sets out the circumstances and the extent to which separation agreements are taken into account. In *Xydhias* v. *Xydhias* [1999] 1 FLR 683, the Court of Appeal stated that the court had an overall discretion and a duty to look at all the circumstance and then upheld an order that was made in the terms that the parties had agreed in correspondence. In *A* v. *B (Financial Relief: Agreements)* [2005] 2 FLR 730, Black J upheld an order that took into account a separation agreement made many years previously and made orders accordingly.

Pre-nuptial agreements that have been carefully drafted have recently carried more weight with the courts than previously. In *M* v. *M (Prenuptial Agreement)* [2002] 1 FLR 654 the pre-nuptial agreement provided that the husband would pay the wife £275,000. The husband's wealth was £7.5m and the wife's £300,000. Connell J held (at [26]):

> I do bear the agreement in mind as one of the more relevant circumstances of this case, but the court's overriding duty remains to attempt to arrive at a solution which is fair in all the circumstances, applying s 25 of the Matrimonial Causes Act 1973. Accordingly I pass to consider the various subparagraphs of subs 2.

He ordered the husband to pay child maintenance of £15,000 per year and a lump sum of £875,000 made up of a housing fund of £575,000 and an income fund of £300,000. In *K* v. *K (Ancillary Relief: Prenuptial Agreement)* [2003] 1 FLR 120 the pre-nuptial agreement provided for a lump sum of £100,000 plus 10 per cent per annum for the wife and reasonable provision for any children and a home. This was not quantified and so, even if the agreement was strictly followed, it was open to the court to set the figures to cover needs. The husband had wealth in excess of £100m. The deputy High Court judge ordered a lump sum of £120,000 accordingly and thereby followed the pre-nuptial agreement to the letter. The judge supplemented this with a housing fund of £1.2m that would revert to the husband on the child's majority and with maintenance.

Although the courts reiterate that there is an overall discretion and all the circumstances must be taken into account, it seems that separation agreements are strongly persuasive and often orders are made in the terms of the agreement. By contrast, pre-nuptial agreements are at most a consideration and may lead to the court taking a more 'needs' based than 'fair share' based approach to the case. They may still lead to a different result, but are hardly enforced in terms.

Of course in any event separation agreements will only be strongly persuasive if they meet the *Edgar* principles, namely:

1. Both parties had independent legal advice.
2. There was full financial disclosure.
3. The agreement was within the realm of what the court would order.
4. There has been no significant change of circumstances.

There is a longer checklist for pre-nuptial agreements in *K* v. *K (Ancillary Relief: Prenuptial Agreement)* [2003] 1 FLR 120 at p.131, which in general terms can be rephrased as follows:

1. Did both partners understand the agreement?
2. Were both partners properly advised as to its terms?
3. Did one partner put the other under any pressure to sign it?
4. Was there full disclosure or at least sufficient disclosure for the purposes of the agreement?
5. Was one partner under any other pressure at the time they signed the agreement?

6. Did they willingly sign the agreement?
7. Did one partner exploit a dominant position, either financially or otherwise?
8. If there are children, were they contemplated in the agreement?
9. Has any unforeseen circumstance arisen since the agreement was made that would make it unjust to hold the parties to it?
10. Is the agreement clear in its meaning?
11. Would upholding the agreement lead to an injustice?

The other points of the checklist relate to legal issues. The judge also held that it would not be right to uphold part of an agreement that precluded maintenance to a mother with minor children.

The question then is of course whether pre-registration agreements are treated any differently from pre-nuptials. As civil partnership is in no way defined to be for life, the public policy argument against pre-nuptial agreements should not be applicable to pre-registration agreements. Nevertheless they will still face the second hurdle that they share with separation agreements. Looking at outcomes, it seems from the case law that this is still a much lower hurdle. There is therefore a case to be made that pre-registration agreements are more likely to be binding and should follow the case law on separation agreements rather than the case law on pre-nuptial agreements. This is, however, largely speculative and the law in the area of pre-nuptial agreements is still in a state of development. This development may be overtaken by legislation although there is no legislation on the horizon at the moment. For couples who would like to protect themselves against the somewhat unpredictable outcome of financial litigation on dissolution, making an agreement is a sensible precaution. It is quite possible that at the time the relationship may break down in years to come the law will have developed further making the agreement enforceable or at least more persuasive. The possible difference in approach set out here should not, however, encourage practitioners to advertise pre-registration agreements as binding. The argument may be persuasive, but it remains to be seen whether it will be followed by the courts. Clients must be warned in the usual way, and anything else may be negligent.

Consideration should also be given to include both a choice of law and a choice of jurisdiction clause for each of:

- dissolution;
- assets;
- maintenance; and
- pensions

because private international law rules may well change the law in future and the partners (together or separately) may move across international borders. The differences in approach between the various different same-sex partnership regimes in each country mean that this is even more important for civil partners than for spouses.

6.4.11   Closeness and type of bond

Although civil partnership is designed as a substitute for marriage for same-sex couples, the definition of civil partnership says nothing about the nature of the relationship and there is no requirement to have a sexual relationship, an exclusive sexual relationship or even an intimate relationship (**1.3.3**). Therefore a wide variety of relationships can be the basis of a civil partnership. While the incidence of close friends registering a civil partnership for pure economic reasons is likely to be small, and the relationship between the partners of a same-sex couple is probably often close to the one that is expected of an opposite-sex marriage, this is by no means guaranteed. Mark Vernon writes:

> The heart of the matter is, I think, that relationships between gay men and women are different from those between married couples. This has nothing to do with children, because clearly some same-sex partners have kids. Neither is it about an idea of complementarity found only in opposite-sex couples. Rather it is about social history and the way in which the personal is political. In marriage, this is still caught up with notions of possession, for all that many would have it otherwise. Witness the persistent nostalgia for acts like the father giving away the bride.
>
> For gay couples there is little sense of this. For example, gay men and women routinely remain friends with former lovers in ways that would be thought dodgy, even treacherous, in the married world. And I am much more likely to do something without my partner, like go on holiday, than my married friends are.
>
> So what is the best model for civil partnerships? In a word, friendship. If erotic love is about having another and them having you, friendship is about knowing another and being known by them: close friends become 'one soul in two bodies', as Montaigne put it – rather different from the nuptial notion of two bodies becoming one.
>
> ('Coming out as friends' *The Guardian*, 28 October 2005)

Not everyone may agree with this and no doubt civil partners will show a wide range of types of relationships with their partners. Nevertheless, the question is whether and how a court should take into account the closeness or type of the bond between the partners when it comes to the discretionary exercise in a financial application.

Example 6.3

Ivy and Joy are both teachers. They met when they were in their early 30s and neither of them had yet found the right man to marry. They were fed up with lodging in other people's homes and decided to rent together. Later they bought a house together. Their friendship developed and not only do they share a house, but they also run the household together: they cook and eat together, Ivy docs the cleaning and washing and Joy does the garden and the odd-jobs. They have no sexual relationship with each other at all and indeed at various stages both have boyfriends but matters have not developed to the extent that either of them decides to marry any of the men they go out with. They go on holiday together, as it is convenient because they have the same interests and have annual leave available at the same time. They are now both in their late 50s and nearing retirement. They greatly enjoy each other's company and regard the other as the person they are closest to. Despite the fact that they both still see men from time to time, they are also confident that neither of them will ever get married or live with a man. They want to continue to live together in the set-up they know. They are concerned that if one of them should die or have to go into a nursing home, the house may need to be sold. In order to protect each other they are thinking about registering a civil partnership.

Although a lot was made of spinsters living together in the passage of the Bill in Parliament, there is no evidence that this type of set-up is widespread. Or consider this:

Example 6.4

Warren and Jeremy are 32 and 35 when they meet. They have both been in long-term relationships before and found that they wanted to have and did have sex with other men during their previous relationships. Therefore from the beginning of their relationship they both think that this is likely to happen in the future in their new relationship. They talk about this and agree that they would accommodate sex outside the relationship as long as it did not jeopardise the relationship itself and happened away from home. They both realise that their relationship with each other is about more than just sex and that sex outside the relationship will not necessarily jeopardise the relationship that they have with each other. For the first few years they fancy each other madly and not much happens sexually with others. At some stage they experiment with looking for a third man, but this does not seem to be what they are looking for as they have different tastes in men. Over the years, their love for each other deepens while their sexual desire for each other wanes. By the time they are in their late 40s, they are not having sex with each other any more at all but still regard themselves as a couple.

There are no known statistics of the incidence of this type of relationship, but from anecdotal experience, it is not an uncommon scenario amongst gay men, although it appears to be different amongst lesbians. At this stage the relationship between Warren and Jeremy is nothing but a very intense friendship. What then is the difference between that and Ivy and Joy's relationship with each other? On the other hand, while gay men may be more open to their friends about such a relationship, is this really a situation that does not occur in married couples? If it does, it is probably kept quiet. Maybe it is different in that in married couples the sex between the spouses may have ceased while

95

there is rarely an open agreement to allow each other to have sex with others, even if it happens and is tolerated silently.

The courts are ill-equipped to enter into an investigation of the nature of the relationship and the reasons behind it. There certainly seems no reason to regard the sexless marriage different from the civil partnership where both men have a healthy sex life, albeit not with each other. When the partners register a civil partnership they are making a commitment. Although there are no vows, they know or should know that they will have to go through a dissolution procedure if matters do not work out and that they will face the court's jurisdiction on finances if they do not come to an agreement amongst themselves. This also of course applies to Ivy and Joy. Therefore unless there is some specific indication to the contrary for example in a pre-registration agreement, the court should not investigate into these circumstances and the closeness and type of bond between the civil partners should not be a factor to take into account.

6.4.12 Chattels

Chattels are something courts and lawyers hate dealing with as it can get extremely messy. They only become interesting when they are valuable antiques or *objects d'art* (*A* v. *A (Financial Provision)* [1998] 2 FLR 180, in which Singer J visited the parties' properties in order to decide on the division of chattels). While in households with children many chattels and furniture may be very functional, which will no doubt to some extent determine where they should go, this is not necessarily the case in childless relationships. With many couples hobbies and interests are different so that, say, the music and book collections are easily divided. The main difference with same-sex couples is probably that interests are often overlapping and it may be difficult to attribute a particular item or collection to one or the other partner (although this can, of course, also occur with married couples). The one area which is unique is the joint wardrobe. If both are of a similar size, some same-sex couples will not only borrow each other's clothes but actually buy together; or one partner may predominately buy clothes for both of them, maybe enjoying the freedom to shop on double the budget. It may then not be easy to divide this up. Whether Singer J or a future judge will make a home visit to decide which ties should go where, remains to be seen.

6.5 INHERITANCE ACT

The Inheritance (Provision for Family and Dependants) Act 1975 (IPFDA 1975) has been amended to add three new categories of claimant, namely:

- civil partners (inserted into IPFDA 1975, s.1(1)(a));
- former civil partners (inserted into IPFDA 1975, s.1(1)(b)); and
- someone who was living in the same household and as the civil partner of the deceased for the two years ending with the death (IPFDA 1975, new s.1(1B)).

The first two are obvious. Spouses and civil partners can claim for more than just maintenance and therefore are in a much better position than cohabitants. This will greatly improve the situation of survivors of same-sex partners, provided that they are civil partners. The last category is clearly distinct from those who have actually registered as civil partners (as they fall into IPFDA 1975, s.1(1)(a)) and refers therefore to people who have not registered. The problem is that civil partners are defined as 'two people of the same sex [who] . . . register as civil partners' (s.1). Therefore all that is then left from the definition for the third category of claimant are 'two people of the same sex'. This is clearly nonsensical as it would apply to many people including lodgers, friends, etc. It may possibly exclude those who are unable to register a civil partnership because they fall into a prohibited degree of relationship, but even this is not clear (and it would not be clear why those should be excluded at all). This is clearly a drafting mistake (see also **1.4.8** and **14.2.1**). What the courts will make out of this is, however, not clear. They should not simply be able to apply the tests that have been set for couples living together as husband and wife, because Parliament went to great lengths to create a statutory regime that is by its very nature not marriage. In practice, it should certainly not preclude a same-sex cohabitant from making the claim.

The Explanatory Notes to the Act make it clear that 'this is done to preserve the effect of the decision in *Ghaidan v Mendoza* [2004] UKHL 30' (at [547]) (*Ghaidan* v. *Godin-Mendoza* [2004] 2 FLR 600). Accordingly, in cases where the deceased died before the CPA 2004 came into force the same-sex cohabitant should still be able to claim under the IPFDA 1975, albeit under s.1(1A). Although *Ghaidan* v. *Mendoza* has now been followed by *Secretary of State for Work and Pensions* v. *M* [2006] UKHL 11 (see **1.2.1**), this should not have changed the position for claimants under the IPFDA 1975.

In any applications under the IPFDA 1975, the same discretionary exercise and factors to be considered apply as set out above for applications for financial provision on dissolution.

6.6 FINANCIAL APPLICATIONS ON DIVORCE

The Matrimonial Causes Act 1973 (MCA 1973) has been amended to provide that maintenance will stop on formation of a civil partnership as it does on remarriage (MCA 1973, ss.28, 35, 38 and 52 as amended by CPA

2004, Sched.27, paras.42–46). This includes almost all overseas regimes of same-sex partnership registration (see **8.4**) but not overseas opposite-sex partnership registrations. By contrast, *Mesher* and *Martin* orders, such as those suggested in precedent 50 of the *Precedents for Consent Orders*, 7th Edn (Resolution, 2005), are not affected. These orders typically provide for the home not to be sold until the youngest child has reached majority, or (usually) the wife's remarriage (or in some cases the wife's death), whichever is the sooner. On sale the husband will then receive a defined share of the equity (the net sale proceeds) from the house. It is a pity that the 2005 edition of the Resolution Precedents has disregarded civil partnership. It can by no means be assumed that just because someone is divorcing and has been in an opposite-sex marriage, that person will always only be in opposite-sex relationships. Indeed, the realisation that they prefer same-sex relationships may be the true (but possibly unknown) reason for the end of the marriage. The trigger events should therefore be worded as follows (changes in bold):

> The property shall not be sold without the prior written consent of both parties or further order until the first to happen of the following events ('the determining events') namely:
>
> i   The [youngest] surviving [of the] child[ren] of the family attaining the age of eighteen years or completing [his] [her] full-time [secondary] [undergraduate] [post-graduate] education [or as appropriate] whichever shall be the later; or
> ii   The death of the [Husband] [Wife]; or
> iii The remarriage **or formation of a civil partnership** [or cohabitation with another person ~~as man and wife~~ for a period of [ ] months in any [ ] month period] of the [Husband] [Wife]

All such orders should include these triggers since at least the date that the CPA 2004 received Royal Assent on 18 November 2004, if not earlier. Failure to have advised the beneficiary of the charge (usually the husband) of this and failure to include this may well be negligent. A formation of a civil partnership may not be included in the wording of 'cohabitation with another person as man and wife' if the former wife is cohabiting with another woman. While the cohabitation definition may have been extended to included same-sex couples by the House of Lords decision in *Ghaidan* v. *Godin-Mendoza* [2004] 2 FLR 600, this was on the ground of the cohabitants' human rights, not because a third party, in this case the former husband, would like the cohabitants' home to be sold. The recent House of Lords decision in *Secretary of State for Work and Pensions* v. *M* [2006] UKHL 11 has shown that there is no universal rule that 'cohabitants' will always include same-sex couples. Indeed, a civil partnership need not mean that the partners in fact cohabit. Even the inclusion of 'or further order' may not help the former husband because in a particular case the court may not order the sale, for example if the wife's new partner is not well off. In any event, the former husband may have to spend considerable amounts to finance a new application to the court for such an order with maybe little prospect of recovering the costs (depending upon how any new costs rules are going to be applied).

CHAPTER 7

Children

7.1 CHILDREN OF SAME-SEX COUPLES

7.1.1 Introduction

With the changes made in the 1980s by the Family Law Reform Act 1987 (which abolished discrimination on the grounds of illegitimacy) and the Children Act 1989 (CA 1989), the question of the parents' status or relationship has become secondary and the welfare of the child has become paramount in questions surrounding all aspects of what was once called custody. As a result the law in England has to some extent been flexible enough to adapt to changing family structures. For example, courts have made residence orders in favour of mothers and married or unmarried fathers, and they have made joint residence orders in favour of one parent and a new partner, whether same-sex or opposite-sex; these orders automatically confer parental responsibility for the time they are in force. Contact orders can (albeit with leave) be made in favour of anyone. There has, however, been and continues to be a lack of recognition of those same-sex couples who have children without the legal involvement of any other adult (see **7.1.2** below and **figure 7.1**). As far as adoption is concerned, the law has until recently lagged behind. The child's welfare was not paramount and adoptions orders could only be made in favour of married couples and single people. This has changed with the Adoption and Children Act 2002, which came into force on 30 December 2005. The CPA 2004 has brought in further changes, recognising same-sex couples as parents.

The remainder of this chapter deals with the following:

- An overview of the multitude of ways that gay men and lesbians and trans people can have and bring up children (**7.1.2**). For the sake of simplicity, the terms 'gay family' and 'gay parenting' will be used without wanting to disparage lesbians or heterosexual trans people.
- A short historical perspective shows the change in the social and legal attitudes towards gay parenting in the last 15 years (**7.2**).

- The changes in the law in 2005 (**7.3**) including adoption (**7.3.2**), residence orders (**7.3.3**), parental responsibility (**7.3.4**), contact and residence orders (**7.3.5**), guardianship (**7.3.6**) and the international dimension (**7.3.7**).
- **Section 7.4** deals with various remaining issues, mainly under the Human Fertilisation and Embryology Act 1990 (HFEA 1990), including status under donor insemination and surrogacy arrangements.

7.1.2 'Gay' families

Social awareness of parenting by lesbians and gay men is lacking. The traditional idea that children are brought up by their mother and their father who are married to each other still prevails in the style of the Ladybird 'Peter and Jane' stories in past decades. In reality, of course, only 58 per cent of families with children in England and Wales are of this type. Seven per cent of parents are cohabiting with the other parent without being married, and a third of families are parents either bringing up children on their own or with a partner who is not a natural parent of their children (source: Office of National Statistics, Census 2001, Table S007). There are no statistics available for 'gay' families and same-sex parenting. In addition, other children are brought up in children's homes or by foster parents. For decades now, some mothers who have brought up children after a divorce from their husbands have gone on to form a relationship with other women. This may still be the most common form of same-sex parenting, where one (or both) of the partners in a female same-sex couple bring children into the family from a previous opposite-sex relationship. This does of course also happen with fathers who form same-sex relationships, but almost certainly less frequently so, probably because after the majority of separations and divorces the children stay with the mother whatever the parents' sexual orientation. Although of course there are single lesbians and gay men who are parents, this chapter will focus on lesbians and gay men who are parenting as couples.

The past two decades have seen continuing acceptance of homosexuality, gay men and lesbians have tended to come out at a younger age, and more and more gay and lesbian couples are setting up home together. With this has come a realisation, certainly amongst lesbian couples, that they also can have children. Some couples, of course, do not want to have children, but those who do will probably have made a very conscious decision to do so. The Human Fertilisation and Embryology Act 1990 regulates fertility clinics and fertility treatment. Section 13(5) provides that the clinic needs to take account of the 'need of that child for a father'. As a result some clinics, especially outside London, will not provide artificial donor insemination to a lesbian woman, whether or not she is in a long-term relationship, although other clinics do provide the service to lesbians. However, as a consequence of this legislation or maybe to save the costs involved with treatment through a clinic, some lesbians decide to have children under informal agreements with male friends. Often the friends are gay men who seek some parenting role or who give their sperm out of friendship or altruism. The parties will almost certainly not have intercourse and the necessary kits are freely available by mail order (but see *Re D (Contact and PR: Lesbian Mothers and Known Father) (No.2)* [2006] 1 FCR 556). Some parents may already be friends, while others may meet through small advertisements for this purpose. Usually, there will have been detailed discussions about whether or not the biological father will have a parenting role, but it is rare that the parties write down their agreement. No law is broken by these arrangements, but to some extent they exist in a lacuna: legally the parents of the child are the biological parents and they are largely treated in the same way as if they had been in an opposite-sex relationship, even if in a very brief one. For example, a drunken night after a raucous party that included heterosexual intercourse and led to an unexpected baby broadly has the same legal consequences as these informal parenting agreements. In that sense, it does not matter whether the mother and the donor agreed that the donor should be a co-parent or that he should have no involvement with the child at all, or whether he should or should not provide financial support. In all these cases, the donor or father of the unplanned baby will be able to apply for contact and residence orders without leave under CA 1989, s.10(4)(a). In this respect, English law ignores the social aspect and simply looks at the biological realities. This contrasts with the situation in the Netherlands where the biological father in such an arrangement was unable to have contact with the child. In *JRM* v. *The Netherlands (sub nom G* v. *Netherlands)* Application No. 16944/90 (1993) 16 EHRR CD 38, the applicant biological father had met a lesbian couple and agreed to donate sperm to one of them, who subsequently gave birth to a child. The Dutch court gave additional guardianship to the mother's partner. The applicant babysat once a week, but when he asked for regular contact, the mothers stopped all contact. The Dutch courts rejected the application for contact. The European Commission for Human Rights rejected the application under Art.8 of the Convention (right to private and family life) on the ground that mere sperm donation did not create family life with the baby.

What order the English court will make will to some extend depend on the quality of the applications and any previous involvement of the father with the child. However, there is a presumption that a child should have contact with their father and a contact order is likely unless there are good reasons not to make it. Scottish law seems to be similar ('Lesbian parents tell of "bullying"', *The Observer*, 10 March 2002). Both donor and father are liable to pay child maintenance under the Child Support Acts and there is no discretion not to make an assessment in these circumstances. There are no reported cases of applications to the court for financial provision under CA 1989, Sched.1 and it is unclear whether the courts would decide not to ask the donor to make provision because there was an informal agreement that he would not do so. The court may be more convinced not to make financial provision if the mother's female partner was party to the agreement and of sufficient means to financially support mother and child herself.

In other cases, the mother and donor have agreed to co-parent the child, a plan which must be difficult from the start as essentially the adults are setting up the scenario of separated heterosexual parents, with contact weekends and so on. Sometimes these plans go wrong, especially when the intentions of the parties were not made clear or they change their mind about what they think they want or is best of the child (*Re D (Contact and PR: Lesbian Mothers and Known Father) (No.2)*, above). Surrogacy is not illegal in English law, but heavily regulated including restrictions on payments to the surrogate mother. It is therefore rare, and there are few known cases of gay men bringing up a child born by a surrogate mother.

For some time now, local authorities have targeted the gay community with advertising to look for foster parents, probably in the knowledge that most same-sex couples do not have children of their own but have the time and energy to parent. While there was a time when this caused a stir in the tabloid press (see *Re W (Wardship: Publication of Information)* [1992] 1 FLR 99), this has now died down and many same-sex couples bring up foster children.

A more permanent and legal bond with a child is of course adoption. Until 2005 it was only possible for a married couple or a single person to adopt (Adoption Act 1976, ss.14–15). Nevertheless, same-sex couples have adopted children, even if only one of them could be the adopter. Of course the local authority assessment of the potential adopter would always involve assessing both members of the couple, and it would be reckless not to do so. Nevertheless, due to the legal constraints, the couple had to make the impossible decision of who should be the adopter. Should it be the wealthier of them (to ensure inheritance), or the main carer, or the older (to ensure they were the next-of-kin in old age), or the younger (who was likely to live longer)? Often the courts realised the reality of the situation and made a joint residence order in favour of the couple (*Re AB (Adoption: Joint Residence)* [1996] 1 FLR 27; see **7.3.3** for residence orders). This has now all changed and under the Adoption and Children Act 2002 (ACA 2002) same-sex couples can adopt children as a couple. Whether this will lead to an increase in adoptions by same-sex couples remains to be seen.

When the ACA 2002 went though Parliament, the focus shifted from gay parenting (the idea of which instilled horror in some and unease in others) to the needs of children whom nobody wanted. It is of course correct to have the welfare of the child in an adoption as the paramount consideration and the ACA 2002 does this for the first time. Nevertheless, it also raises the question of whether the unspoken intention behind allowing gay couples to adopt was to enable the local authorities to find families for disabled children or older children with a difficult background and history. While it may be true that those couples making a conscious decision to parent may be able to make a decision to adopt or foster a disabled child and may then be prepared,

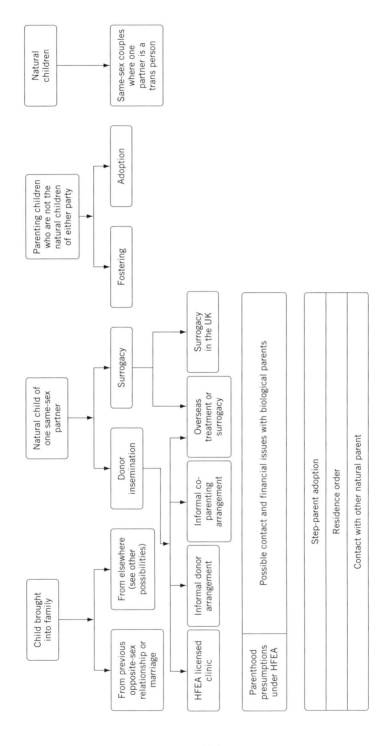

Figure 7.1 Possibilities for 'gay' parenting

at least to some extent, for the task they face, offering gay men and lesbians only disabled or difficult children for adoption would be discriminatory and wholly inappropriate. One can only hope that in practice this will not happen.

The Gender Recognition Act 2004 opens up the possibility of same-sex couples who can conceive naturally (see **5.4.4**). How a registrar will deal with the issue when registering the birth of a child by two men (who may or may not be civil partners) remains to be seen. There is no reason why the registrar should not simply register the birth in the normal way, but record two fathers. The same would apply to two women in the corresponding situation.

7.2   SOCIO-LEGAL ATTITUDES TO GAY PARENTING

7.2.1   The historical attitude

Until very recently homosexuality was seen as undesirable by the courts and indeed potential exposure to homosexuals was seen as a danger to children. In *Re D (An Infant) (Adoption: Parent's Consent)* [1977] AC 602 the House of Lords overturned the Court of Appeal and reinstated the first instance order dispensing with the father's consent to the adoption of his son by his former wife, the mother, and her new husband. The court regarded the fact that the father was 'a self-confessed practising homosexual' as a major factor, for which before the marriage 'he had received voluntary treatment'. Their Lordships found that the trial judge had been right in concluding that the reasonable father would have agreed to the adoption. Wilberforce LJ commented:

> I think that the reasonable parent in the circumstances here shown would inevitably want to protect his boy from these dangers [of being exposed or intro-duced to ways of life which, as this case illustrates, may lead to severance from normal society], that this parent, to his credit, recognised this, and that the trial judge so decided.

In *S* v. *S (Custody of Children)* (1980) 1 FLR 143 the Court of Appeal in a decision on 21 June 1978 dismissed the mother's appeal against the order giving custody to the father because she lived in a lesbian relationship, which she had previously denied. The main reason was that one of two experts (the expert for the father, who had not seen the children or either party) thought that the children could experience 'social embarrassment and hurt' because of the mother's sexual orientation. The argument that children would be harmed by society's reaction to their parent's sexual orientation was compared with the similar one used against giving parents care and control of their children if they had formed mixed-raced relationships. Susan Boyd in 'What is a "Normal" Family?' [1992] MLR 269 remarked that 'this argument allows one discriminatory act (homophobia in the community) to condone another (depriving lesbians and homosexual men of custody)'.

In *Re P (A Minor) (Custody)* (1983) 4 FLR 401 the children lived with the mother after the parents divorced but then the girl returned to live with the father. She then made unspecified allegations against the father and the father no longer sought custody, but said that the girl should be brought up in a local authority home rather than live with the mother and her female partner. French J at first instance gave custody to the mother. He is quoted as saying that the mother 'tells me that she is not one of those homosexuals who, as many do nowadays, flaunt their homosexuality not only in the face of those who are interested to know but also of those to whom it is of no concern whatsoever'. The Court of Appeal dismissed the father's appeal because 'there is in the interests of the child no other acceptable alternative form of custody' (per Watkins LJ).

7.2.2 Changes in the 1990s

These attitudes changed in the 1990s mainly thanks to sociological studies that could show that the fears on which the courts had based their judgments were unfounded prejudices. The change is probably best shown in the case of *C* v. *C (A Minor) (Custody Appeal)* [1991] 1 FLR 223, in which the Court of Appeal heard the father's appeal against an order giving care and control of a 6½-year-old girl to the mother who lived in a lesbian relationship. The girl had grown up with the mother after the parents separated when she was 18 months old. The judge at first instance stressed that the mother's relationship was not 'the normal'; he considered that since contact had been agreed, the girl would find out about her mother's sexual orientation sooner or later anyway and that the strong bond between daughter and mother outweighed all other factors. The Court of Appeal accepted the appeal. Balcombe LJ said:

> The fact that the mother has a lesbian relationship with Ms A does not of itself render her unfit to have the care and control of her child. It is, however, an important factor to be taken into account in deciding which of the alternative homes which the parents can offer the child is most likely to advance her welfare.

At the rehearing Booth J gave care and control to the mother (*C* v. *C (Custody of Child) (No.2)* [1992] 1 FCR 206). This time the girl was represented by the Official Solicitor who had instructed an expert on homosexuality. The court was reassured by the expert that living with the mother would not lead the girl to become a lesbian too. Although the expert accepted that the girl might be taunted about her mother's sexual orientation, the fact that the father had told friends about it led the court to conclude that the girl would be better off dealing with the mother's homosexuality if she grew up with the mother, who accepted expert help to deal with the issues, than in the father's home, where especially the father's new wife was extremely hostile to homosexuality. The expert also reassured the court that the girl would not be involved in the mother's sexual activities. Several studies, led by Professor Golombok, came out in the early 1990s and helped shift the courts' attitudes from one that would order children to live with the other parents because the mother was a lesbian, via one that gave a residence order to the mother despite her sexual orientation, to one that ignored this (see also Boyd, above and *Lesbians in Residence and Parental Responsibility Cases* [1994] Fam Law 643).

In *B* v. *B (Minors) (Custody, Care and Control)* [1991] 1 FLR 402, Calman J granted care and control of a seven-year-old boy to the mother who was living in a relationship with another woman following divorce. The two elder children were living with the father and his new wife and it had been agreed that there should be joint custody. The court went against the recommendation of the court welfare officer and followed a consultant psychiatrist's report to the effect that there was no indication that the boy would be either unduly stigmatised or that his psychosexual development would be distorted. The judge was comforted by the 'boyish appearance' of the child and in the belief that the mother and her partner were not 'militant lesbians who try to convert others to their way of life'. Still, in *Re W (Wardship: Publication of Information)* [1992] 1 FLR 99 the Court of Appeal overturned an injunction against the publication by the *Daily Mirror* of the fact and circumstances that a 15-year-old gay boy had been placed with a gay couple as foster parents by the London Borough of Southwark because 'this was a matter of great public interest and concern'. In *Re H (A Minor) (Section 37 Direction)* [1993] 2 FLR 541 Scott Baker J said 'The fact that they are lesbians does not, according to the evidence that I have heard, make it any less likely that the placement will succeed than if they were an ordinary heterosexual couple'.

In *Re E (Adoption: Freeing Order)* [1995] 1 FLR 382, CA, E, a girl of 12½ was freed for adoption and the mother's consent to the adoption was dispensed with. Her objection on the ground that the adopter was a lesbian was found not to tip the scales. The adopter was 'of mature years, an experienced social worker who had worked with children displaying behavioural problems'. E had severe behavioural difficulties and had previously been rejected by four married couples who had looked into adopting her. The judge at first instance, Judge Baker QC, had heard expert evidence including from Professor Golombok. He had found that 'Prima facie, it is undesirable that E should have gone to a lesbian . . . but this case is a special one. E is a special girl who has had a specially unhappy past and has an unusual and unique opportunity now'. The order was therefore still made very much despite the fact that the adopter was a lesbian and only because nobody else wanted to look after E. Only two years later in *Re W (Adoption: Homosexual*

Adopter) [1997] 2 FLR 406 Singer J freed a child for adoption against the wishes of the parents who objected because the adopter was a woman living in a relationship with another woman. He recognised that since the earlier cases 'times, and the attitude of adoption agencies, have clearly changed, and whereas it has not been commonplace for children to be placed in the care of homosexual carers whether for fostering or prospective adoption purposes, it is by no means unknown'. He found that there was nothing in law to prevent adoption by homosexuals. 'Any other conclusion would be both illogical, arbitrary and inappropriately discriminatory . . .' There have been fewer cases reported recently, probably because these issues did not come to the higher courts but were dealt with sensibly at the level of district judges in county courts.

Courts have made joint residence orders in favour of same-sex couples routinely at first instance for many years now. The only cases that have been reported are those where same-sex parents have separated. In *G* v. *F (Contact and Shared Residence: Applications for Leave)* [1998] 2 FLR 799) the mother's former partner applied for leave to apply for contact. Bracewell J held that 'The fact that the relationship between the applicant and the respondent was a lesbian relationship . . . is to be seen as background circumstances of the case and there is no basis for discriminating against the applicant in her wish to pursue these proceedings on the basis that she and the respondent lived together in a lesbian relationship'. More recently in *Re G (Residence: Same-sex Partners)* [2005] 2 FLR 957 the Court of Appeal granted a joint residence order in a case where the mother and her partner had separated because otherwise the mother's former partner, the non-birth mother, would not have had parental responsibility. Subsequent to that decision by the Court of Appeal the mother breached the order by moving the children to Cornwall and reducing contact with the non-birth mother. The matter came before the Court of Appeal again in early 2006 and the court upheld an order by Bracewell J who, as a consequence of the mother's behaviour, had ordered that the children's main home should be with the non-birth mother (*CG* v. *CW & G (Children)* [2006] 1 FCR 681). The judgment of Thorpe LJ shows that the children's interests were placed ahead of any considerations of blood relationship. He said:

> 41. To further illustrate my doubt take the heterosexual couple whose desire for a family has been frustrated by the wife's infertility. They opt for IVF treatment with donated eggs. The eggs are fertilised by the husband's sperm. Should the relationship founder some years after the birth of the child or children, it would seem to me of little moment if the father in any ensuing dispute were to assert some enhanced position resulting from the biological connection.
> 42. Again, in the case of the male homosexual couple who enter into a surrogacy agreement in order to parent, I do not consider that a decisive distinction is to be drawn subsequently on the basis that one of the contenders for care supplied the

sperm. I also instance the known example of a lesbian couple where in the use of IVF treatment, the eggs of one are implanted in the womb of the other.

43. These instances simply demonstrate that we have moved into a world where norms that seemed safe twenty or more years ago no longer run.

Comparing the opposite-sex and the same-sex parents as alike is extremely enlightened and bodes well for future jurisprudence.

7.2.3 Gay men and lesbians as the non-resident parent

The courts are of course not only dealing with same-sex couples who are parenting children, but are also faced with gay and lesbian parents in situations where the child is not living with them and they are asking the courts to rule on contact, parental responsibility or other CA 1989, s.8 orders (specific issue, prohibited steps and residence). This may arise in the context of a separating opposite-sex couple, a separating same-sex couple or a co-parenting arrangement.

In the context of the divorce or separation of opposite-sex parents, the gay or lesbian parent may have finally come out after many years of agonising over their sexual orientation. Sometimes they may have succumbed to societal pressures and married young and only later discovered their sexuality; in other cases they may have tried to suppress their sexuality; in yet others, they may have been open about their sexual orientation with their opposite-sex partner all along. Even if the heterosexual parent generally showed a gay-friendly attitude, this may change when confronted with the shock of separation and divorce. The gay or lesbian parent may feel guilty. Often the heterosexual parent will feel that the child is best brought up by them and/or in a heterosexual family. Sometimes irrational fears and arguments such as HIV infection, taking the child to gay clubs, introducing the child to 'unsuitable friends', etc. will be brought up. In all these situations it is important when acting for either party to put the child's interests at the centre. When acting for the gay or lesbian parent, it will be important to keep any evidence focused on the child and at the same time include issues that will pre-empt such irrational fears, for example by showing that the sleeping arrangements for overnight contact are such that there is no chance of the child walking in on the gay or lesbian parent and their partner. Suspicion of new partners may be higher than in a heterosexual context, especially if meeting the new partner provided the momentum for the gay or lesbian parent to come out.

When a same-sex couple separates, issues about contact or residence may arise in a similar way as for an opposite-sex couple. In the vast majority of cases where an opposite-sex couple is separating, it is still uncontroversial that the children will live with the mother, who in the majority of cases will have been the main carer. By contrast there are further complications in same-sex parenting, partly because these gender-stereotypical roles seldom apply and partly because the main carer may not be the biological (or legal) parent of the child. Two women may live together and one of them may care for their children, but the other (or both if more than one child) may be the biological parent of a child. If a couple adopted a child, until 2005 only one of them could be the adoptive parent and that may not be the person who mainly looks after the children. See also *Re G (Residence: Same-sex Partners)* and *CG* v. *CW & G (Children)* above and *G* v. *F (Contact and Shared Residence: Applications for Leave)* above. Co-parenting arrangements are discussed in **7.1.2** above.

7.3 LEGAL CHANGES IN 2005

7.3.1 Introduction

Two major changes came in at the end of 2005. While other minor but significant changes were made by the CPA 2004, the main development with regard to children was of course the ACA 2002, which finally came into force on 30 December 2005. Although not intended as legislation for gay equality, this for the first time introduces the possibility of joint adoption by same-sex couples and therefore the possibility that a child can have two mothers or two fathers. Conceptually this is a big leap. The concept of legal adoption has been around for a long time, although there is of course no biological foundation for the creation of legal parent–child relationships. Equally, the deeming provisions under the HFEA 1990 create legal parent–child relationships often without any biological connection (see **7.4.1**). However, both adoption and the provisions under the HFEA 1990 were until then restricted to opposite-sex couples, and the ACA 2002 broke out of this mould.

In addition to adoption, the ACA 2002 introduces extended joint residence orders (**7.3.3**) and parental responsibility agreements for step-parents (**7.3.4**).

7.3.2 Adoption

While there is a great demand for adoptive children in the UK, this is predominantly from opposite-sex couples who are unable to have children themselves, and the demand is mainly for white babies. Social services find it difficult to find adoptive parents for older children, who may be traumatised by their early experiences; for disabled children; for siblings; and for children from ethnic minorities, whom the agencies tend to try to place with parents from the same or similar ethnic background. The focus in Parliament was therefore to some extent on allowing same-sex couples to adopt in order to find adoptive parents for these children. Many same-sex couples have chosen to foster or adopt children from these categories, maybe because they do not necessarily have an image of a stereotypical heterosexual family with a baby that they are trying to fulfil by adopting, and because they will have given parenting a lot of thought. This is also reflected by the circumstances of *Re E (Adoption: Freeing Order)* [1995] 1 FLR 382 and the quotes from a Government report by Singer J in *Re W (Adoption: Homosexual Adopter)* [1997] 2 FLR 406 (**7.2.2** above). Nevertheless adoption by same-sex couples is of course not confined to such children. It is likely that initially the majority of same-sex couples who adopt will be those where one of the couple is already the parent of the child or children, either biologically or by previous adoption. Whether adoption agencies will treat same-sex couples and gay and lesbian potential adopters in the same way as they treat opposite-sex couples and heterosexual people remains to be seen. That adoption by gay men and lesbians cannot be taken for granted is shown in the case of *Fretté* v. *France* (Application No.36515/97) [2003] 2 FLR 9 where the European Court of Human Rights rejected the application by a gay man against the ban on adoption by single people in French law. Many countries who introduced same-sex registered partnership years before the UK expressly excluded adoption from the remit of the regime, although some have introduced it since (e.g. Sweden).

Adoption is the only way to create a legal parent–child relationship. It is easy to ignore the importance of adoption from the viewpoint of a family lawyer, who will often be confronted with acute problems arising from separation and family breakdown. Parental responsibility may give the parent the same rights and duties as any other parent to make decisions about the child's life, but it does not make the adult a parent of the child. The legal relationship may be important in a variety of contexts, including:

- later on in life when the adult may be mentally incapacitated, in hospital or dying and the then grown-up child wants to act as next-of kin;
- when the adult child may be mentally incapacitated, in hospital or dying and the parent wants to act as next-of-kin;
- death of the adult, which is particularly important if the adult dies intestate or when domiciled in a country where there are compulsory inheritance shares for children (and there are other children or other relatives who will take priority), as well as in the context of foreign inheritance tax;
- death of the child (whether under or over the age of majority) and the consequential inheritance and other issues.

Although adoption is a lengthy and cumbersome as well as an intrusive process, it is worth considering it even if a same-sex couple do not in the first instance contemplate it. The details of the procedure under the ACA 2002 are beyond the scope of this book and parents in this situation should in the first instance look at information that is publicly available from social services and consult specialist practitioners. Adoption is unlikely, however, to be an option if there is another parent (such as one mother's former husband or a sperm donor who co-parents). In these situations other ways of regularising the relationships between the parents and the children will need to be considered (see below). As the adoption process takes a relatively long time, the adopters should be advised of other ways to acquire parental responsibility in the meantime (see below).

Adoption is now possible by a couple or a single person (ACA 2002, ss.50 and 51 respectively). A couple is defined in ACA 2002, s.144(4) as a married couple, civil partners (inserted by CPA 2004, s.79(12)) or 'two people (whether of different sexes or the same sex) living as partners in an enduring family relationship'. The advantage for civil partners is that they do not need to show that their relationship is 'enduring'. However, in practice this may not be of great relevance. Civil partners are generally treated in the same way as spouses for issues such as single adoption (which is only possible in certain circumstances if the adopter is in a civil partnership: ACA 2002, s.51(3A)) and a prohibition against adopting a former civil partner (ACA 2002, s.47(8A); amended by CPA 2004, s.79). This will have marginal significance because an application for adoption in English law must be started while the child to be adopted is under 18.

Step-parents can now adopt without the need for the existing parent to adopt their own children (ACA 2002, s.51(2)).

7.3.3 Residence orders

Residence orders have long been the only way that same-sex parents were both able to have parental responsibility because they confer parental responsibility for their duration. While they were first granted only with reluctance, recent experience shows that courts make them willingly and judges are generally delighted to deal with parents who agree rather than disagree with each other, as most of those coming before the courts do. However, the power of joint residence orders is limited because:

1. Parental responsibility stops when the joint residence order stops. Therefore, if the parents separate, the courts may contemplate continuing a joint residence order where they would not do so if the non-resident parent had parental responsibility already in some other way (for example by being the biological father or an adoptive parent). This was the issue in *Re G (Residence: Same-sex Partners)* [2005] 2 FLR 957 (see **7.2.2** above; see also *Re H (Shared Residence: Parental Responsibility)* [1995] 2 FLR 883).
2. Joint residence orders end when the child reaches the age of 16. The Children Act 1989, s.12(5)–(6) inserted by ACA 2002, s.114 gives the courts power to direct that the residence order (whether joint or not) should continue until the age of 18 if it is in favour of someone other

than a parent or guardian of the child, and this may only be varied with leave of the court. This closes the lacuna between those ages. Existing residence orders are not affected and a fresh application is necessary.

3. Parental responsibility does not create a parent–child relationship (see adoption at **7.3.2**).

Civil partners and former civil partners will not need leave to apply to the court for a residence order.

7.3.4 Parental responsibility

Mothers have parental responsibility automatically (CA 1989, s.2(1) and 2(2)(a)) as do fathers who:

- are married to the mother at the date of birth (CA 1989, s.2(1));
- married the mother subsequently (Legitimacy Act 1976, s.2); or
- are named as the father on the birth certificate if the birth was registered after 1 December 2003 (see CA 1989, s.4(1) as amended by ACA 2002, s.111).

Other fathers have been able to acquire parental responsibility through a parental responsibility agreement in the prescribed form or by court order (CA 1989, s.4). No other person could acquire parental responsibility as such, but a residence order confers parental responsibility for its duration (see **7.3.3**). A new s.4A is inserted into the CA 1989 by ACA 2002, s.112 which allows step-parents to acquire parental responsibility by parental responsibility agreement or court order, and this is extended to civil partners by CPA 2004, s.75(2). This applies to the husband or wife or civil partner of either parent, not only the parent the child lives with, and irrespective of whether there is a residence order. The agreement needs to be signed by all parents with parental responsibility. That means that if the father does not have parental responsibility (for example an unmarried father or a donor friend to a lesbian mother), only the mother needs to sign the agreement to confer parental responsibility to her civil partner or husband. It is likely that the courts will be more reluctant to remove parental responsibility from a step-parent who has acquired it through an agreement without good reason. On the other hand, it is not necessarily a given that the step-parent would be granted parental responsibility by court order. Therefore a father without parental responsibility should apply for it if the mother is planning to marry or register a civil partnership and if he does not necessarily want the mother's husband or civil partner to have parental responsibility. Any father or step-parent who has acquired parental responsibility through an agreement or court order or an unmarried father who has parental responsibility by virtue of being on the birth certificate can lose it through an order of the court. However, this is likely to be extremely rare.

Through the obvious biological constraints, the majority of civil partners with children will be in a situation where one is a step-parent of the child or children (except if one partner has changed gender, see **5.4.4**). Therefore the new parental responsibility agreement option for step-parents is extremely important for civil partners. Remarried mothers may not be able to use this option because the child's father may not willingly agree to sign it. By contrast, in many cases children of mothers in a civil partnership do not have a (legal) father or none with parental responsibility and therefore the mother and her civil partner can use this option without having to consult another adult. There is no fee and the form is available from the court service website or from any family court. The procedure is slightly complex but it is explained on the reverse of the form. The form has to be signed at a court office and the agreement has to be lodged at the Principal Registry afterwards. Therefore this is an option that does not have to involve solicitors and is free of charge to the parents. The parents should, however, be aware that parental responsibility does not make the adult a parent of the child (see **7.3.2**).

7.3.5   Contact, residence orders and other s.8 orders

Civil partners will be able to apply for contact and residence orders in respect of their stepchildren without leave of the court (CA 1989, s.10(5)(aa) as amended by CPA 2004, s.77). See also **7.2.3** above. This does not apply to specific issue and prohibited steps orders, although leave should usually be granted without much effort.

7.3.6   Guardianship

Any parent who has parental responsibility for a child may appoint someone else as guardian. The appointment will take effect on the parent's death if (CA 1989, s.5(1)):

• the deceased parent has a residence order in their favour, or
• there is no other parent with parental responsibility.

Otherwise the appointment takes effect on the death of the other parent. It does not matter if a step-parent has parental responsibility, nor if a non-parent has a residence order in their favour.

Example 7.1

Lucy lives with her mother and stepfather and there is a residence order in their favour. The mother has appointed her mother (Lucy's grandmother) as guardian. The appointment takes effect on the mother's death because of the residence order. Lucy's father then appoints his civil partner as guardian. On

Lucy's father's death both the maternal grandmother and the father's surviving civil partner will have parental responsibility.

If the adults cannot work together the court can bring the guardianship to an end (CA 1989, s.6(7)). It would seem that if there is a joint residence order in favour of both (separated) parents, the appointment of a guardian by the first parent to die will take effect on the death of that parent, whereas it would not take effect if there was no residence order at all. Most appointments are made in a will but they can be made independently from any will. They are often forgotten, but are another way of protecting the child in case of a parent's death. The Children Act 1989, s.6(3A) (inserted by CPA 2004, s.7) provides that an appointment of the other civil partner will end with the dissolution of the civil partnership, as is the case for marriage.

7.3.7   Relative

Section 75(4) of the CPA 2004 changes the definition of 'relative' in CA 1989, s.105 to include 'a grandparent, brother, sister, uncle or aunt (whether of the full blood or half blood or by marriage or civil partnership) or step-parent'. Step-parents include the civil partners of parents (s.75(2) amending CA 1989, s.4A(1)). This means that these relatives through civil partnership can receive local authority support under CA 1989, s.23 and do not count as private foster carers or childminders under Parts 9 and 10A of that Act.

7.3.8   The international dimension

Within the EU (except Denmark) the revised Brussels II (EU Regulation 2201/2003) provides that the courts in the country where the child is habitually resident shall have jurisdiction. The Regulation does not apply to adoption, 'the establishment or contesting of a parent-child relationship', or the names of a child. Paternity and adoption are generally governed by the law of the parent's domicile or nationality and a detailed investigation is beyond the scope of this work. Where such issues of paternity or parentage are dependent on a civil partnership and this is not recognised in another country, there may be uncertainty whether the parentage is recognised. Parental responsibility agreements or orders should fall within the remit of Brussels II and should therefore be recognised. Outside the EU, other treaties may apply. Detailed advice will be required if a couple in a civil partnership with children plan to emigrate.

While adoption by same-sex parents who are both domiciled in the UK should be recognised if the family moves to another country, this is by no means guaranteed. Another issue altogether is inter-country adoption where a child is brought from one country to another for the purposes of adoption or where a UK-resident person goes abroad to adopt and comes back with the child. Many overseas countries will not allow adoption by a single person or same-sex couples and this, for example, includes China. Again, detailed advice and guidance will be necessary in these cases as it may be easy for the prospective adopters to unwittingly commit an offence.

For the purposes of Art.3(a) of the Hague Convention of 25 October 1980 on the Civil Aspects of International Child Abduction, 'rights of custody' equate to parental responsibility in English law. It may nevertheless not be easy to convince a foreign court that the non-birth parent in a same-sex relationship has rights of custody under the Convention and it may be wise to apply for a declaration to that effect in the English courts at the earliest opportunity. If a court orders a civil partner to disclose information about a child's whereabouts under the Child Abduction and Custody Act 1985, s.24A, the fact that this may incriminate the civil partner is not an excuse for not disclosing the information (Child Abduction and Custody Act 1985, s.24A(2), as amended by CPA 2004, Sched.27, para.110).

7.3.9   Courts

Although all family courts can deal with applications under the CA 1989 by same-sex couples or civil partners, only a small number of courts have so far been designated civil partnership courts for dissolutions, etc. of civil partnership. It is likely that more courts will be designated in due course and the limited number reflects the fact that in the early life of the Act there will be few such applications. Nevertheless, the designations go in parallel with judicial training and it may therefore be advisable to make applications under the CA 1989 in those courts where the judiciary and the staff are more likely to have received training on civil partnership and awareness of same-sex partners (see **4.5.2**).

7.4   OUTSTANDING ISSUES

7.4.1   Donor insemination

The Human Fertilisation and Embryology Act 1990, s.13(5) provides that:

> a woman shall not be provided with treatment services unless account has been taken of the welfare of the child who may be born as a result of the treatment (including the need of that child for a father), and of any other child who may be affected by the birth.

This has been interpreted by some clinics as prohibiting treatment of lesbians. This decision would obviously be discriminatory unless it was based on scientific research that showed that being brought up by a lesbian (couple) was detrimental to a child's welfare. In fact, research shows that a child's welfare is not negatively affected if the child does not have a father. The restrictive interpretation of HFEA 1990, s.13(5) is a contributing factor to the informal parenting arrangements entered into by many lesbians (see **7.1.2**). The recent Government consultation *Review of the Human Fertilisation and Embryology Act*, which closed on 25 November 2005 (at para.3.27) invited comment on this point and pointed out that studies do not support the notion that children raised by mothers alone are adversely affected as a result. It is possible therefore that the entire welfare consideration may be changed and this provision may be dropped.

Under HFEA 1990, ss.27 and 28 a mother who carries a child following fertility treatment in a licensed clinic is legally the mother of the child (even if the egg was donated by another woman). Her husband will be the legal father (unless he did not consent to the treatment), even if the sperm was donated by someone else (HFEA 1990, s.28(2)). The mother's unmarried male partner will be the legal father if the mother and her male partner were treated together (HFEA 1990, s.28(3)). The Civil Partnership Act 2004 does not make any changes to the HFEA 1990. When the conceptual hurdle has been crossed that a child can have two mothers, there seems little sense in not extending the provisions for deemed legal parentage under the HFEA 1990 to same-sex couples so that the mother's civil partner or same-sex partner will automatically be regarded as the child's mother too. Indeed, this was mooted in the Government's consultation on the HFEA 1990 (para.8.19 onwards). It is likely therefore that the revised Act will provide for this, at least if the measures find parliamentary time and get past both Houses of Parliament.

7.4.2 Surrogacy

Under HFEA 1990, s.30 the court can make a parental order in favour of a married couple to make them the legal parents of a child where the child was carried by a surrogate mother with either the egg of the wife or the sperm of the husband. Effectively this is a form of fast-track adoption with another name. No provision is made for parental orders for unmarried couples or any same-sex couples. Since surrogacy is the only way a male same-sex couple can have natural children, this is of course an important issue. The law surrounding surrogacy is complex and there are a number of offences in relation to surrogacy including negotiating a surrogacy agreement on a commercial basis (which probably includes lawyers) and advertising for surrogate mothers (Surrogacy Arrangements Act 1985, ss.2 and 3). Parental orders cannot be made if the surrogate mother has been paid money over and above her reasonable expenses unless the court authorises that payment. For these reasons surrogacy in the UK is rare. The Government's consultation on the HFEA 1990 (see **7.4.1**) also mooted changing the provision to extend parental orders to civil partners and unmarried and unregistered couples.

CHAPTER 8

International aspects

8.1 WHAT IS INTERNATIONAL ABOUT CIVIL PARTNERSHIP?

8.1.1 Introduction

This chapter will bring together all international aspects of civil partnership, most of which are set out in Part 5 of the CPA 2004. The main points covered are:

- capacity and domicile (**8.2**);
- registration of a UK civil partnership in UK consulates, etc. (**8.3.1**);
- registration by soldiers, sailors and airmen abroad (**8.3.2**);
- overseas relationships that are recognised here, the conditions and the way they are recognised including potential problems and pitfalls (**8.4**); these arise mainly from the fact that a number of overseas regimes are much weaker than marriage or UK civil partnership but will be recognised as civil partnerships here;
- jurisdiction for dissolution and stays of proceedings (**8.5**); this is largely modelled on divorce law, but there are problems resulting from the lack of mutual agreements and the lack of rules of conflict and jurisdictions in foreign regimes;
- the recognition of overseas dissolutions (**8.6**); again this is modelled on the recognition of overseas divorces, but again there are some problems arising from the fact that some overseas regimes can be dissolved fairly easily;
- a comparison table, comparing the law relating to civil partnerships with marriage and divorce law (**8.7**).

For a brief discussion of the international aspects of the law relating to children see **7.3.8**.

8.1.2 Other countries

Although out of nearly 200 countries and territories in the world only a minority have any recognition of same-sex partnership, this is growing steadily and rapidly. It started in 1989 with registered partnership in Denmark, which was followed during the 1990 by the other Nordic countries. Belgium, the Netherlands, Finland and Germany enacted similar schemes around the turn of the century. France and some Spanish regions have enacted somewhat weaker schemes since the late 1990s. In Canada and Vermont, civil union schemes were enacted after legal challenges in the early years of this century. The last three years have seen an acceleration in the creation of statutory registered partnership schemes as well as the judicial and statutory extension of the definition of marriage. Currently about 25 countries or US states have some form of same-sex partnership registration scheme that confers some or all of the rights of marriage to couples who register.

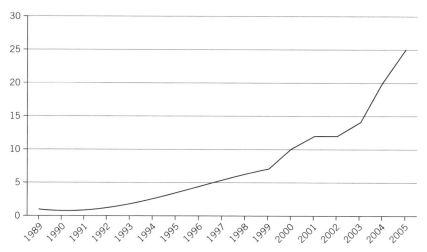

Figure 8.1   Registered partnership regimes including marriage (numbers of countries or territories)

A non-exhaustive list of countries and territories that have same-sex partnership regimes is provided at **8.4.4**.

8.1.3   Significance of international law

Marriage is a universal concept and divorce is almost universal (Malta being the obvious exception), even if in some countries either or both may be governed by religious laws rather than state laws. Opposite-sex couples coming to the UK from abroad, whether as tourists or to settle here, can marry either in their home country or in the UK (subject to residence requirements and immigration control, see **Chapter 11**), and the marriage will generally be recognised in the other country. Most countries also have mature conflict of laws rules to determine which law governs a particular individual's status and the courts of this country have jurisdiction to entertain applications for divorce. None of this exists in a similar way for same-sex partner-

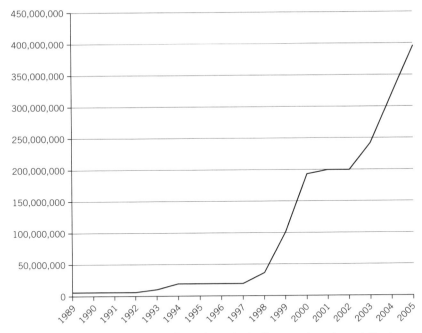

Figure 8.2   Registered partnership regimes including marriage (population)

ship. Those countries that allow same-sex marriage will probably treat same-sex spouses like opposite-sex spouses for international law, but most countries have no same-sex partnership regimes and those that do generally lack conflict of laws rules. The regimes differ widely in their legal consequences, ranging from merely conferring tax and social security benefits through to the inclusion of all the rights and duties of marriage including inheritance and succession rights, duties to maintain each other and provision for sharing assets after the breakdown of the relationship.

There is probably a higher proportion of foreign nationals amongst gay men and lesbians in the UK (especially in London and the big cities) than in the heterosexual population. This may be because gay men and lesbians are more mobile because they tend to have weaker family ties and are less likely to have children. It may also be because Great Britain, and especially London, is a place where one's sexual orientation becomes less important and gay men and lesbians can live a freer life than in, say, a small village or town of a religious country (see for example 'Polish leader's anti-gay stance threatens EU voting rights', *The Guardian*, 25 October 2005). While foreign nationals and ethnic minorities in the UK often marry within their community for a variety of reasons, including religion and family expectations, these constraints have little or no impact on lesbians and gay men, who may be more likely to take partners from a different background from their own.

While a fair proportion of foreign gay men and lesbians are from EU countries and will not need a visa to come to the UK, others may come here for a short stay and are then required to leave. If they have formed a relationship with a British or EU citizen, one of the considerations as to whether or not the couple should register as civil partners may therefore be the immigration issues (see also **Chapter 11**). For all these reasons, it is expected that the international issues are likely to play a more important role in civil partnership law than in matrimonial law.

Finally, many international family law issues are probably glossed over by the courts and by practitioners because under English conflict rules English courts always apply English law to divorce and the consequences of divorce. Therefore even if the parties are foreign nationals or foreign domiciled, foreign law will probably not come into any of the advice or considerations on a divorce. However, this may change under EU proposals in the next few years, and whether or not this will include civil partnership remains to be seen.

8.2   CAPACITY AND DOMICILE

The test of whether prospective civil partners have capacity to enter into a civil partnership is entirely based on English law (or Scottish or Northern Irish depending on where the couple registers) and not on the law of the party's nationality or domicile (see also **3.3**). This makes it easier to check capacity and is more straightforward than the law in this area for marriage. The basic rule for the recognition of marriages is that the parties have to have capacity to marry according to their ante-nuptial domicile (*Dicey and Morris on the Conflict of Laws*, 13th Edn (Sweet & Maxwell, 2000), rule 68). However, a marriage will also be regarded as valid if:

- the parties had capacity under the law of the jurisdiction with which they have the most real and substantial connection, i.e. usually their intended matrimonial home (*Lawrence* v. *Lawrence* [1985] Fam 106, CA);
- one party was English domiciled and both would have had capacity under English law (*Sottomayor, otherwise De Barros* v. *De Barros (No.2)* (1879–80) LR 5 PD 94);
- a party's first marriage was dissolved or annulled in England (or such a divorce or nullity is recognised here) even if it is not recognised under the law of that party's domicile (Family Law Act 1986, s.50); the same applies to Scotland and Northern Ireland;
- in an exceptional case, to give recognition to the foreign law would be unconscionable (*Cheni (otherwise Rodriguez)* v. *Cheni* [1965] P 85, per Sir Jocelyn Simon P at 98).

Therefore in both statute and case law the general principle has been rather watered down. These cases concerned spouses who were divorced abroad when the law of their domicile did not recognise divorce (*Lawrence*, above) or spouses who were related in a degree that prohibited marriage under the law of their domicile but not under English law (*Sottomayor* and *Cheni*, above). Nevertheless, it is arguable that the last principle should also apply to a case where the foreign law would be unconscionable on, say, human rights grounds, for example if it prohibited marriage between people of different ethnic origin (as the law of some US States did as recently as 1967, see *Loving* v. *Virginia*, 388 US1 (1967)). Such a law would clearly be 'unconscionable' (*Cheni*).

There is no reference to foreign domicile in the CPA 2004 for civil partnership registration. The result is that anyone can register a civil partnership here provided:

- they have the requisite visa (see **Chapter 11**); and
- they have capacity under English (or Scottish or Northern Irish) law.

It may be argued that it would not be wise to allow people to marry in the UK when that marriage would clearly not be recognised in their home country (*R* v. *Brentwood Superintendent Registrar of Marriages, ex parte Arias* [1968] 2 QB 956). However, as far as civil partnership is concerned, this does not exist anywhere apart from the UK, and reliance on domicile would therefore preclude any foreign domiciled person from registering here. In that case immigration law based on civil partnership would be pointless and the large number of foreign lesbians and gay men living in the UK would be denied equality. Theoretically, there could have been a restriction preventing those people who have no connection at all with the UK from registering a civil partnership, or even a similar restriction on people domiciled in a country that does not recognise any form of registered partnership (say Italians). However, there are so many possible reasons for registration where there is only a slight connection with the UK (a dormant pension, property that could be inherited, etc.) that it would be impossible to define the class of people who have no legitimate interest in registering a civil partnership here. It also raises issues of discrimination on nationality under EU law. The upshot of this is that, for example, theoretically two 16-year-old Greek lesbian tourists could register a civil partnership in Scotland. There is, of course, little harm in this because for Greek law it is of no consequence anyway. This chapter is mainly concerned with the question of whether a civil partnership, an overseas relationship or a dissolution or annulment is recognised in the UK, not whether it would be recognised in other countries. The law on this will vary from country to country and is unlikely to be consistent in any event.

8.3 REGISTERING A UK CIVIL PARTNERSHIP OUTSIDE THE UK

8.3.1 Registration in a UK diplomatic mission abroad

It is possible to marry in some UK overseas missions, for instance in the Embassy in Riyadh in Saudi Arabia. As marriage is freely available world-wide, in almost all countries this provision is not necessary. Saudi Arabia is one of a few exceptions, where this option is available to help non-Muslim expatriates who would otherwise have difficulty marrying there. With civil partnership a similar issue does of course arise in many more countries. Even in those countries where similar regimes exist, British expatriates may not be able to register or marry because the host country may only allow citizens to do so. Civil partnership does of course have far-reaching consequences including, for instance, succession free from inheritance tax (see **Chapter 13**) and access to dependants' pensions (see **Chapter 9**). In certain cases where the life of one partner is at risk, waiting to register a civil partnership until a return to the UK may not be a viable option, or would be a high-risk strategy. In other cases it may not be possible to come to the UK, for example if a non-British partner cannot obtain a visa for the UK or if one of the partners is unable to travel because of ill-health. Therefore CPA 2004, s.210 includes the facility to allow registrations to take place in overseas diplomatic missions. The details are set out in the Civil Partnership (Registration Abroad and Certificates) Order 2005, SI 2005/2761.

The conditions for registration are as follows (s.210(2) and (3)):

1. At least one of the partners is a UK national (also art.4(2)(a) of the Order).
2. The partners are eligible to register in the part of the UK (Scotland, Northern Ireland or England and Wales) which they have chosen on the notice of the proposed civil partnership (art.5(3)(f) of the Order). There is no requirement for a connection, so that a couple may chose Scottish law for example if one of them is 16 or 17 to avoid having to obtain parental consent (also art.4(2)(b) of the Order).
3. The authorities in the host country 'will not object to the registration'. It is unclear what this will mean in practice. On the one hand, it could mean that the authorities are asked about the idea of having registrations in the British consulate or High Commission in general and if they object, it is taken no further. On the other hand it could mean that the authorities will be asked about every single registration giving the names of the prospective partners. The wording of the CPA 2004 would imply the latter ('not object to the registration' as opposed to 'not object to civil partnership registrations'); however, the former would make more sense and would no doubt also be in the interest of any couples who would not want their sexual orientation to be outed, especially in countries where objections are likely. According to the website of the British Consulate

General in Hong Kong, the authorities there were asked and objected, but the consulates in the following countries offer registrations: Australia*, Belarus, Colombia, Costa Rica, Croatia*, Israel*, Japan, Moldova, South Africa, Switzerland*, Turkmenistan, United States*, Venezuela and Vietnam. Specific rules apply in (*) asterisked countries (source: **www.fco.gov.uk**, updated 13 April 2006). Of course this could mean that the host country is first of all asked in general terms and if the authorities object in general terms, the matter rests there. However, if the authorities approve in general terms, they might still be asked to consent to the registration of the particular couple, who as a result might face persecution. This would be deeply unsatisfactory. Any couple wishing to register a civil partnership overseas should ascertain in advance who will be asked for approval and whether their names will be put forward to the host country's authorities (also art.4(2)(c) of the Order).

4. 'Insufficient facilities exist' for the couple to register an overseas relationship there. This should include both the case where there is no regime that would be recognised in the UK at all, and the case where the local regime is not available to the particular couple, for example because it is exclusive to nationals of that country. This problem has been ignored by the Foreign and Commonwealth Office and art.4(4) of the Order specifically provides that any country or territory listed in Sched.20 to the Act 'has sufficient facilities to allow entry into an overseas relationship' when this is clearly not the case (see Katharina Boele-Woelki and Angelika Fuchs (eds), *Legal Recognition of Same-Sex Couples in Europe* (Intersentia, 2003), Part 2; also art.4(2)(d) of the Order).

5. The particular registration would not be 'inconsistent with international law or the comity of nations'. This is extremely vague and it is not really clear how a private registration which is in the realm of the private law on personal status or possibly the law of obligations could be inconsistent with the law of nations. This condition has not been further specified in the Order, other than that the officer can refuse to register a civil partnership on this ground (s.210(4) and art.4(6) of the Order). There is an appeal to the Secretary of State against such a refusal (art.4(7) of the Order).

The Order sets out a procedure largely following the registration under English law including:

- a requirement to have been resident in the consular district for the seven days before notice is given and a 14-day waiting period (art.5);
- parental consent for 16- and 17-year-olds (art.7, but not if the partners elected Scotland as the relevant part of the UK, which makes this provision in practice redundant);
- objections (art.8);
- registrations only between 8am and 6pm local time, by signing the document (art.10) and only within three months from the notice or from when

the couple were notified that the registration could go ahead after an appeal or objection (art.9(1)).

Article 13 allows the Secretary of State to waive some or all of the formal requirements as to residence, notice and waiting period. This will accommodate people who are seriously ill or house-bound.

For the purposes of UK law, the civil partners are then treated as if they had registered in the part of the UK they elected (art.18). The fees can be found in the Consular Fees Order 2005, SI 2005/1465, as amended by the Consular Fees (Civil Partnership) Order 2005, SI 2005/2762.

8.3.2 Registration by armed forces personnel abroad

While most British expatriates are probably able to travel to the UK to register (subject to ill-health or a foreign partner's immigration problems), soldiers, sailors, airmen and other armed forces personnel will be bound by duty to serve abroad, maybe for several months at a stretch. If they form a relationship or their duties turn from support or peacekeeping to combat, they may want to register as soon as possible in order to protect their partners rather than wait until a return to the UK. Section 211 of the CPA 2004 and the Civil Partnership (Armed Forces) Order 2005, SI 2005/3188, provide for registration abroad or on naval ships for couples, one of whom is a member of the armed forces, employed by the armed forces or a child of such people. Children include children who were treated as children of a family (married or civil partners: s.211(3)). Article 4 of the Order defines who counts as employed by the armed forces for the purposes of these provisions. The provisions do not apply to the armed forces of other countries including commonwealth countries (CPA 2004, s.245(2) and Army Act 1955, s.225(1)).

The section follows provisions under the Foreign Marriage Act 1892, s.22 as amended by the Foreign Marriage Act 1947 and the Foreign Marriage (Amendment) Act 1988, which provide for marriages under UK law abroad for military and civilian armed forces personnel and their children. The couple have to choose whether they want to register under English, Scottish or Northern Irish law (art.6(g)) and there are no restrictions on this. The provisions are again similar to those of a registration in England and Wales including:

- notice to be given (art.6);
- parental consent for 16- and 17-year-olds (art.7, but not if the partners elected Scotland as the relevant part of the UK, which makes this provision in practice redundant);
- publicity (art.9);
- objections (art.10); and
- registrations by signing the civil partnership register (art.12).

In contrast to the provisions for registration in diplomatic missions (see **8.3.1** above) the notice must state the occupation rather than the nationality of the partners (art.6(2)(c)), the registering officer may require proof of ID (art.8), and only the names have to be publicised, but then for 15 rather than 14 days (art.9). The registration can take place within a period of 12 months from the notice or last notice (art.11(4)), but there are no provisions for the waiting period to be shortened as there are in art.13 of the Civil Partnership (Registration Abroad and Certificates) Order 2005, SI 2005/2761. This is regrettable, especially considering that in a number of situations this could be vital, such as notice to a soldier to move to a combat situation within days or where a wounded soldier may not survive.

Article 2(2) specifies the areas where registrations can take place, namely in Australia, Canada, the Falkland Islands, Germany, Gibraltar, Nepal, the United States of America and the Sovereign Base Areas of Akrotiri and Dhekelia in Cyprus. In addition registrations can take place on naval ships which are 'for the time being in the waters of a country or territory outside the United Kingdom' (s.211(5)). It is unclear from the wording whether this includes ships on the High Seas. Unfortunately these provisions leave out many areas where British armed forces are currently based, including large contingents in Afghanistan, Bosnia, Kosovo and the Middle East (Iraq and surrounding areas) as well as smaller contingents in Belize, Brunei, Kenya and Sierra Leone and over 60 other countries around the world (see **www.mod.uk**). This means that the main centres of combat and therefore danger to personnel are excluded. Cyprus, a country generally not perceived as looking favourably on equality for lesbians and gay men, is not, strictly speaking, included as Akrotiri and Dhekelia are sovereign and therefore the Cypriot government has no say in the matter. As with registrations in overseas diplomatic missions, art.13 provides that the registration is deemed to have taken place in a part of the UK chosen by the couple.

8.4 OVERSEAS RELATIONSHIPS

8.4.1 Provisions

Chapter 2 of Part 5 of the CPA 2004 makes provision for recognition of overseas same-sex registered partnership and marriage subject to some minimum standards. The regimes that are recognised are either those set out in Sched.20 (s.213) or they have to fulfil the general conditions set out in s.214. The general problem with this is that the regimes that will be recognised may be far weaker than civil partnership, or the partners may never have envisaged entering a relationship where they have, say, duties to maintain each other or where intestacy provisions apply.

An overseas relationship is recognised if it is between two people of the same sex and either it is one of the regimes specified in Sched.20 (s.213) or it meets the general conditions of s.214. There are provisions for people who have changed their gender (s.216) and minimum requirements as to capacity (ss.214 and 217) as well as a public policy exception (s.218).

On the face of it, this may exclude regimes that are hybrid regimes, either because they are available to both same-sex and opposite-sex couples (such as the French Pacs or the Dutch registered partnership) or because they are formed by either a registration process or de facto cohabitation (e.g. the Catalan regime). Since several regimes that are also open to opposite-sex couples are in fact included in Sched.20, however, these conditions must be interpreted to apply to the individual relationship to be recognised rather than to the regime as a whole. Therefore the fact that a regime is open to opposite-sex couples or also applies to couples who have lived together for a certain number of years without registering still means that this regime is included, but only for same-sex couples who have gone through a registration procedure. Opposite-sex registered partners are not recognised in the UK nor are overseas de facto regimes.

The CPA 2004 provides for two types of regimes that are recognised:

1. Those in Sched.20, which can be amended by statutory instrument (and which has already been so amended: see the Civil Partnership Act 2004 (Overseas Relationships and Consequential, etc. Amendments) Order 2005, SI 2005/3129 and the Civil Partnership Act 2004 (Overseas Relationships) Order 2005, SI 2005/3135 – see the bold entries in **8.4.4** below for a list incorporating these two amendments).
2. Those that meet the general conditions (s.214), which are:

    (a) that the relationship is of indeterminate duration;
    (b) that the parties are treated as a couple generally or for specified purposes or as married; and
    (c) that the process of entering into the relationship requires a registration with the authorities in that jurisdiction.

The conditions for recognition are set out in **figure 8.3**.

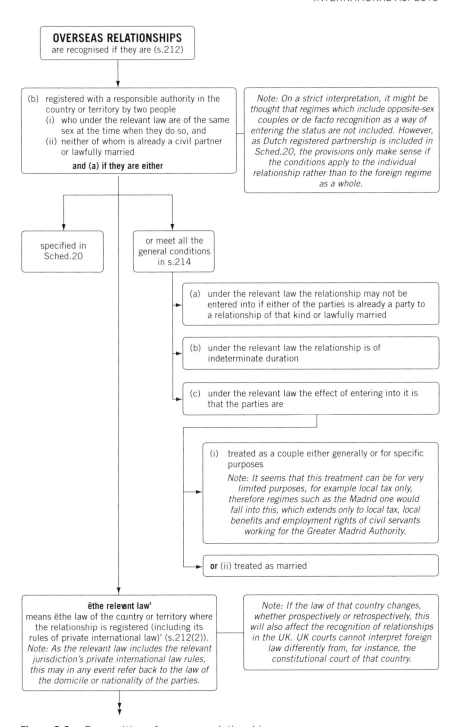

Figure 8.3 Recognition of overseas relationships

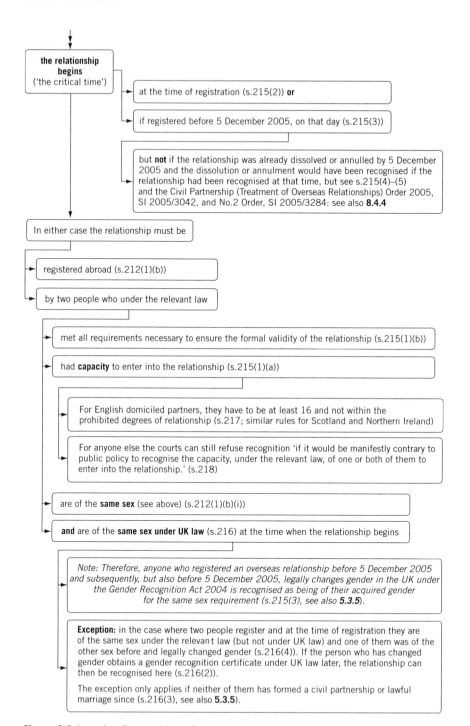

Figure 8.3 (*cont.*)   Recognition of overseas relationships

8.4.2 Problems

There are a number of problems with the way that the Act recognises foreign regimes:

- it creates uncertainty, including to the extent that some couples may not even suspect that they are regarded as civil partners;
- the regime that the parties entered into may be quite different from civil partnership, which will then apply to them;
- it creates bizarre situations in some circumstances;
- it sits uneasily with gender recognition;
- there are likely to be legacy regimes that will remain to be recognised here as civil partnerships long after they have ceased to have much significance in their own country.

Uncertainty

If a regime is listed in Sched.20, the couple can be reasonably certain that it will be recognised. However, the reverse is not true: even if a regime is not included in Sched.20, it may still fulfil the general conditions of s.214. This may apply whether the foreign law came into force (or was affirmed or created by a court decision) after the CPA 2004 (and the latest update of Sched.20) and was not included for that reason, or whether it already existed before the Act came into force and was overlooked or was not included because the Secretary of State believed that it did not meet the general conditions, maybe because it was impossible to find enough information about the overseas regime. Even if a regime is removed from Sched.20, this does not mean that it does not fulfil the general conditions. There is no list of regimes that *do not* fulfil the general conditions. Ultimately recognition is a matter for the courts, not for the Secretary of State, although if a regime is included, it definitely qualifies. The courts could then only refuse recognition of the partnership of an individual couple on public policy grounds under s.218. If a regime is not included in Sched.20, an overseas couple coming to the UK will face great uncertainty. They may, for instance, find that HM Revenue and Customs asserts that they are not civil partners (and therefore, capital gains tax is payable on a transfer of an asset between them). If they then decide to register as civil partners, the registrar may refuse to register them, arguing that they are already civil partners because of the overseas relationship. Some limited certainty may be provided by the provisions of art.15 of the Civil Partnership (Registration Abroad and Certificates) Order 2005, SI 2005/2761 under which the foreign consulate, embassy or High Commission will transmit the foreign certificate to the relevant Registrar General in the UK. The certificate has to be accompanied by a translation and there is a fee of currently £23.50 (Consular Fees (Civil Partnership) Order 2005, SI 2005/2762). If the consular officer transmits the certificate in this way, a certified copy obtained from the register office in the UK is sufficient proof of civil partnership (art.15(6)). It is, however, at least doubtful that consular officers will transmit certificates of regimes that are not listed in Sched.20.

The correct approach would then of course be to apply to the court for a declaration of validity under s.58(1), a costly and cumbersome procedure. Therefore the only easy way out of this conundrum may be to register again (which may not be possible if the couple are truthful on their notice (s.8) and as a result the registrar refuses to register their civil partnership under s.3(1)(b)). Another option may be to enter into another overseas relationship that is definitely recognised in the UK. This would have to be one where there are no residence requirements for entering into it and where the existing overseas relationship would not be a bar to the formation of the new relationship in the other country. One example would be marriage in Canada. It is understood that there are no, or only very lax, residence requirements for marriage in Canada and it is unlikely that a registered partnership from another country by the same couple is a bar to marriage as marriage is a higher status. If the couple manage to register a civil partnership in the UK, they should have total certainty about their status (because either their overseas relationship or their UK civil partnership is valid). At worst, they will have wasted the fee because the registration is a nullity (cf. *Marks* v. *Marks (Divorce: Jurisdiction)* [2004] 1 FLR 1069, at 7 per Thorpe LJ).

As long as the couple are still together and want to be civil partners, there are the various, albeit complicated, ways in which this can be achieved. However, the situation becomes complex if the couple have since separated or one partner has died and the former partners (or the deceased's family) do not agree on whether the relationship is recognised or not.

Example 8.1

Juan and James, a Spanish man and an English man living in Spain, entered into a union in Madrid in 2003. They were recognised as a couple by the Madrid regional government and for the working rights of civil servants working for that government, for the provision of public services, social benefits and regional taxation, but for nothing else. This saved them a small amount of tax but they both understood that the registration had largely symbolic character. They subsequently moved to London and, without their knowledge (and without there being a specific provision stating so), it may be that their registration will be recognised in this country with all the obligations for maintenance and financial provision that this entails. James believes that he is free to marry or enter into a civil partnership with a new partner and may do so not knowing that his new relationship will not be recognised (at least in the UK). If James dies intestate, there is likely to be a question over whether the regime fulfils the general conditions of s.214 as part of the litigation between James' family and Juan.

Differences in the regimes

Overseas regimes vary widely, ranging from marriage (currently Belgium, Canada, Massachusetts, the Netherlands and Spain, and from December 2006, South Africa) to regional registrations with very limited legal consequences (e.g. Madrid). Even some of the regimes included in Sched.20 do not come close to the rights and responsibilities that come with civil partnership and typically exclude inheritance rights or financial consequences on dissolution (other than maybe sharing the home or household goods, e.g. French Pacs). A couple who have registered such a partnership may not necessarily ever have wished the full duties of marriage or civil partnership to apply to them. Recognition certainly does not meet such a couple's legitimate expectation. In the above example, Juan may find that if James applies for dissolution in England, he will have to pay maintenance. This was never something that Juan and James signed up to when they registered in Madrid. The problem is that, almost inevitably, some couples will want to have the maximum amount of rights and responsibilities, while others do not.

English conflict of laws rules either recognise a foreign marriage or they do not. If they do, English courts apply substantive English law to that marriage and any divorce and its consequences. Civil partnership law follows this lead and therefore only allows for either recognition of the overseas regime as a civil partnership or no recognition at all. Other countries by contrast apply the law of the parties' joint nationality or, if different, post-marital cohabitation (or similar), to a marriage. Thus the divorce or property regime of two Italians will be decided under Italian law whether they divorce in Germany, Italy or Holland. In the same way, rules for same-sex partnership regimes (where they exist) provide that the regime remains the same when the couple or one partner crosses a border and will not change from, for example, a Pacs into a Dutch marriage or registered partnership. The main problem with the UK approach is that the parties involved are unlikely to be aware of the fact that they are civil partners under UK law. It is therefore essential that practitioners fully advise clients who are foreign nationals or who have lived abroad on the possibility that a foreign registered partnership regime may or may not be recognised in the UK.

Bizarre circumstances

It is common knowledge that if a couple are married they will need to get divorced (or have their marriage annulled) before remarrying, and this is a condition for a marriage (and this question is explicitly asked) worldwide (ignoring for the moment polygamous marriages where these are possible). However, the system of recognising almost all forms of overseas registered partnerships between same-sex partners is unique to the UK. Most countries have no provisions for recognition of such partnerships, and some only recognise a limited number of regimes (e.g. New Zealand). Others recognise a foreign partnership as a foreign partnership rather than as a partnership under domestic law.

This raises the possibility that someone may be able to register a series of partnerships or marry in different countries and have various partnerships recognised in various countries, creating limping marriages and partnerships.

Example 8.2

Annelie and Barbara enter into a Pacs in France. Later they separate and Barbara marries Clara in Spain before they both move to England. Annelie meets Deirdre, a New Zealander and they move to New Zealand and register a civil union there (Civil Union Act 2004). This relationship also breaks down and Deirdre marries her new partner Elizabeth in Massachusetts. In time, Barbara's relationship with Clara and Deirdre's relationship with Elizabeth both come to an end. Elizabeth meets Clara on an all-lesbian skiing holiday, and Elizabeth and Clara now want to know whether they can register a civil partnership in England or whether they have to divorce first. It is assumed that all registrations were possible in the relevant countries because either the previous registrations were no bar or the authorities did not know about them.

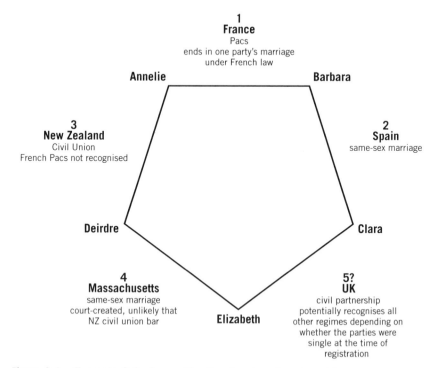

Figure 8.4   Example 8.2 of a multinational series of partnerships

Quick analysis:

- Annelie's and Barbara's Pacs is recognised in the UK as an overseas relationship (listed in Sched.20). It is not recognised in New Zealand (see Civil Unions (Recognised Overseas Relationships) Regulations 2005, SR 2005/125). It is probably no bar to marriage in Spain or Massachusetts.
- Barbara's and Clara's marriage is recognised in the UK and probably in Massachusetts. However, the Spanish marriage would probably be void from a UK point of view, unless the Spanish marriage automatically dissolved the French Pacs from an English point of view (see also **8.6.4**). France may view Annelie as single, but probably would not if it does not recognise the Spanish same-sex marriage (which it is understood it does not). The UK would then still recognise the Pacs.
- Annelie's and Deirdre's civil union in New Zealand would be recognised in the UK if the French Pacs was by this time dissolved. It is unlikely that it is recognised in Massachusetts or Spain or France.
- Deirdre's marriage to Elizabeth in Massachusetts would probably be recognised in Spain as well as in the UK (provided Deirdre was free to marry) but not in New Zealand or France. Therefore if the French Pacs was dissolved by Barbara's marriage to Clara and therefore the New Zealand civil union is recognised in the UK, the Massachusetts marriage is void in the UK. Otherwise, it is recognised here.
- If the French Pacs ends by Barbara's Spanish marriage to Clara and if this is recognised in the UK, Clara's marriage will in turn be recognised in the UK and therefore she would need to get divorced first to be able to register a civil partnership with Deirdre. If the Spanish marriage is void in UK law, she would not need to do anything.
- Conversely Elizabeth would need to divorce Deirdre only if the French Pacs still persists and was not dissolved by Barbara's marriage to Clara because then the New Zealand civil union between Annelie and Deirdre is void under UK law and Deirdre's marriage to Elizabeth is valid under UK law.
- France would probably recognise none of the overseas marriages. Spain would recognise the Spanish marriage and probably the Massachusetts marriage and New Zealand would recognise its own civil union and probably the UK civil partnership between Elizabeth and Clara, even if neither of them gets divorced first (because New Zealand would not recognise the same-sex marriages).

Gender recognition

If a person has legally changed gender in a foreign country, this is not recognised here (see **5.3.5**). So if subsequent to the foreign gender recognition the trans person registers a same-sex partnership overseas, it is not recognised here as a same-sex partnership (although if it is a marriage, it may be recognised as an opposite-sex marriage). The trans person can then apply for gender recognition in the UK and if granted, the same-sex overseas relationship will be recognised, but only if neither party has since entered into a new relationship or marriage with anyone else. See **5.3.5** for examples of the absurdities that may result. From these examples, it can be seen that the initially laudable desire to recognise as many overseas regimes as possible is likely to create a number of limping and doubly-limping relationships. This situation will only be avoided if all countries that have same-sex partnership regimes enter into multilateral agreements for mutual recognition or at least provide that neither the prospective partner nor spouse can be in any of the other regimes.

Legacy regimes

There are several countries where individual territories enact regimes and where later the federal government enacts a regime for the whole country. In Switzerland the cantons of Geneva, Neuchatel and Zurich have their own regimes with more limited consequences than the federal regime, which will come into force in 2007. Some cantons will retain their regimes while others may abolish theirs. However, whilst it may be that no new couples will be allowed to register, those couples who have already registered are likely to retain their status. The situation is similar in Spain (where there has been same-sex marriage since 2005) and in Canada. Over time, the regional regimes may become less and less relevant. However, it is unlikely that a regional registration would be converted into the new national regime. Therefore, for any couples who come into contact with the UK, it will be necessary to find out whether or not that regime fulfils the general conditions. It is quite possible that for reasons of clarity the government will remove a regime from Sched.20 when it is superseded and closed to new registrations. This will not, however, automatically convert those couples who are already registered overnight into single people.

8.4.3 Special rules for overseas relationships

Existing overseas relationships are deemed to be formed on 5 December 2005 (s.215(3)) but not if the relationship was already dissolved or annulled on that date and the dissolution or annulment would have been recognised if the relationship had been recognised at that time. Such people are then regarded as 'single' rather than 'civil partnership dissolved'. Nevertheless, either former partner can apply under Sched.7 for financial relief after overseas dissolution. The overseas relationship is also treated as a civil partnership for some provisions under the Marriage Act 1949 (including kindred and affinity), the Inheritance (Provision for Family and Dependants) Act 1975, the Fatal Accidents Act 1976, certain provisions of bankruptcy law, Sched.1 to the Children Act 1989, some provisions under Part 4 of the Family Law Act 1996 and ss.9, 65 and 68 of and Sched.1 to the Civil Partnership Act 2004 (Civil

Partnership (Treatment of Overseas Relationships) Order 2005, SI 2005/3042, art. 2). Under the same Order, for a variety of provisions existing overseas relationships are deemed to be formed at the time when they were actually formed.

1. The one year required for divorce under s.41 will be calculated from the actual registration overseas (art.3(1)).
2. The provisions for contributions to property improvement under s.65 (following the provisions of the Matrimonial Proceedings and Property Act 1970, s.37: see **6.2.1**) apply to overseas relationships ignoring the deeming provision (art.3(2)).
3. Instead of the duration of the civil partnership under Scheds.5, 6 and 7, the court will need to consider the duration of the overseas relationship (art.3(3)–(4)).
4. Section 18B of the Wills Act 1837 (inserted by CPA 2004, Sched.4, para.2) provides that existing wills are revoked automatically if the testator forms a civil partnership. This follows the law on marriage. However, this would mean that if someone made a will after registering a partnership (or marrying) overseas but before 5 December 2005, that will be revoked automatically on 5 December 2005 because the relationship is recognised as a civil partnership and deemed to have been formed on 5 December 2005 (s.215(3)). Article 4 of the Civil Partnership (Treatment of Overseas Relationships) Order 2005, SI 2005/3042, was meant to remedy this by providing that any will made after the overseas registration would survive the recognition on 5 December 2005. However, that is not what it said, and it was superseded just in time for the commencement of the Act by the Civil Partnership (Treatment of Overseas Relationships No.2) Order 2005, SI 2005/3284. As a consequence, any will made before 5 December 2005 will survive. This means that any will made before the registration of the overseas relationship will also survive and not have been revoked on registration by operation of law.

Example 8.3

Rob is English domiciled and lives in Toronto. He made a will in 1995 when he was 22 leaving all his estate to Greenpeace. In 2004 he marries Andrew in Ontario, Canada. The Canadian marriage would be recognised as a civil partnership, but deemed to be formed on 5 December 2005. If Rob and Andrew had, instead, married in 2006, Rob's will would have been revoked and he would have died intestate. However, in this situation his 1995 will expressly survives because the Wills Act 1837, s.18B does not apply to wills made before 5 December 2005 for overseas registrations before that date. So rather than dying intestate, all of Rob's estate will go to Greenpeace. However, Rob is unlikely to be aware of this.

---

5. For any marriages or civil partnerships that are registered in whichever country after 5 December 2005, the first in time will be recognised and any later one will not (s.212(1)(b)(ii)). However, for overseas relationships registered before 5 December 2005 two different rules apply: same-sex relationships entered into before that date rank in time, but any opposite-sex marriage made even on 4 December 2005 will have priority (Civil Partnership (Treatment of Overseas Relationships) Order 2005, SI 2005/3042, art.5). This is no doubt meant to create certainty for those opposite-sex couples that are married on 5 December 2005, but it creates other uncertainties and anomalies.

Example 8.4

In 1997 Ulla and Anna register a partnership in Gothenburg. In 2002 Ulla marries Linda in Amsterdam. UK law recognises the Swedish registered partnership and not the Dutch marriage because Ulla fails to meet the revised s.212(1)(b)(ii) under art.5 of the Order. If Ulla had instead married Gerd in Amsterdam, UK law would recognise the marriage between Ulla and Gerd and not recognise the registered partnership between Ulla and Anna. Nor could Anna avail herself of any of the exceptions listed above because the Swedish registered partnership would not fall into any of them. It simply does not exist for UK law and never has.

8.4.4   Countries with same-sex partnership regimes

The following countries and territories have same-sex partnership regimes. Those that are listed in the amended Sched.20 are marked in bold; the others arguably meet the general conditions of s.214. This list is non-exhaustive as this is an ever-changing target and information, especially on regional regimes, is often difficult to obtain.

COUNTRY OR TERRITORY	SAME-SEX PARTNERSHIP REGIME
Andorra	**unió estable de parella**
Argentina: Capital Territory	
Argentina: Rio Negro	
Australia	**Tasmania significant relationship**
Belgium	**the relationship referred to as cohabitation légale, wettelijke samenwoning or gesetzliches zusammenwohnen**
Belgium	marriage
Canada	marriage
Canada: Nova Scotia	domestic partnership
Canada: Quebec	**the relationship referred to as union civile or as civil union**

Czech Republic	(recently enacted)
Denmark	**registreret partnerskab**
Finland	**the relationship referred to as rekisteröity parisuhde or as registrerad partnerskap**
France	**pacte civil de solidarité**
Germany	**Lebenspartnerschaft**
Greenland	**arguably included by inclusion of the Danish regime**
Iceland	**staðfesta samvist**
Luxembourg	**the relationship referred to as partenariat enregistré or eingetragene partnerschaft**
Netherlands	**geregistreerd partnerschap**
Netherlands	**marriage**
New Zealand	**civil union**
Norway	**registrert partnerskap**
Slovenia	
South Africa	Marriage from 1 December 2006 (following *Minister of Home Affairs* v. *Fourie and Bonthuys*, South African Constitutional Court, Case No.CCT 60/04, 1 December 2005)
Spain	**marriage**
Spain: Aragon	
Spain: Asturias	
Spain: Balearic Islands	
Spain: Catalonia	
Spain: Madrid	
Spain: Navarra	
Spain: Valencia	
Sweden	**registrerat partnerskap**
Switzerland	Federal regime (coming into force on 1 January 2007)
Switzerland: Geneva	
Switzerland: Neuchatel	
Switzerland: Zurich	
United States of America: California	**domestic partnership**
United States of America: Connecticut	**civil union**
United States of America: Hawai'i	Reciprocal beneficiary relationships
United States of America: Maine	**domestic partnership**
United States of America: Massachusetts	**marriage**
United States of America: New Jersey	**domestic partnership**
United States of America: Vermont	**civil union**

8.5 JURISDICTION AND STAYS

8.5.1 Jurisdiction for dissolutions

Jurisdiction is dealt with in Chapter 3 of Part 5 of the CPA 2004 and the provisions for the three UK jurisdictions are separate, although it appears that the Northern Irish provisions are identical and the Scottish are similar to those for England and Wales. The Civil Partnership (Jurisdiction and Recognition of Judgments) Regulations 2005, SI 2005/3334 (the Regulations), made under powers conferred by s.219 make rules for jurisdiction following the revised Brussels II (EU Regulation 2001/2003 which substitutes Regulation 1347/2000) these are supplemented by s.221. Accordingly the English court has jurisdiction for dissolution, separation and nullity of civil partnerships (including, of course, overseas relationships, see **8.4**) if:

1. Any of the following grounds based on habitual residence apply (reg.4):

    (a) both civil partners are habitually resident in England and Wales;
    (b) both civil partners were last habitually resident in England and Wales and one of the civil partners continues to reside there;
    (c) the respondent is habitually resident in England and Wales;
    (d) the petitioner is habitually resident in England and Wales and has resided there for at least one year immediately preceding the presentation of the petition; or
    (e) the petitioner is domiciled and habitually resident in England and Wales and has resided there for at least six months immediately preceding the presentation of the petition.

2. If neither Scotland (under the Civil Partnership (Jurisdiction and Recognition of Judgments) (Scotland) Regulations 2005, SSI 2005/629) nor Northern Ireland (under the Civil Partnership (Jurisdiction and Recognition of Judgments) Regulations 2005, SI 2005/3334, reg.5) has jurisdiction under identical provisions, England has jurisdiction if:

    (a) one civil partner is domiciled in England and Wales (s.221(1)(b)); or
    (b) the civil partnership was registered in England and Wales and 'it appears to the court to be in the interests of justice to assume jurisdiction' (s.221(1)(c)).

The Act and the Regulations are drafted to follow the law on divorce jurisdiction, which was of course changed by the EU Brussels II Regulation. The first fall back position as at 2(a) above is the same as for divorce under the Domicile and Matrimonial Proceedings Act 1973 (DMPA 1973), s.5.

The supplemental ground for jurisdiction in 2(b) above is new for civil partnership law. It deals with the scenario where a couple register in England but by the time their relationship ends, neither party is habitually resident or domiciled in the UK and the country they have moved to either does not have any regime similar to civil partnership or their courts have no jurisdiction to dissolve the English civil partnership, possibly for lack of jurisdiction rules. This problem does not arise on marriage and divorce in the same way because both are more or less universal concepts.

Example 8.5

Giovanni and Paolo are both Italian. Giovanni is studying for a PhD at Imperial College in London and Paolo works in London as a fashion designer. They meet and register a civil partnership in London. Many years later they move back to Italy together for early semi-retirement in a converted mill in the hills of Umbria. When their relationship breaks down neither of them is habitually resident or domiciled in any part of the UK. They could therefore not apply for a dissolution under any of the grounds in 1(a) to (e) or 2(a) above, but could nevertheless apply under 2(b) asking the court to assume jurisdiction because they cannot dissolve their civil partnership in Italy, as Italy does not have any such concept.

For nullity proceedings there is a further ground for jurisdiction, namely in the case where either civil partner has died, sole domicile, or one year's habitual residence of either civil partner at the date of death (s.221(2)(b)). This applies to void civil partnerships only because (as for marriage) no posthumous application is possible in cases of voidable civil partnerships because it would be pointless since an order annulling a voidable civil partnership only ends it from the date of the order. Jurisdiction for presumption of death orders can be based on sole domicile or one year's habitual residence of the applicant or registration in England and Wales (s.222). Applications of validity can be heard in England and Wales on the basis of one civil partner's sole domicile, habitual residence for one year or registration in England and Wales. As for nullity, there are the additional grounds for jurisdiction for declarations of validity based on sole domicile or one year's habitual residence at death if one civil partner has died (s.224).

8.5.2   Problems with jurisdiction rules

Mirroring EU Brussels II Regulation in civil partnership law makes little sense because UK law cannot legislate for other EU member states and only regulates how business is allocated between the three UK jurisdictions. The fallback positions therefore apply even if other EU jurisdictions would have jurisdiction on grounds similar to the ones in Civil Partnership (Jurisdiction and Recognition of Judgments) Regulations 2005.

Example 8.6

Nikki and Rebecca are civil partners. Nikki is English domiciled and Rebecca is Irish domiciled. As they then lived in Edinburgh they registered their civil partnership there. They then moved to Amsterdam. Neither England nor Scotland (under the equivalent rules) has jurisdiction based on habitual residence (1(a)–(e) above). Therefore the fallback position of sole domicile gives England jurisdiction (s.221(1(b), 2(a) above) and Scotland also has jurisdiction under the equivalent of 2(b) above (s.225(1)(c)). If instead they were a married couple neither England nor Scotland would have jurisdiction because the Netherlands would have jurisdiction based on their joint habitual residence there.

There is no rule of precedence as regards to first to issue as in Brussels II and no automatic stay. So even if there were proceedings for dissolution in the Netherlands already, England could still proceed with the dissolution (and *forum conveniens* principles apply: see **8.5.3**). These would even apply if there were competing proceedings in Scotland and England in this example because the obligatory stay rules would not apply. Further and more serious problems arise when it comes to the question of recognition of dissolutions from other EU member states (see **8.6.2** below).

8.5.3　Stays

The Family Proceedings (Civil Partnership: Staying of Proceedings) Rules 2005, SI 2005/2921, made under s.223 mirror DMPA 1973, Sched.1. Obligatory stay rules apply for certain proceedings in related jurisdictions (i.e. other parts of the UK, and even the Isle of Man and Channel Islands, which do not have same-sex registered partnership: r.3). Proceedings must be stayed under r.3 where there are proceedings in a related jurisdiction, and the parties have lived together in that jurisdiction following the formation of their civil partnership at the time when the proceedings began or when they separated (if earlier), and either party was habitually resident in that jurisdiction throughout the year ending with the date on which they last lived together. Rule 11 provides that for overseas relationships that were registered before 5 December 2005 the cohabitation requirement relates to the time after the overseas registration rather than the deemed formation on 5 December 2005.

If a UK case does not fall into these limited criteria, and for all other cases, the English court has a wide discretion under its power to stay the proceedings based on the balance of fairness (including convenience – often referred to as the *forum conveniens* principle: r.4, cf. DMPA 1973, Sched.1, para.9). This also applies to EU countries and therefore the Brussels II first-come rule for divorce and nullity proceedings doos not apply. Rules 6 to 9 provide for limited power to make financial orders when proceedings are stayed in favour of another British jurisdiction.

To facilitate the stay jurisdiction in family cases the English High Court has additional powers under its inherent jurisdiction to order a party to a divorce not to pursue competing proceedings abroad (*Hemain* v. *Hemain* [1998] 2 FLR 388; *Bloch* v. *Bloch* [2003] 1 FLR 1). There is no reason why this should not also apply to proceedings to end a civil partnership.

8.6 RECOGNITION OF OVERSEAS DISSOLUTIONS

8.6.1 General principles

The recognition of orders other than dissolutions is generally the same or similar and this part will refer to 'dissolutions, etc.' throughout. Sections 233 to 238 make provision for recognition of overseas dissolutions similar to Part II of the Family Law Act 1986. For EU countries the provisions are also in the Civil Partnership (Jurisdiction and Recognition of Judgments) Regulations 2005, SI 2005/3334 (see also **8.5** above). There are three different categories of countries (see **figure 8.5**):

- other UK jurisdictions (Scotland and Northern Ireland);
- the EU (including this time Denmark); and
- the rest of the world.

Essentially, the further the country is away from England and Wales, the more stringent are the conditions for recognition.

Special provisions have been made for special cases under powers in s.237 in the Civil Partnership (Supplementary Provisions relating to the Recognition of Overseas Dissolutions, Annulments or Legal Separations) (England and Wales and Northern Ireland) Regulations 2005, SI 2005/3104. These include provision for cases:

- where the dissolution, etc. was made according to the law of a territory and not a whole country, e.g. a State of the US or a Swiss canton (s.237(2)(a); SI 2005/3104, reg.2);
- where a civil partner is domiciled in a country whose law does not recognise same-sex registered partnership (s.237(2)(b)(ii)); SI 2005/3104, reg.3) see **8.6.4** below;
- where there are cross-proceedings (s.237(2)(c); SI 2005/3104, reg.4);
- where dissolution follows legal separation (s.237(2)(d); SI 2005/3104, reg.5); and
- for questions of proof of relevant facts (s.237(2)(e); SI 2005/3104, reg.6).

No provisions were made for overseas dissolutions of overseas relationships under powers in s.237(2)(b)(i).

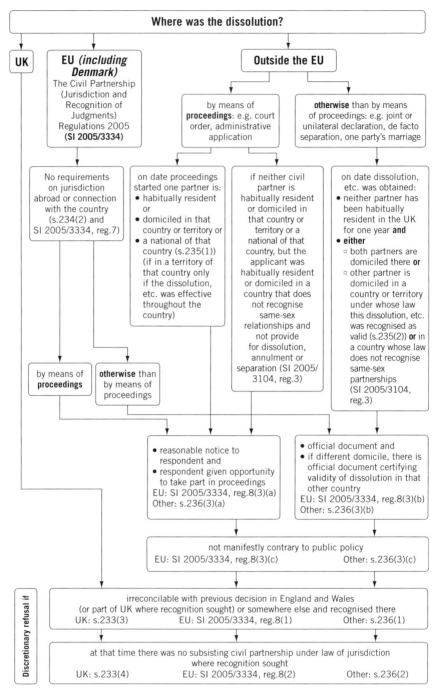

Figure 8.5 Recognition of overseas dissolution, annulment or separation orders

---

Special cases: (The Civil Partnership (Supplementary Provisions relating to the Recognition of Overseas Dissolutions, Annulments or Legal Separations) (England and Wales and Northern Ireland) Regulations 2005 **(SI 2005/3104)**):

- for references to 'territory' see SI 2005/3104, reg.2 made under s.237(2)(a)
- overseas relationships dissolved overseas (s.237(2)(b)(i)) – no regulations have been made
- where a civil partner is domiciled in a country that does not recognise same-sex relationships (s.237(2)(b)(ii)): see above (SI 2005/3104, reg.3)
- cross-proceedings (s.237(2)(c)): SI 2005/3104, reg.4
- conversion of legal separation (s.237(2)(d)): SI 2005/3104, reg.5
- proof of findings of fact made in proceedings outside the UK (s.237(2)(e)): SI 2005/3104, reg.6

Figure 8.5 *(cont.)*   Recognition of overseas dissolution, annulment or separation orders

United Kingdom jurisdictions

UK decisions can only be refused recognition if:

- they are irreconcilable with a previous decision made in England; or
- they are irreconcilable with a previous decision recognised in England; or
- under English law there was at that time no longer a civil partnership (s.233(3) and (4)).

This follows the law on recognition of divorces in the Family Law Act 1986 (FLA 1986), s.51(1)–(2). As the law for the whole UK is practically the same, any of these cases is unlikely.

Foreign jurisdictions

For all other cases, whether in the EU or not, there is a distinction between dissolutions, etc. obtained by means of proceedings (which do not have to be at a court) and dissolutions, etc. obtained otherwise than by means of proceedings, which for divorce is, for example, a bare talaq that is available under pure Sharia law. For civil partnership dissolution this may for example be a unilateral declaration (maybe notarised), de facto separation for a certain period, or by one party's marriage (e.g. French Pacs). The only, but extremely significant, difference is that for EU countries there is no requirement that either party has any connection with the jurisdiction. For non-EU countries there are also requirements for a connection with the jurisdiction. The following jurisdictional requirements do therefore not apply to EU countries.

By means of proceedings

Dissolutions, etc. obtained by means of proceedings outside the EU are only recognised if the foreign court had jurisdiction (under UK law, irrespective of whether the foreign court based its jurisdiction on those grounds) based on either party having been (s.235(1) following FLA 1986, s.46):

- habitually resident there;
- domiciled there (under English law or the law of that country); or
- a national of that country.

If the dissolution is made under the law of a territory of a country (such as a US State), the third category is varied slightly to say that if one party was a national of that country and the dissolution is effective throughout that country, it will also be recognised here (SI 2005/3104, reg.3).

This on its own excludes for example cases where a foreign court solely based its jurisdiction on:

- the civil partnership having been registered there (but see the power to include this under s.237(2)(b)(ii) and the issues set out in relation to SI 2005/3104, reg.3 at **8.6.4** below);
- the parties' choice of jurisdiction or choice of law; or
- no apparent connection at all.

Otherwise than by means of proceedings

Dissolutions, etc. otherwise than by means of proceedings outside the EU will only be recognised if neither party was habitually resident in the UK for one year and either:

- both are domiciled in the jurisdiction where the dissolution was obtained at the time it was effective; or
- one is domiciled there and the other is domiciled in a jurisdiction that recognises as valid the dissolution, etc. (s.235(2)).

Procedural safeguards

These are grounds for refusing recognition and they are discretionary. They apply to dissolutions, etc. in both EU and non-EU jurisdictions. Dissolutions, etc. may be refused recognition if certain minimum requirements of due process were not met (s.236(3); SI 2005/3334, reg.8(3) for EU, following FLA 1986, s.51(3)(a)). For dissolution, etc. by means of proceedings the other partner has to be given notice of the proceedings and a reasonable opportunity to take part in them. For dissolution, etc. obtained otherwise than by means of proceedings there has to be an official document of the dissolution, and if either partner was domiciled in another jurisdiction there has to be an official document certifying that the dissolution is recognised under that law. There is also a public policy exception for both forms of dissolution (s.236(3)(c); SI 2005/3334, reg.8(3)(c) for EU). In addition recognition of foreign dissolutions, etc. may be refused if (SI 2005/3334, reg.8(1)–(2) for the EU and s.236(1)–(2) for other countries):

- they are irreconcilable with a previous decision made in England; or
- they are irreconcilable a previous decision recognised in England; or
- under English law there was at that time no longer a civil partnership (s.233(3) and (4)).

This follows the rules on refusal of recognition of decisions from other UK jurisdictions (above). Recognition will not mean recognition of orders on maintenance, custody or other ancillary matters (s.237(6)).

8.6.2 Problems with recognition of EU dissolutions

The Civil Partnership (Jurisdiction and Recognition of Judgments) Regulations 2005, SI 2005/3334 try to follow Brussels II by establishing mirroring grounds of jurisdiction (reg.4) and defining 'member states' although there is nothing to be a member of. Regulation 6(3) lists all EU Member States including Denmark (which is not part of Brussels II), curiously in no particular order. In alphabetical order they are: Austria, Belgium, Cyprus, the Czech Republic, Denmark, Estonia, Finland, France, Germany, Greece, Hungary, Ireland, Italy, Latvia, Lithuania, Luxembourg, Malta, the Netherlands, Poland, Portugal, Slovakia, Slovenia, Spain and Sweden. In this way, EU countries are made members of a 'club' they never chose to join. The Regulations then go on to provide that all EU judgments are recognised without questioning the basis of their jurisdiction at all (regs.7, 9 and 10). It inserts some basic safeguards mirroring again the provisions of s.236 in reg.8.

The problem with this is that the Regulations do not (and cannot) provide for the grounds on which other EU states base their jurisdiction. The regimes that are recognised under s.212 are diverse and a large number have no rules for mutual recognition of regimes, let alone for mutual recognition of dissolutions or rules of jurisdiction. Where Brussels II sets uniform rules for jurisdiction across the EU (except Denmark), the Regulations only set them for England and Wales and for Northern Ireland and similar rules apply in Scotland (Jurisdiction and Recognition of Judgments) (Scotland) Regulations 2005, SSI 2005/629).

If the assumption has been made that EU Member States generally have comparable laws which mean that their judgments should be recognised here without being questioned, this assumption is basically flawed. It is clear that they do not necessarily have comparable laws in the area of same-sex registered partnership since 13 out of a total of 25 EU Member States do not have such regimes at all, while others have very weak regimes. On the other hand, there appears to be no reason why countries such as Iceland, Norway and Switzerland should be excluded, as they have registered partnership regimes and legal regimes that are generally recognised here. The inclusion of Denmark is also odd, as Denmark is not part of the Brussels II regime.

For the purposes of EU law, registered same-sex partnerships may fall under the Brussels I Regulation (Council Regulation (EC) No.44/2001 on jurisdiction and the recognition and enforcement of judgments in civil and commercial matters; for Denmark the Brussels I treaty) as a simple civil judgment or outside EU law. The question is whether civil partnerships are a matter of 'status or legal capacity of natural persons, rights in property arising out of a matrimonial relationship' under Art.1(2)(a) of the Brussels I Regulation. If, as some believe, it does fall into Brussels I, English courts would have to recognise foreign EU judgments that comply with the Brussels I criteria superseding a large part of the CPA 2004 and the Regulations.

As it is, nothing prevents the courts in any EU country from assuming jurisdiction on tenuous grounds, such as simply one party's choice. If dissolution in a country is possible simply by filing a notice at a court or maybe even a register office and on the unilateral decision of one party, any English civil partner could have their civil partnership dissolved there. This would have the effect of depriving the other civil partner not only of the limitations that s.44 places on dissolutions, but also making any financial applications subject to leave of the court under Sched.7 and severely restricting any financial provision.

8.6.3 Problems with overseas dissolution of overseas relationships

After submissions made by the Lesbian and Gay Lawyers Association the Government seemed to recognise that the Act as drafted means that the UK recognises a wide range of overseas regimes without necessarily recognising the way the regime is dissolved. This includes, for example, a French Pacs which is dissolved by one party marrying a third party or the Catalonian regime, which is dissolved by de facto separation for a certain period. Because of lack of time, a provision was inserted to deal with this by way of a future statutory instrument (s.237(2)(b)(i)).

Example 8.7

Monika and Sabine enter into a registered partnership in Zurich. Monika lives in Zurich and is a Swiss national. Sabine is Austrian but also lives in Zurich. The registered partnership is recognised in England. They separate and Sabine returns to live in Austria. Later, Monika marries Anthony and they move to London. Under the Zurich law, Monika's marriage to Anthony dissolves the registered partnership.

English law would almost certainly recognise the registered partnership. However, under the Act it would not recognise the dissolution, which is otherwise than by means of proceedings, because Sabine is domiciled in

Austria and Austrian law will not recognise the dissolution as it does not recognise any form of same-sex partnership (s.235(2)(b)(ii)). Even if Sabine was Swiss, recognition may be refused if there is no official document certifying that the dissolution is effective under the law of the country in which it was obtained (s.236(3)(b)). It is not clear whether the Zurich state chancellery would issue any document at all. At first sight, SI 2005/3104, reg.3 may come to Sabine's help because she is domiciled in Austria, which does not recognise legal same-sex partnerships. However, this is not the case because:

1. There is no official Austrian document certifying that the dissolution is valid under Austrian law (s.236(3)(b)(ii)). Of course there would not be. The part of SI 2005/3104, reg.3 dealing with dissolutions otherwise than by means of proceedings is therefore effectively redundant.
2. Monika may not actually be domiciled in Zurich under English law (she may be originally from, say, Bern and may have moved back there), nor under Zurich law (see SI 2005/3104, reg.3).
3. If the wedding takes place in Las Vegas, the territory where the dissolution took place is arguably Nevada and the dissolution is not 'effective' under Nevada law (s.235(2)(a)).

Accordingly, Monika's and Anthony's marriage would not be recognised in England, but would be recognised everywhere else. Monika would find herself married to Anthony in Switzerland and in a registered partnership with Sabine at the same time under English law. This would cause problems, for instance, if years later Monika died in England without leaving a will because if Monika died domiciled in England under English law Sabine would be the main beneficiary of Monika's estate as her civil partner under the intestacy provisions. If Monika was not domiciled in England at the date of her death, under Swiss law Anthony would probably inherit.

8.6.4 Recognition where one party is domiciled where there is no legal recognition

English courts have jurisdiction to hear applications for dissolution, etc. if the civil partnership was registered here and cannot now be dissolved elsewhere in the UK (see **8.5.1** and **example 8.5** above; s.221(1)(c)). This is supposed to cater for the situation where neither civil partner is domiciled or habitually resident in the UK and the civil partnership could not be dissolved (because they live in a country that has no same-sex partnership regime or has no provision for the dissolution of UK civil partnerships).

Conversely if another country has a similar provision, a dissolution obtained there would not be recognised here under the CPA 2004 if there is no other connection to that country.

Example 8.8

Mustafa and Kemal (two Turkish men) register a partnership in Iceland. They later move to Turkey (which does not recognise same-sex partnerships). Years later after separation, they are able to obtain a dissolution in Iceland (assuming that Iceland allows this).

Without further provision a dissolution in a country that had assumed jurisdiction because the couple registered there would not be recognised in the UK if there was no connection via habitual residence, domicile or nationality or (for dissolutions otherwise than by means of proceedings) if the other partner was not domiciled in a place that also recognised the dissolution. German law, for example, allows dissolutions of German-registered partnerships in any event (Zivilprozessordnung, §661(3)1(b)). It also recognises dissolutions from any country or territory provided they are recognised in the place where the partnership was registered (Zivilprozessordnung, §661(3)3). This would have seemed the obvious solution to the entire problem that arises for dissolutions made in a place with which the couple have no connection via habitual residence, domicile or nationality.

Instead, s.237(2)(b)(ii) allows for regulations to be made by statutory instrument to provide for recognition of dissolutions 'where a civil partner is domiciled in a country or territory whose law does not recognise legal relationships between two people of the same sex'. Provisions in the Civil Partnership (Supplementary Provisions relating to the Recognition of Overseas Dissolutions, Annulments or Legal Separations) (England and Wales and Northern Ireland) Regulations 2005, SI 2005/3104, reg.3 mean that the UK would now recognise the dissolution of Mustafa's and Kemal's partnership, although there is no other connection between Iceland and either of the two individuals.

Instead of a straightforward approach like the one taken in Germany, reg.3 makes very complicated provisions. For dissolutions, etc. by means of proceedings the conditions for recognition are that the applicant for the dissolution, annulment or legal separation is either habitually resident or domiciled in a country or territory (reg.3 inserted by subsection (1A)(c)):

- whose law does not recognise legal relationships between people of the same sex; *and*
- does not provide for dissolution, annulment or legal separation as regards such relationships.

The first oddity is that the country or territory does not have to be the one where the relationship was registered. The second is the connection between the two conditions, which both need to be fulfilled. The consequence of this is that if the country where the applicant is habitually resident recognises legal relationships between people of the same sex, but does not allow for a dissolution of the relationship in question, the dissolution obtained elsewhere would not be recognised in the UK.

Example 8.9

Kai and Stan register a partnership in Switzerland in 2007. Kai is Swiss and Stan is an American citizen domiciled in New York State. The both live in New York City at the time of registration and register in Switzerland because this is the only place available to them. In 2008 Kai naturalises as an American citizen and (at least from an English law perspective) acquires New York domicile. There is no concept of domicile under Swiss law and the nearest would be more akin to residence, which is clearly New York. Sometime in the following years the New York State Supreme Court follows the example of Massachusetts and legalises same-sex marriage. However, as in Massachusetts, New York law does not recognise the Swiss-registered partnership and does not offer any way to dissolve it in the New York courts. When the relationship breaks down in 2010 Kai is unable to obtain a dissolution in New York, but can obtain a dissolution in Switzerland because that is where he registered (Bundesgesetz vom 18. Dezember 1987 über das internationale Privatrecht, SR 291, Art.65b). The dissolution will not be recognised in the UK because neither Kai nor Stan has any connection with Switzerland (habitual residence, domicile or nationality) nor would this case meet the conditions of SI 2005/3104, reg.3 set out above because New York State does recognise same-sex partnerships in the form of marriage. This is obviously already a mistake in the enabling provisions in s.237(2)(b)(ii). Assuming that instead of Switzerland, the couple had registered in Germany, the dissolution would be recognised regardless of whether the parties had any connection with Germany, but only because Germany is part of the EU and a 'member state' under Part 2 of the Civil Partnership (Jurisdiction and Recognition of Judgments) Regulations 2005, SI 2005/3334.

Even where the law of the country of the applicant's domicile or habitual residence does not recognise legal same-sex relationships, it may still offer to dissolve overseas relationships. The applicant may still want to go back to the country of registration because that is where the question of dissolution is most important. The way the regulation is worded also means that if the country of the applicant's domicile or habitual residence does not recognise legal same-sex relationships, but offers (only) to grant a separation order for foreign-registered couples, this will mean that the dissolution in the country of registration will not be recognised. Similar problems arise for dissolutions otherwise than by means of proceedings. None of these issues do, of course, arise in this way in the case of marriage and divorce because there is only one type of marriage and one type of divorce rather than this multitude of regimes.

If the enabling provision was wider, it could be reworded to change the 'and' to an 'or', which would already help. If the application was limited to overseas relationships (and UK civil partnerships were expressly excluded), the provisions could be made under s.237(2)(b)(i) instead of (ii), where there is no condition in about the parties' domicile.

The relevant part of reg.3 could therefore read (changes in bold):

(c) at the relevant date the party seeking the dissolution, annulment or legal separation was either habitually resident or domiciled in a country whose law –

　　(i) does not recognise legal relationships between people of the same sex **or**
　　(ii) does not provide for dissolution, annulment or legal separation (**as the case may be**) as regards such relationships.

The far easier solution for this issue and for the issue of overseas dissolution of overseas relationships (see **8.6.3** above) could have been resolved by following the German and Swiss examples and simply providing that a dissolution, etc. of any form of overseas relationship will be recognised here if it has been obtained in the country or territory of registration, or if has been obtained elsewhere and is recognised in the country or territory of registration.

Since the requirements on jurisdiction are worded in a way that if the other country has jurisdiction a decision 'is to be recognised', the wording of the statute does not exclude the courts from recognising decisions that are outside the list. The requirements as to due process allow courts to refuse recognition and they may still recognise a decision even if it does not meet the criteria (see **example 8.7**). One would hope, therefore, that the courts take a commonsense approach to this area and try to fill the gaps this legislation has left. Nevertheless, in the interests of legal certainty a clearly worded Act would have been preferable.

8.7 MAIN DIFFERENCES FROM MARRIAGE AND DIVORCE LAW

International family law is complicated. Because civil partnership is not a universal concept and there are a multitude of different regimes, the international aspects of civil partnership are even more complicated than those for marriage and divorce. Nevertheless, it is highly important because some people will inevitably move around and register in countries they do not necessarily have the closest connection with in a variety of regimes. The legislator tried to follow the existing body of family law in this area but in the course of doing so achieved more confusion and some undesirable and bizarre results.

Some of the main points are summarised in the table below.

Area of law	Civil partnership, in comparison with marriage
Capacity and domicile	There is no requirement for capacity under the partner's domicile as there (at least theoretically) is for marriage (see **8.2**).
Registration in UK consulates	Will probably be more widely available (see **8.3.1**).
Registration by armed forces abroad	Same as for marriage (see **8.3.2**).
Recognition of overseas relationships	As with marriage, a wide range of overseas relationships are recognised, although 'polygamous' relationships are not. The problems lie in the details (see **8.4**).
Jurisdiction for dissolution	Tries to be the same as for divorce, there are some problems in the detail; additional ground for civil partnerships registered here (see **8.5.1–8.5.2**).
Stays	Same as for divorce (see **8.5.3**).
Recognition of overseas dissolutions	Intended to be the same as for divorce, but several problems arise because of the nature of the variety of relationships recognised (see **8.6**).

CHAPTER 9

Pensions

Bridget Garrood

9.1 INTRODUCTION

The degree of equality, approximation or continuing discrimination in the pension entitlement available to civil partners and surviving civil partners differs widely depending on the type of pension involved. Despite the general equality policy behind the CPA 2004 and the widest powers available under s.255 to amend existing pension law, for many years to come significant differences will remain between the pension rights of civil partners and their surviving partners on the one hand, and those of spouses and widows or widowers on the other. This raises important issues under the Human Rights Act 1998, particularly with reference to the amended Employment Equality (Sexual Orientation) Regulations 2003, SI 2003/1661. Amendments to pension legislation can be found in a variety of locations:

- s.255, which enables amendments to be made to pension legislation by statutory instrument;
- Sched.24, which amends a large variety of social security legislation including legislation relevant to state pensions;
- Sched.25, which amends certain Acts of Parliament relating to pensions; and
- a variety of statutory instruments made either under powers under the CPA 2004 or under existing powers.

Pensions are manifold and complicated. They have been changed and tinkered with by almost every post-War government. This chapter is therefore written to give an insight into the basics of the different types of pensions while highlighting the changes for civil partners and where discrimination persists. It does not claim to be a complete guide for every type of pension. Advisers will need to distinguish the particular types of pension schemes which are set out in more detail in this chapter. All those affected must obtain independent legal and financial advice and have their own state, occupational and private pensions calculated specifically for them before making any decisions on investments or elections.

9.1.1 The state pension scheme

For details, see **9.2** below.

Basic state pensions

A person's basic state pension based on his or her own national insurance contribution (NIC) record (Category A pension) will not be affected by registration as a civil partner. However, a former civil partner's contribution record may be used by surviving and former civil partners if this is more favourable. Civil partners will not normally qualify for any additional allowance for a dependent civil partner until 2010. A (surviving) civil partner of either gender will be in an identical position to that of a married man or widower for this and for many other purposes in relation to the state pension. Unlike a married woman, neither a male nor a female civil partner who reaches state pension age before 6 April 2010 will therefore receive a Category B(L) pension based on their living civil partner's NIC record. Civil partners whose partners were born on or after 6 April 1950 will be able to claim Category B(L) pensions in the same way as wives when they retire. In practice male civil partner couples will have to wait longer for equality to reach them, because women born on 6 April 1950 will be able to retire when they reach 60 on 6 April 2010, but the men born on that date will not be able to retire until they reach 65 in 2015. The introduction of this type of pension for civil partners happens at the same time that the state pension age for women born between 5 April 1950 and 5 April 1955 will rise gradually from age 60 to 65, between the years 2010 and 2020, in accordance with a sliding scale of ages (set out in Pensions Act 1995, Sched.4).

Survivor pensions

The same principle in terms of conferring upon civil partners more limited rights than those available to married women applies to the inheritable and other survivor aspects of the state scheme (including inheriting the additional state pension SERPS/S2P). A surviving civil partner gains the survivor rights of a widower rather than those of a widow and the position will only change on 6 April 2010. Until then, surviving civil partners, like widowers, will only become entitled to a pension equal to the deceased partner's if both were over state pension age at the date of death (CPA 2004, Sched.24, para.28) (Category B pension). There are limited circumstances where a surviving civil partner can claim a Category B pension now: surviving civil partners can use the substitution provision to use their late partner's contribution record for their own pension now as long as both parties have reached state pension age at the date of the death. Whenever a surviving civil partner inherits a full basic state pension from his or her civil partner, this will also be topped up by any inheritable SERPS/S2P and Graduated Retirement Benefit (see **9.3**).

9.1.2 Public sector occupational schemes

Surviving civil partners' pensions in the public sector (see **9.4**) will also mirror widowers' but not widows' rights. Only periods of service by the deceased pension member since 6 April 1988 will count in the calculation of their surviving civil partner's entitlement. This will mean that a male member who accrued pension rights in the public sector before 6 April 1988 will not be able to leave a pension to his surviving civil partner of the same amount as would pass to his widow if they were married.

9.1.3 Private sector employers' occupational schemes

Contracted-out schemes (or parts of schemes) (see **9.5**) will be required to provide survivor benefits for civil partners on the basis of deceased members' rights accrued since 6 April 1988. Final salary schemes, or average salary schemes, or similar, will only be required to provide survivor pensions to surviving civil partners built up from periods of pensionable service or contributions paid by the deceased scheme member from 5 December 2005. Schemes which already provide benefits to surviving same-sex partners will be obliged to continue to do so for civil partners. Employees retiring on or after 5 December 2005 in a defined-benefits occupational pension scheme may invoke the protection against discrimination under the Employment Equality (Sexual Orientation) Regulations 2003, reg.3(3) requiring benefits available for surviving spouses to be made available to surviving civil partners. In many schemes a dependant's pension is only paid to a dependant who was the member's spouse or civil partner during active membership. This discriminates against civil partners because they were unable to register until late 2005. Anyone in this situation who retired (or changed career) before that date may have lost out.

9.1.4 Personal pension plans

For further details on this see **9.6**. These may include a protected rights fund derived from contracting out of SERPS/S2P. On the death of a member before retirement the contracted-out part of the fund must be used to buy an annuity for the surviving civil partner to the extent that the deceased member's rights have accrued from 6 April 1988. Other funds may pass tax-free to any person who was nominated by the deceased member, usually at the trustees' discretion depending on the scheme's rules. Any survivor benefits payable on death after retirement will depend on the specific rights which the member opted to buy on retirement. It is possible that a dependant's pension and/or the balance of any guaranteed pension period may be payable to the surviving civil partner if named as the beneficiary, depending on what type of annuity was bought.

9.1.5 State pension scheme – summary

Pension type	Rights for civil partners	Date of change	Year by which discrimination phased out*
Category A basic state pension	Use former civil partner's national insurance contribution (NIC) record.	5 December 2005	2005
Category A basic state pension	Use late civil partner's NIC record.	5 December 2005	2005
Category B(L) basic state pension	60% of partner's state pension supplemental to own (but capped) – if civil partner born on or after 6 April 1950.	2010–2015	Statistically in 2045, or later when all people born before then and their surviving civil partners will have died.
Category B basic state pension	Can receive on basis of partner's NIC record after partner's death (inherited pension) at their rate: if *both* are above state pension age when first one dies or if in receipt of certain benefits or allowances.	5 December 2005	None
Category B basic state pension	Can receive on basis of partner's NIC record after partner's death (inherited pension) at their rate:	6 April 2010	Statistically in 2030–2035 or later when all people born before 1950 (women) and 1945 (men) will have died.

	if reached state pension age after 6 April 2010 and over state pension age at date the other dies *irrespective of deceased's age at death.*		
SERPS/S2P	Inherit part of partner's: same as Category B	2005–2010	Statistically in 2030–2035 or later when all people born before 1950 (women) and 1945 (men) will have died.
Contracted-out SERPS/S2P	Survivor's pension.	5 April 1988	None
Public sector occupational pension	Survivor's pension.	5 April 1988	Statistically in 2067 or later when all people who started their working life before 1988 and their civil partners will have died.
Private sector occupational pension	Survivor's pension.	5 December 2005	Statistically in 2085 or later when all people who started their working life before 2005 and their civil partners will have died.

* Based on average life expectancy of 85 years and 10 years' age difference between partners.

9.2 BASIC STATE PENSION

The UK basic state pension is a non-means-tested contributory scheme. Employers, employees and the self-employed are required to make national insurance contributions (NICs), on which a number of state benefits are based. The state pension scheme is part of the contributory welfare benefits system. These contributory benefits arc supplemented and complemented by means-tested benefits such as Income Support, Housing Benefit and tax credits as well as Pension Credit (see **10.6**). The present state pension system was devised in 1948 at a time when the vast majority of married women were housewives and the men were the family breadwinners. It has been amended over the decades, but the scheme remains different for men and women, not least in the different state pension age, which is currently 65 for men and 60 for women. From 2010 to 2020 this difference will be phased out by raising the state pension age for women born between 5 April 1950 and 5 April 1955 gradually from 60 to 65. Currently, wives and widows also have greater rights than husbands or widowers, because traditionally women do not have the same level of NICs that men have.

Initially the Government suggested that no provision for civil partners and surviving civil partners should be made in the state pension scheme until the equalisation of the state pension age and the rights of husband and wives plus widows and widowers. In the White Paper (Women and Equality Unit (WEU) *Civil Partnership: A framework for the legal recognition of same-sex couples* (June 2003) at 7.25) the Government said that 'introducing changes before this time would create new inequalities within the state pension system'. The Government was faced with the question of whether to treat civil partners as husbands or wives (and widows or widowers). Should all women be treated as widows because they are women, or as widowers because they are claiming on their female partner's NIC record? Similar issues arise for male civil partners. Following consultation, the Government conceded that there was no logical reason why the more limited state pension rights available to husbands and widowers should not be made available to civil partners immediately. Equal rights will come in between 2010 and 2020, but discrimination will not be phased out until later this century. Even now, there are some adult dependency allowance rights available to married pensioners which are not extended to civil partners, as they are considered too complex. (See **9.2.1**.)

9.2.1　Category A basic state retirement pension

A Category A retirement pension is the pension paid when a person reaches state pension age primarily on the pensioner's own NIC record. The full rate is £84.25 per week for 2006/07. As for spouses, surviving civil partners can already use their late partner's NIC records to substitute these for their own if the partner dies before they themselves reach state pension age. The period for which NIC records can be substituted ends at the end of the tax year in which the deceased died. There is a choice of starting point: either for all the tax years from the date of registration of the civil partnership; or for all the tax years of the surviving civil partner's working life (Social Security Contributions and Benefits Act 1992, ss.48 and 121). A similar substitution provision exists for former civil partners on dissolution. They can use their former civil partner's NIC record even if the civil partnership is dissolved after they have reached state pension age. However, in that case the period they can substitute will end with the tax year when they reached state pension age. If they marry or form a new civil partnership before reaching state pension age, they lose this right. If they do so after they have started claiming their pension on the substituted NIC records, they do not then have their pension reduced. Many divorced women and widows who need to rely on their husband's NIC record will typically have worked up to the date of marriage and then stopped working soon afterwards to look after children and the household. In practice, for such women there is often little difference between using the record for the marriage or for the husband's working life until divorce or death. By contrast, for civil partners this is vital, as otherwise a long relationship where one partner may have looked after the household or children before 2005 would be ignored if only the length of the civil partnership itself were counted.

The loss of the option to substitute a former spouse's NIC record on remarriage or civil partnership registration causes particular problems for civil partners, especially of course women who may not have a full NIC record in their own right. The idea behind the rule that the former spouse's record is lost on remarriage is that the new spouse's NIC record may suffice for a full state pension. These provisions were designed for dependent women and, assuming that more men than women have nearly full NIC records, this makes sense. Women who remarry are also protected because they can top up their own state pensions with Category B(L) pensions, which married men and civil partners will not be able to do until 2010 (for women) and 2015 (for men – see **9.2.2**). This means that if a divorced person who does not have a full NIC record in their own right is in a same-sex relationship, and is approaching state pension age, they may want to consider waiting to register a civil partnership. This will in particular affect women who brought up a family and were married.

Example 9.1

Sonia was born in 1949 and is 56 years old in 2005. She married George in 1967 when she was 18 and was a housewife bringing up their only child. Although they separated in 1985 George and Sonia did not divorce until 1998. George is 10 years older than Sonia and his NIC record until 1998 includes 40 years' contributions. Sonia formed a relationship with Anne in 1988 and they have been living together since. Anne also had children from an earlier relationship, who were teenagers when Sonia started living with her. Anne went back to work while Sonia stayed at home running the household. She has done odd jobs, but has no NIC record to speak of. Anne's NIC record is a lot less than George's record, which would provide Sonia with a full Category A state pension of £84.25 (2006/07) per week. If Anne and Sonia register a civil partnership in 2006, Sonia will lose her right to use George's NIC record instead of her own.

She cannot get a Category B(L) pension from Anne so her state pension will be low. However, if she waits until she is retired in 2009 and then registers the civil partnership, she will continue to receive her Category A pension based on George's NIC record for the years up until 1998.

A husband can also receive a dependency increase on his state pension for his wife who has not yet reached her state pension age provided she does not earn more than a specified amount. The dependency increase is paid at the same rate as a Category B(L) pension, i.e. 60 per cent of the full pension (£50.50 for 2006/07). From 2010 dependency increases will be equally available to wives and to civil partners even if they had already retired earlier. A civil partner receiving the pension who has already retired in 2010 will probably have to ask the pension service to claim the dependency increase as the pension service may be unlikely to work it out without being reminded to do so. Wives can only get a dependency increase for their husband if they received incapacity benefit including a dependency increase immediately before retirement. Civil partners cannot even get this at the moment.

9.2.2 Category B(L) wives' pension

A Category B(L) pension is paid to a married woman based on her husband's NIC record. It becomes payable to her once she herself reaches state pension age and can give her up to 60 per cent of the full basic state pension during her husband's lifetime (£50.50 per week for 2006/07). For husbands and civil partners this does not apply unless the wife or civil partner was born on or after 6 April 1950. In practice, this means that female civil partners will achieve equal rights with their married contemporaries from 2010 while men (who if born on 6 April 1950 will not reach state retirement age until 2015) will achieve it in 2015.

If the wife has a state pension of her own, which is lower than the full Category B(L) pension, the two can be combined, but the total is capped at the full Category B(L) pension. If her own Category A pension is higher than the full Category B(L) pension, she gets no Category B(L) pension.

9.2.3 Category B survivor's pension

A Category B pension is paid to a surviving spouse or civil partner to top up their own pension. If the deceased had a full NIC record, the survivor will also get a full pension, currently £84.25 per week (2006/07), otherwise the survivor will receive less. The survivor effectively 'inherits' the deceased's state pension at the rate of payment to which the deceased was entitled before the death (or would have been entitled to after state pension age). Currently all widows who are over state pension age at the date of their husband's death receive a

Category B pension irrespective of their deceased husband's age. This will also apply to widows and civil partners who reach state pension age after 6 April 2010. Until then widowers and civil partners only receive a Category B pension if both spouses or both civil partners were over state pension age at the date of death.

Example 9.2

Paul (75) and Geoffrey (66) are civil partners. Geoffrey worked abroad all his working life as a freelance holiday rep and has no UK state pension entitlement; Paul receives a full state pension (Category A). Paul dies in 2007. Geoffrey will receive a state pension of the same amount as Paul's basic state pension (Category B: Social Security Contributions and Benefits Act 1992, s.51(1A)). If Geoffrey had instead been Paula's widower, he would have received the same state pension.

While widows receive a Category B pension even if their husband died before he reached state pension age, civil partners will continue to lose out for some years.

Example 9.3

Janet was married to Richard and brought up their children for many years. She did not work and has no NIC record. They divorce when the children have grown up and she marries Joseph in 2006 when she is 59 years old. Joseph has always worked and paid NICs. When Joseph dies aged 57 in 2008 Janet (then aged 61) receives a Category B state pension based on Joseph's NIC record. If Janet had instead registered a civil partnership with Josephine she would receive no Category B state pension and would need to rely on her own negligible NIC record. If Janet and Josephine had not registered a civil partnership Janet could have used Richard's NIC record for a Category A state pension in her own right when she retired at age 60 in 2007. However, since she was in a civil partnership at that time, she lost that right, retired on a low Category A pension in her own right and lost out on the Category B pension from Josephine because Josephine was below state pension age when she died. Women who can substitute a former husband's NIC record and are born before 6 April 1950 should think carefully before deciding to register a civil partnership before 2010. They may lose out on a large part of the state pension as a result.

Widows, widowers and surviving civil partners can also receive a Category B pension if they are receiving Widowed Parent's Allowance when they reach state pension age or if at some time in the past they were entitled to Bereavement Allowance or Widowed Parent's Allowance when they were over 45. The pension is reduced on a sliding scale if the survivor was between

45 and 54 when the other died (Social Security Contributions and Benefits Act 1992, Sched.4A, para.1; see also **Chapter 10**).

If the surviving partner received a Category A state pension in his or her own right and inherits a Category B state pension, the survivor can then receive a composite pension, which is capped at the full basic state pension rate of £84.25 per week (2006/07). As an alternative the surviving partner can use the late partner's NIC record, but not both. The pension service will calculate both alternatives and use the one more favourable to the pensioner. Surviving civil partners should check that this has indeed happened. Usually for widows, it is more favourable to use the composite method than the substitution method. Substitution is, of course, currently available equally for civil partners whereas Category B pensions are not.

Example 9.4

Jenny and Matthew married in their early 20s. Jenny stopped working to have children and never worked again. Matthew had a period where he did not work and receives about 70 per cent of a full state pension after retirement. Jenny receives a small Category A state pension (about 30 per cent of the full rate) in her own right. If after Matthew's death Jenny substitutes his record for hers, she would probably receive a little more than the 70 per cent of the full state pension (because as a woman she only needs 39 years of NICs instead of 44, although this will of course phase out). If she receives a composite pension, she will effectively receive the full Category A state pension rate.

9.2.4   Deferment of retirement pension

It is possible to defer receiving a Category A or Category B retirement pension beyond state pension age. If the pension is deferred, the pensioner becomes entitled to a higher rate of pension at a later date. There was a five-year maximum time limit for such deferment, but this was abolished from 6 April 2005 when the incremental increase in the deferred pension became slightly more generous. The changes were brought in under the Pensions Act 2004, which also enables people to defer state pension in return for a taxable lump sum in certain circumstances. Because deferred rights are inheritable by spouses, civil partners will have the same rights as widowers. They also have to consent to the deferment where it affects their rights.

9.3   ADDITIONAL STATE PENSION SERPS/S2P

9.3.1   Graduated Retirement Benefit

The state pension is very basic and currently below what the Government deems to be the minimum necessary income for pensioners (see **10.6**). From

1961 to 1975 people could therefore make special graduated (earnings-related) contributions in addition to the flat rate NICs at the time. Half of the deceased spouse's or civil partner's Graduated Retirement Benefit entitlement comes with a Category B pension (see **9.2.3**). Therefore all widows and those widowers and civil partners entitled to Category B retirement pension may receive this now (National Insurance Act 1965, s.37 and the Social Security (Graduated Retirement Benefit) (No.2) Regulations 1978, SI 1978/393, Sched.1). In future, all widowers and civil partners will also be able to receive this when they become entitled to Category B retirement pensions. No Graduated Retirement Benefit is inherited from the deceased's former spouse or civil partner.

These provisions are set out in the Social Security (Retirement Pensions and Graduated Retirement Benefit) (Widowers and Civil Partnership) Regulations 2005, SI 2005/3078. In the explanatory memorandum to these regulations it is expressly stated that:

> This alignment of the role for civil partners with the widower's inheritance position rather than that of widows mirrors the policy as reflected in the amendments made to other state pensions legislation. The policy underpinning this is to avoid creating inequalities in the state pension scheme.

9.3.2 SERPS and S2P

From 1978/79 employees had to pay higher Class 1 NICs, which entitles them to an additional state pension measured on their contributions in relation to average earnings. This is earnings-related and was called the State Earnings-Related Pension Scheme or SERPS. It is not available to the self-employed. Since April 2002, the rules are based on what is known as the State Second Pension (S2P). This is more generous than SERPS and simpler to operate. Certain carers and people with long-term disabilities also qualify. Along with certain low-paid employees, they will be deemed to have a minimum level of earnings (around £12,500 for the tax year 2006/07). SERPS/S2P are inherited with a Category B pension (see **9.2.3**) and therefore all widows, but only a limited group of widowers and surviving civil partners will currently receive it through survivorship. The percentage of SERPS inherited is reduced from 100 per cent to 50 per cent over a period from 2002 to 2010 (depending on the date the contributor reached state pension age). The rate of S2P that can be inherited is always 50 per cent. No SERPS/S2P is inherited from a former spouse or civil partner of the deceased.

9.3.3 Contracting out of the additional state pension scheme (SERPS/S2P)

Employees pay Class 1 NICs at 11 per cent of earnings between a lower threshold and an upper earnings limit and 1 per cent of the earnings above the upper limit. Since 1988 employees can elect to contract out of SERPS/S2P. Instead of accruing (full) entitlement to SERPS/S2P they pay lower NICs of 9.4 per cent for employees and the difference is paid into either their employer's occupational pension scheme or their private pension scheme (see below). Contracted-out schemes (or the contracted-out part of a scheme) must offer special benefits in place of the additional state pension benefits. These rights are known as protected rights. In a defined-contributions scheme, they will be identifiable in a protected rights fund. Contracted-out survivor's pensions are lost on marriage (or remarriage) and registration of a (new) civil partnership and cohabitation.

In consultation the Government considered the potential effect of the unexpected loss of these survivor pensions for widows and widowers who would stand to lose their pension if they are already in a same-sex relationship or subsequently form a civil partnership or start to live together with another person as though they were civil partners. The Government noted that 'if we allowed schemes to apply the new rules for cessation of survivor benefits immediately, this would have meant an alteration to the terms on which the survivor benefit had originally come in to payment and the potential loss of the survivor benefit in circumstances that had not been envisaged' (DWP Consultation Document, *Occupational and Personal Pensions: the Civil Partnership (Amendment of Provisions Relating to Contracted-Out Occupational and Appropriate Personal Pension Schemes) (Surviving Civil Partners) Order 2005* (March 2005), paras.19–21). As a result transitional provisions now in the Pension Schemes Act 1993, s.17(4B) provide that people who were widows or widowers of contracted-out scheme members who died before 5 December 2005 do not lose these pensions as a result of registering a civil partnership. Although they would lose their pensions if they remarried, the Government concluded that 'this potential difference in treatment can be justified when weighed against the unforeseen loss of a benefit' (Consultation Document, at para.21).

9.4   PUBLIC SECTOR OCCUPATIONAL PENSION SCHEMES

Public sector occupational pension schemes are generally defined-benefits (final salary) schemes. The schemes are unfunded, which means that today's pensions are paid for by the contributions currently paid by scheme members supplemented by funds out of general taxation. No money is put aside. These schemes include the armed forces schemes, the Teachers Pension, the NHS Superannuation Scheme, local government and civil service pension schemes, police and fire-fighters' pensions and others. Some statutory schemes were amended directly by the CPA 2004 (e.g. Fire Services Act 1947, House of Commons Members Fund Act 1948), but most schemes are set up under secondary legislation and amendments were made to those schemes under delegated powers. As with civil partners' rights within the state pension scheme, the entitlement to a survivor's pension will also broadly reflect widowers' rights. Pensionable service and contributions accrued since 1988 will count in the calculation of these survivor pensions, as for all contracted-out schemes. This is because public sector pensions extended full surviving spouses benefits to widowers in 1988, when all female employees in the public sector, for example teachers, had to start making the same contributions as male members. Individual features characterise the various public sector schemes.

The power to amend pension schemes conferred by CPA 2004, s.255(1) is exercisable under s.255(4)(b) 'with a view to ensuring that pensions, allowances or gratuities take account of rights which accrued, service which occurred, or any other circumstances which existed before the passing of this Act'. However, s.255(4)(a) provides that the provision for civil partners 'may be the same as, or different to, the provision made with respect to widows, widowers or the dependants of persons who are not civil partners'. This is significant for public sector pension members because pensionable service under public sector schemes will include years before 2005, but it will only count to the extent that it relates to service after 5 April 1988. Most male members contributed a higher amount to their pensions since the late 1970s or earlier and some female members also contributed higher amounts before 1988, in both cases in order to start accruing rights to widow's or widower's pensions for their surviving wives or husbands. By way of example, male teachers made higher pension contributions to have widows' pensions rights included from 1 April 1972. Those members who have not married but now register as civil partners will effectively have wasted those additional contributions and will never receive a benefit for them in return. It must be questionable whether the policy of counting years of service for a surviving spouse's pension but ignoring the same years to calculate pensions for surviving civil partners is compliant with the Human Rights Act 1998. It is an important issue that will need to be tested in the courts. If someone who has paid for a widow's or widower's pension in years before 1988 wants to safeguard a potential future claim by their surviving partner as a surviving spouse, they could marry abroad (for example in Canada, where residence requirements do not seem to be stringent) instead of registering as civil partners in the UK. The Canadian marriage would be recognised as a civil partnership, but the couple could alternatively claim that they should be recognised as spouses and therefore a widow's (or widower's) pension based on the full contributions should be paid to the survivor.

Example 9.5

Jonathan was born in 1950. He registers a civil partnership at age 56 with Paul (age 43) in 2006. Jonathan started working as a teacher in 1972. He paid contributions to the Teachers Pension scheme to include a widow's pension from the start. However, the first 16 years of Jonathan's pensionable service are entirely ignored for the purposes of calculating a survivor pension for Paul if he survives Jonathan. If Jonathan works until he is 60 years old, his own pension will be based on his years of service divided by 80, thus $38/80 \times$ salary (say £30,000, thus £14,250 per year). A widow's pension would be based on all those years divided by 160, i.e. half of Jonathan's pension, or £7,125. Paul, however, will only receive a pension based on years from 1988, thus $22/160 \times £30,000 = £4,125$ per year, i.e. £3,000 less than Jonathan paid for.

In many schemes members or surviving civil partners have a limited time to buy back past years, i.e. they can elect to pay the difference between the contributions paid in years before 1988 that did not include a dependant's pension and the contributions that included a dependant's pension. The time limits are extremely tight: for some schemes the election has to be made shortly after April 2006 or shortly after registration of a civil partnership or by the surviving civil partner (if the member dies within that period) within weeks of the member's death. Affected people should contact their pension scheme urgently. The irony is, of course, that members will pay contributions that they have already paid for (see e.g. a time limit of six months and three months respectively for the Teachers Pension scheme: Teachers' Pensions (Amendment) Regulations 2005, SI 2005/2198, reg.32).

Consultation to amend a pension scheme under s.255 is only necessary amongst such persons as the relevant minister may consider appropriate, and may be dispensed with altogether if it would be expedient to do so due to urgency. It is likely, therefore, that almost all public sector pensions will have been amended by statutory instrument without much consultation.

The Government is keen to change a variety of pension schemes, both to take some pressure off the public purse and to allow employees to elect to have dependant's pension rights for cohabitants. Several schemes, such as the Armed Forces Pension Scheme (Armed Forces Pension Scheme Order 2005, SI 2005/438) and the Parliamentary Contributory Pension Fund (Parliamentary Pension (Amendment) Regulations 2005, SI 2005/887) were changed in 2005. Both new schemes provide reduced benefits to surviving adult dependants who are more than 12 years younger than the deceased. This does not however apply to the pension of an adult survivor under the Parliamentary scheme if the scheme member was a participant in the scheme before 3 November 2004 and married or registered a civil partnership with the survivor before 1 May 2006, or made a declaration under sub-paragraph (1)(a) of reg.K2A of the Parliamentary Pensions (Consolidation and Amendment) Regulations 1993, SI 1993/3253, as amended.

Following consultation, the National Health Service Pension Scheme Regulations 1995 were amended in November 2005 by the National Health Service (Pension Scheme, Injury Benefits, Additional Voluntary

Contributions and Compensation for Premature Retirement) (Civil Partnership) Amendment Regulations 2005, SI 2005/3074. The amended scheme provides similar benefits on the death of scheme members based on membership from 6 April 1988. Current members will also have a time-limited option to buy survivor pension cover for membership prior to 1988. An irrevocable notice must be given under amended reg.G12(3)(a) not later than 28 February 2007, which specifies the period in respect of which the election is made by the member, who must be of 'sound health for his age'.

The Local Government Pension Scheme Regulations 1997 (and related regulations) were amended in November 2005 after an eight-week consultation period. Many of the respondents commented on whether it was desirable to extend the provision to allow membership before 6 April 1988. Unlike the amendments to the National Health Service scheme referred to above, there is no statement of compatibility with the European Convention on Human Rights, since the Local Government Pension Scheme instrument does not amend primary legislation and is therefore subject to the negative resolution procedure. The Local Government Pension Scheme is however a statutory pension scheme for employees of local government. Civil partners will be eligible for the payment of a death grant where the member dies from a work-related injury or disease with effect from 5 December 2005. There will be parity of treatment for gratuities.

9.5 PRIVATE SECTOR EMPLOYERS' OCCUPATIONAL PENSION SCHEMES

A large number of private sector employers offer their employees membership of an occupational pension scheme. Usually the employer makes contributions to the scheme and for almost all schemes the employee also contributes. In addition, contracted-out NICs can be paid into the scheme (see **9.3.3**). Employees' contributions are made from gross income (basic rate income tax is paid directly into the scheme and the additional 18 per cent higher rate income tax can be reclaimed) and there is no tax on the capital accumulating inside the pension fund. On retirement part of the pension may be in form of a tax-free lump sum; the monthly pension that pensioners then receive is subject to income tax. Since this is usually less than the salary paid while working and therefore taxed at a lower marginal rate, the whole scheme is tax-advantageous.

The attraction for employers is that they can offer their employees an additional benefit, often at a lower cost than contributions into a personal pension scheme and with tax advantages. The contributions made every month are invested and the investments pay out pensions to retired employees. The fund may be invested in assets such as stocks and shares, but also property and art. Traditionally most occupational pension schemes are defined-benefits schemes where the future pensions are paid out based on a final or average salary, e.g. 1/80 of the average salary over the last three years of service for every year of membership. When share prices boomed in the 1990s a number of funds were thought to be worth a lot more than the pensions they would have to pay out in the future and employers were allowed to take out the apparent surplus. When stock markets collapsed with the dotcom bubble at the turn of the century, many schemes found that they were in fact under-funded and would not be able to pay out the pensions that the employees will be entitled to in the future. As a result, a number of employers have introduced defined-contributions schemes where the pension paid out is directly linked to the contributions paid in, similar to a private pension scheme ('80% of final pay schemes at risk', *The Guardian*, 19 November 2004). These are also called money purchase schemes (group schemes). Some occupational pension schemes have only ever been money purchase schemes. In most cases existing employees are able to remain in the old defined-benefits scheme. Often the existing final salary scheme will not have the option to allow a dependant's pension for an unmarried (or unregistered) partner. So if members want this as part of their scheme, they will have to leave the security of the final salary scheme and opt for the lesser benefits of the defined-contributions scheme.

Since occupational pensions (whether defined-benefits or defined-contributions) are part of the benefits remuneration package provided by employers, they fall under the EU non-discrimination rules (Council Directive 2000/78/EC, 27 November 2000), which were implemented into UK law by the Employment Equality (Sexual Orientation) Regulations 2003, SI 2003/1661. These have been amended by the Civil Partnership Act 2004 (Amendments to Subordinate Legislation) Order 2005, SI 2005/2114, Sched.17, para.7. A new reg.3(3) prohibits discrimination against civil partners compared to spouses and makes it clear that the difference is not a 'material difference' which would justify different treatment. The revised reg.25 provides that discrimination is not unlawful if it relates 'to a benefit by reference to marital status where the right to the benefit accrued or the benefit is payable in respect of periods of service' before 5 December 2005; nor is it unlawful to confer benefits to spouses and civil partners only and not to cohabitants. This means that pensions for surviving civil partners do not need to be backdated and that spousal rights do not need to be extended to cohabitants. Schemes or part of schemes which are not contracted out of the additional state pension SERPS/S2P will therefore only be required to provide survivor pensions to surviving civil partners built up from contributions since 5 December 2005. For membership after that date benefits to surviving civil partners will need to be equivalent to those for widows or widowers. If, however, the scheme has made provision for unmarried opposite-sex surviving partners, it is also required to make the same provision for same-sex partners for periods of pensionable service or contributions from 1 December 2003.

Benefits for surviving civil partners based on the member's contracted-out rights will be identical to the rights available to widowers (Civil Partnership (Contracted-Out Occupational and Appropriate Personal Pension Schemes) (Surviving Civil Partners) Order 2005, SI 2005/2050, amending the Pension Schemes Act 1993). Contracted-out occupational and personal pension schemes are required to provide survivor benefits for surviving civil partners based on the member's contracted-out rights accrued from 6 April 1988. As this is when contracting out began, there will be no discrimination. In the summary of the responses to the Government's consultation on the Order, it was made clear that reg.9A of the Employment Equality (Sexual Orientation) Regulations 2003 directly binds all pension trust managers and trustees of occupations pension schemes even if the scheme rules themselves are not amended. This applies to all contracted-out schemes or parts of schemes, whether they are part of a defined-contributions or a defined-benefits scheme.

The most limited rights of all, at least in statutory legal terms, are likely to persist in private sector occupational schemes. Although many such schemes already allow provision for unmarried partners, including same-sex partners, such provision is discretionary, which distinguishes it from the mandatory nature of survivor benefits for widows, widowers and surviving civil partners. The scheme will inevitably, however, have been set up under a trust deed, which advisers should check carefully to see whether the trustees have a discretion to pay benefits to the surviving civil partner as a cohabitant. The tax advantageous status of pensions requires that benefits are paid to the member, their spouse (and now their civil partner) or people who are financially dependent on the member. The discretion available to trustees in administering survivor benefits to unmarried partners and their dependants gave considerable scope for discrimination on the basis of sexual orientation. A number of trustees interpreted the position in a way that no benefits could be paid to a surviving partner who was not financially dependent, i.e. those who had their own pensions, which excluded many same-sex partners. The lobbying group Stonewall achieved an important breakthrough in 1999 when the Inland Revenue was persuaded that such discretion could extend to unmarried partners (including same-sex partners) whose relationship was one of financial interdependence rather than financial dependence.

Not requiring membership of a pension scheme before 2005 to count for benefits to a survivor's pension means in practice that only those leaving school at 16 and starting off in their careers in 2005 (i.e. born after about September 1989) will definitely not be affected by residual discrimination. The discrimination will continue to have effect until all older colleagues and their dependants have died, which could be well towards the end of this century.

9.6 PERSONAL PENSIONS

Private ('personal') pension schemes are money purchase schemes. The member makes regular or one-off payments into the pension, which are then invested in a fund that is intended to grow. This can be in share portfolios (unit trusts, etc.), commercial property, corporate bonds and the like. Contributions are made from gross income (basic rate tax is paid by HMRC to the pension provider, higher rate tax can be reclaimed at the end of the tax year) and the fund grows tax free. On retirement the member can elect to receive 25 per cent of the fund as a tax-free lump sum. The rest (or the whole fund if no such election is made) must be used to buy an annuity that pays a monthly pension. This is taxed as income.

Personal pension schemes have been available since 1 July 1988, and were introduced to provide more flexibility and mobility within the pensions system. Before 1988 only the self-employed could have personal pensions, which were called retirement annuity contracts. Since then employees can also have personal pensions. Since personal pensions were often sold by brokers who then received commission, the provider would front-load the costs, which would then be repaid over time. As a result a large part of contributions in the early years would go towards repaying charges so that funds grew slowly. Partly to change this, the Labour Government introduced stakeholder pensions through the Welfare Reform and Pensions Act 1999. Stakeholder pensions are intended to be a simpler version of the personal pension scheme, where charges are limited to 1 per cent of the fund per year. If employers do not offer any occupational pension scheme they must offer their employees access to a stakeholder pension scheme, but there is no obligation on employers to contribute into the scheme. Non-working people can also have stakeholder pensions and the Government pays into their schemes as if they had paid tax at the basic rate even if they have no income of their own. So a husband can, for example, pay into a stakeholder pension in the name of his wife. The Pensions Act 2004 made further changes to personal pensions allowing investment in a wider range of assets, within self-invested personal pensions (SIPPS). Many of the changes came into force in April 2006. Whether they are called retirement annuity contracts or stakeholder pensions, they are all essentially different types of personal pension schemes. Many personal pension schemes were set up solely as vehicles for contracting out of SERPS/S2P. They may also be used to collect and administer additional voluntary contributions (AVCs). Personal pensions, including stakeholder pensions, are usually set up with insurance companies or investment managers, often via a financial adviser or pension consultant.

At the time they buy an annuity, those with personal pension schemes can choose whether or not they want to have a dependant's pension. They can elect to have a dependant's pension, which can be nominated to a specific beneficiary, or to have none, which means the monthly pension payment from the annuity is higher. This has been commonly used by unmarried and same-sex couples to provide survivor benefits for the other. The survivor's pension is therefore entirely a matter of choice. Not all annuity providers offer dependant's pensions for unmarried or same-sex partners, but in most cases the pension holder can shop around. One exception is where there are guaranteed annuity rates, which exist under some old schemes, especially retirement annuity contracts. They are attractive because annuity rates have fallen significantly in recent years. In such cases civil partners or other people in same-sex relationships are faced with a dilemma if their provider does not offer dependant's pensions. Until there is a general anti-discrimination law (and these schemes are not excluded), this will remain a problem. In such a situation the costs of transferring the pension to a different provider must be weighed up against the cost of making alternative financial provision for their partner. An additional issue is that because of the longer life expectancy of women, private pension providers are likely to offer a worse deal to a female member who is in a civil partnership than to one who is married. Whether this then means that providers are going to offer a better deal to men in civil partnerships than to those in marriages remains to be seen. This would be an extension of the fact that annuities for women are more expensive than for men, as women are likely to live longer. This is of course the other side of the coin of the cheaper life insurance available for men. Although the EU contemplated making this sex discrimination illegal, the proposals were dropped. Nevertheless, in practice it will mean that female civil partners will need to accumulate a larger fund to receive the same monthly payments than those that male civil partners or spouses would need to accumulate.

In addition to voluntary contributions by pension scheme members, or by their employer, members who are employees can also elect to opt out of the additional state pension (SERPS/S2P) and have payments made into their personal pension scheme instead (see also **9.3.3**). These must be invested in a separate protected rights fund. It is not possible to commute any part of the protected rights pension benefits for a tax-free lump sum payment because protected rights are treated more rigidly. Protected pension rights must be taken in a prescribed form including a compulsory pension for the surviving spouse or civil partner in circumstances where the member dies whilst in receipt of a protected rights pension. From 5 December 2005 an election for the purchase of survivor benefits may include benefits for a surviving civil partner.

9.7 PENSIONS FOR TRANS PEOPLE

People who obtain legal recognition of their acquired gender under the Gender Recognition Act 2004 will be treated for all purposes as their new gender, including in respect of their pensions (see generally **Chapter 5**). This means that a 63-year-old trans man who has so far been treated as a woman and who is given a gender recognition certificate in 2006 will lose his state pension until he is 65 and a trans woman of the same age will be able to claim her state pension immediately (but cannot backdate it to the age of 60). Consistently with that principle, occupational pensions should treat the trans person as their new gender. So if a trans woman marries a man, she should be entitled to the same widow's pension as any other woman who married that man would have been.

What is unclear is whether a trans man who is a member of an occupational pension scheme in which women started contributing at a much later date than men for dependant's pensions will now have service from the earlier or the later date counted for a widow's pension for his spouse. As these entitlements are based on contributions, the later date would be the logical conclusion. This would sit uneasily with the way civil partners are treated (see **9.4** and **9.5** above).

9.8   THE POLICY

The question the Government seemed to have problems with was whether to treat surviving civil partners in the same way as widows or as widowers: should all female surviving civil partners be regarded as widows and all male surviving civil partners as widowers? Pensions can of course be regarded as an investment or insurance scheme where benefits depend on the contributions made over a period of time. This is obvious in the case of personal pension schemes, but the analogy also works with defined benefit schemes which characterise public sector pensions. From this point of view it becomes clear that if members of a pension scheme increased their monthly contributions to acquire a dependant's pension as part of their benefits (whether out of choice or as a requirement of the rules of the scheme), this should be granted irrespective of the dependant's gender. So surviving civil partners should be treated in the same way as surviving spouses. This would mean that a male civil partner who is the surviving partner of a male member of a pension scheme would be treated in the same way as the member's widow. A surviving female civil partner of a female member would be treated in the same way as her widower.

So if, for instance, a male teacher started paying higher monthly contributions to have a widow's pension as part of his benefits in 1972, there is no reason why his civil partner should not receive a dependant's pension if he forms a civil partnership instead of getting married (see **example 9.5** above). Although the life expectancy of men and women is different (women tend to live longer), this issue is unlikely to matter much to the scheme if it can be assumed that roughly equal numbers of men and women will form civil partnerships. This seems to be the way that the issue has been treated for people

173

who change gender under the Gender Recognition Act 2004 (see **9.7**). Therefore using 1988 as a start date for all dependants' pensions for surviving civil partners leaves discrimination for those scheme members who made higher contributions to their pension before that date. It leaves it open to any affected couples or surviving civil partners to challenge the law under the Human Rights Act 1998 as being discriminatory. One option would be for the couple to marry abroad and try to get the marriage recognised as a marriage rather than a civil partnership (see **9.4**).

The issue with the basic state pension is more complicated. The scheme was set up at a time when women were often wholly financially dependent as wives and marriage was far more likely to be terminated by death than by divorce. Until 1979, married women could choose to pay NICs at a reduced rate to save money, but these do not count for the state pension. Some women still do so today. These are the remnants of outmoded assumptions about female dependency, which were made by the architects of the welfare state. As a result only 17 per cent of women who retired in September 2004 received a full state pension based on their own records. A further 6 per cent received a full state pension based on their husband's or former husband's records. Men have a significantly higher basic state pension entitlement (DWP, *Women and pensions – the evidence* (November 2005), available from the DWP's website **www.dwp.gov.uk**). If a woman in the remaining 76 per cent is married to a man with a full or almost full state pension, she will of course inherit this on his death if she survives her husband.

The Government estimates that the percentage of women who have a full state pension in their own right (or via their husband's contributions) is rising steadily and that there will be no gender inequality for those retiring in 2025 (*Women and pensions*, above). Women who have spent time after 1978 looking after children or caring for relatives may be able to make use of Home Responsibilities Protection, which will in effect reduce the years in which they are supposed to accrue NICs (and therefore weigh their NICs higher). However, they still need to accrue some years of NICs in their own right. The problem of low state pensions for women is obviously higher in older women, those who have looked after the home or the family, and first-generation immigrants (who may not have spent all their working life in this country). A minimum income for people of state pension age is guaranteed via the Pension Credit, which is effectively a form of means-tested welfare benefit similar to Income Support (see **10.6**).

Under the changes made to the state pension regime for civil partners, surviving female civil partners will be significantly worse off than widows. However, it is likely that those female civil partners who lose out (retiring before 2010) are affected by the same issues as married women and will be on low pensions. In a generation when homosexuality (for men) was still illegal and it was stigmatised for all, many women will have brought up a family and only come out as lesbian later in life. If they were married, they may be able to avail themselves of their former husband's NIC record for the time of the marriage, but this will not cover them for post-divorce childcare years. The costs of bringing female civil partners into the same situation as widows would have been low as Pension Credit tops up the income of those who have no full state pension provision and the number of women registering a civil partnership of that generation is also likely to be low compared to the general population (see the Government's own estimates for projected take up in WEU, *Civil Partnership: A framework for the legal recognition of same-sex couples* (June 2003)). Not having done so will mean that female civil partners are left disproportionately poor (see **example 9.3** above). Of course if the Government had extended the existing provision for wives and widows to female (surviving) civil partners, male civil partners would have been in a worse position than female civil partners. However, this discrimination would have been similar to the ongoing discrimination between married men and women. While occupational and private pensions are fundamentally based on the contributions made (and therefore a survivor's pension should be dependent on the gender of the pension scheme member), the substitution of one spouse's or ex-spouses NIC record to enhance state pension for the financially weaker spouse is a logical way of compensating for the other spouse's lower contributions, and can therefore justifiably be treated differently. As it is, female civil partners are worse off than wives and widows without any justification for this discrimination. It is not logical that two groups of people should be discriminated against because discrimination against one group cannot be ended immediately.

Although the Employment Equality (Sexual Orientation) Regulations 2003 make discrimination against civil partners, as compared with married spouses, unlawful in the area of employment, and although this extends to pensions entitlement, it only applies to periods of service and contributions paid into non-contracted-out schemes from the commencement date of the CPA 2004, i.e. 5 December 2005. No period of service or contributions before 5 December 2005 is required to count towards the calculation of survivor benefits for civil partners. It makes no difference to the pension available to the surviving civil partner whether the deceased had been a member of the relevant pension scheme for 48 hours or 48 years before 5 December 2005. Only service between 5 December 2005 and the date of death of the pension member will accrue entitlement for the surviving civil partner.

The ongoing discrimination, especially under occupational pensions and SERPS/S2P raises human rights issues similar to those which were identified by the Joint Committee on Human Rights when the Bill was considered during its passage through Parliament (Fifteenth Report of Session 2003–04, 15 July 2004, HL Paper 136, HC 885). This focused on the rights under public sector pension schemes, for which originally only service after 5 December 2005 was intended to count.

The Government had argued that there was no discrimination because extensions to pension rights were never introduced retrospectively. It was, for example, pointed out that survivor benefits in the public sector were only made available to widowers in 1988 and widowers' pensions were only calculated with reference to contributions of a female scheme member from 1988 whereas for widows of male members a longer period of contributions was taken into account. The Joint Committee took the view, however, that a proper comparison for the purposes of considering equal treatment should be drawn in terms of how a relevant comparator would be treated today, not how that comparator was treated at some point in the past. The Joint Committee argued as follows:

> The relevant comparison appears to us to be between a surviving civil partner whose partner dies the day after the Act comes into force, after having made identical contributions . . . and a married survivor whose partner dies on the same day with exactly the same contribution record.

It was considered necessary by the Joint Committee (at para.[38]) to:

> distinguish between the content of the right to which the Human Rights Act gives rise, and the date upon which that right became available in the UK. The issue of retrospectivity arises not in relation to the content of the right (to what benefit or protection does the human rights claim give rise?) but in relation to the availability of that right (when must the relevant events have taken place in order to be able to rely on the right?).

The Committee concluded that a surviving civil partner should therefore receive the same entitlement as a surviving spouse in an analogous position in the absence of any objective reason for the content of that entitlement to be different.

As a result the Government agreed to count service or contributions from 1988 towards survivors' pensions for public sector schemes and SERPS/S2P. This is of course a half-way house and ignores survivors' pension rights accrued for spouses before that date.

The Employment Equality (Sexual Orientation) Regulations 2003 have been amended to provide that private occupational pension schemes will need to provide survivors' pensions but only from service from 5 December 2005 onwards. Similar arguments as were brought forward by the Joint Committee on Human Rights may well be used to argue that this provision is a breach of the Human Rights Act 1998 and should be set aside.

9.9 POINTS TO NOTE FOR PRACTITIONERS

- Pension provision for civil partners and surviving civil partners is usually less than that for spouses and widows or widowers.

- This discrimination will continue well until the end of the twenty-first century.
- There may be arguments under the Human Rights Act 1998 to challenge all or some of the discriminatory provisions made (see **9.8**).
- Depending on their age, their former husband's NIC record and the NIC record of their partner, divorced women (and sometimes men) born before 6 April 1950 should consider waiting until after retirement before registering a civil partnership (see **9.2.1**).
- Men who were members of public sector pension schemes before 1988 and anyone who was a member of a private sector defined-benefits pension scheme before 5 December 2005 which does not have same-sex partner benefits for the full period of membership, may wish to consider marrying their same-sex partner in a country where this is possible (for example Canada). This would allow them to argue at a later date that they should be recognised as a married couple rather than civil partners, so that their surviving civil partner is entitled to the same pension that a widow would be entitled to (see **9.4**).
- When obtaining pension information for the court in connection with a financial application on a dissolution, the provider will probably often need to be specifically told that information is required for pensions for surviving civil partners rather than spouses. Although the pension information form P1 requires this information for surviving spouses and surviving civil partners, it is unlikely that all providers will indeed furnish the information as it is likely that in most cases it will need to be calculated manually for civil partners. Requesting information for civil partners may involuntarily 'out' clients' sexual orientation to their pension providers and therefore to their employers (for an occupational pension). The client's consent should be obtained for this. To avoid drawing attention to individual clients, practitioners may decide to insist on receiving the information for surviving civil partners in all cases and to refuse to reply to the question of whether this is really necessary (see **6.4.9**).

CHAPTER 10

Social security, tax credits and child support

Keith Puttick

10.1 INTRODUCTION

10.1.1 General observations

This chapter deals with changes to social security, tax credits and child support, and focuses on their impact on the main entitlements, rights, responsibilities and liabilities of:

- civil partners; and
- same-sex cohabitants.

The Civil Partnership Act 2004 clearly resulted in swings and roundabouts for those in same-sex relationships. Despite the extension to civil partners of the same benefits rights previously only available to married couples, there have also been some very negative effects produced, including reductions in state financial and other support as a result of attributing 'couple' status to civil partners living in the same household, and same-sex partners 'living together'. As Brenda Hale (Baroness Hale of Richmond) put it when describing civil partnership:

> The legal consequences both during and at the end of the partnership will be virtu-ally identical to those of marriage. These include the disadvantages as well as the advantages – principally being treated as a couple rather than two people for benefit purposes.
>
> ('Unmarried couples and the law' [2004] Fam Law 419 at 424)

In a later commentary on the changes, in *Secretary of State for Work and Pensions* v. *M* [2006] UKHL 11, at para.101, she observed that Government policy-makers 'knew full well' what they were doing when making changes to the state benefit and child support systems, some of which would be disadvantageous. She added:

So too did those in the lesbian and gay community who were campaigning for the change. To people who have traditionally been excluded by society and the law, what matters most is equal dignity, being taken seriously on the same terms as the traditionally included, unless there is a good reason for making a difference.

The legislation affects civil partners and unregistered, same-sex cohabitants in many other ways, as considered in this chapter.

10.1.2   The main changes

1. Civil partners gain access to the full range of contributory, non-contributory, and other benefits, on the same basis as married couples. In some cases, for example elements of state retirement pension, the new benefits are subject to an implementation timetable (see **Chapter 9**).
2. Civil partners are treated as a single family unit for most purposes.
3. Cohabiting, unregistered same-sex couples are generally assessed and treated as a single family unit in the same way as unmarried cohabiting opposite-sex couples.
4. Same-sex couples' rights and responsibilities, and procedures for adjudicating these, are aligned with those of opposite-sex couples in relation to benefits, tax credits, and relevant parts of the child support system.

This chapter covers the following areas:

*   the old law and the need for reform (**10.2**) including the advantages (**10.2.1**) and disadvantages (**10.2.2**) of the old law, and the reforms made by the CPA 2004 (**10.2.4**);
*   the changes to 'couple' status (**10.3**);
*   means-tested benefits (**10.4**) including relevant aspects of Income Support, income-based Jobseeker's Allowance, Housing Benefit and Council Tax Benefit;
*   non-means-tested benefits (**10.5**) including incapacity and bereavement benefits and state retirement pension benefits (see also **9.2**);
*   Pension Credits (**10.6**);
*   tax credits (**10.7**) including Working Tax Credit and Child Tax Credit;
*   Child Benefit and child support (**10.8**); and
*   cohabitation and 'living together' rules (**10.9**).

10.2   THE OLD LAW AND THE NEED FOR REFORM

10.2.1   Advantages of the old law

Under the old law same-sex partners were treated as two separate people. This meant:

1. Same-sex partners were not within the definition of a married or unmarried couple, so their *capital resources* (including realisable assets) were not aggregated and deemed to be available to both of them. They could continue to receive means-tested benefits like Income Support (IS), income-based Jobseeker's Allowance (JSA (IB) – replacing means-tested unemployment benefit), Housing Benefit (HB) and Council Tax Benefit (CTB) as individuals, without being affected by capital limits.
2. *Partners' income* was not combined as part of a joint claim or otherwise treated as 'available' to the claimant of such benefits (Working Tax Credit (WTC), Child Tax Credit (CTC), and Pension Credit (PC)).
3. If one of the same-sex partners was engaged in *remunerative work* the other partner was not barred from claiming IS or JSA (IB), or prevented from receiving those benefits after the partner started work.
4. In the *community care system* a same-sex couple was not generally treated as a couple or a family unit for the purpose of means-testing services, access to support for fees for accommodation, etc. However, practices have varied (and still vary) between authorities.
5. Women and men receiving *bereavement benefits* after the death of their spouses could cohabit with a same-sex partner without those benefits being stopped (as would happen in an opposite-sex relationship).
6. *Civil and criminal liabilities* which applied to opposite-sex cohabitants after adverse cohabitation decisions did not apply to same-sex cohabitants.

Overall, same-sex couples enjoyed rights and immunities that were *not* available to married or unmarried couples.

10.2.2   Disadvantages of the old law

Pursuing the swings and roundabouts theme, under the old law same-sex cohabitants were disadvantaged in a number of ways. For example, they were barred from important rights that were available to spouses, such as:

- bereavement benefits;
- adult dependency increases paid with certain benefits;
- state retirement pension and related benefits;
- the ability to use a former or deceased partner's National Insurance Contribution (NIC) record to assist a claim for contributory benefits such as state retirement pension.

10.2.3   'Couple' and 'married couple' status

Like most European legal systems UK law traditionally confined the legal definition of a 'couple' to a man and a woman, and in many cases a *married* couple. The effect was to make opposite-sex marital status a gateway to many benefits and welfare services – and to relegate two major groups, same-sex couples and unmarried opposite-sex couples, to the margins of the social welfare law system. Unfortunately, this injustice has sometimes been reinforced by decisions of the European Court of Human Rights in Strasbourg, as in *Shakell* v. *United Kingdom* (Application No.45851/99), 27 April 2000; (2001) *Welfare Benefits Law and Practice* Vol.8, Issue 1). In that case the court upheld UK law which prevented the surviving partner of a long-term, opposite-sex relationship receiving bereavement benefits because the partners were not spouses. This was in spite of the fact that NICs had been paid over a lengthy period. Despite this, the applicant was unable to bring the case within the protection normally given to 'possessions' under Art.1 of Protocol 1 of the European Convention on Human Rights. The key point was that the court, in effect, accepted that States could legislate to discriminate in favour of the institution of marriage and spouses, and in a way that treated survivors of other types of domestic partnership less advantageously. *Shakell* has been applied in later cases by tribunals and Social Security Commissioners; for example by Mr Commissioner Lloyd-Davies in Commissioner's Case CG/1259/2002 (12 June 2003) (see **www.osscsc.gov.uk**). There are, no doubt, many survivors of long-term same-sex relationships who have also experienced such discrimination in recent years. Whilst civil partners have gained comparable rights to the survivor of a married couple, the survivor of an unregistered, same-sex couple relationship will continue to be ineligible for bereavement benefits even where NICs have been paid.

10.2.4 Reform through the Civil Partnership Act 2004

Such disparities in treatment came under close scrutiny with the introduction of civil partnership status. Apart from the need to redress the inherent injustices involved, the position was almost certainly incompatible with the European Convention on Human Rights after the enactment of the Human Rights Act 1998 (HRA 1998). The Government realised it would become increasingly difficult to defend proceedings even with the assistance of the 'justification' defence and the statutory defences in HRA 1998, s.6 because of the development of Convention rights in the area of social security in the UK courts through a series of successful claims. Those claims have relied in particular on:

- Article 8 of the Convention (the right to family life);
- Article 14 (on discrimination); and
- Article 1 of Protocol 1 prohibiting interference in 'possessions', especially contributory benefits and now most kinds of state benefits (*Koua Poirrez* v. *France* (2005) 40 EHRR 34 at 45, para.37; and *Stec and Others* v. *United Kingdom* (2005) 41 EHRR SE18, Application No.65731/01).

The Government's vulnerability had already been illustrated by cases like *Willis* v. *United Kingdom* [2002] FLR 582, ECtHR, where it was held that disparity in treatment necessitated implementation of equal treatment of widowers and widows with effect from 9 April 2001. The case also highlighted the scale on which institutionalised gender-based discrimination permeated the UK's state welfare system.

10.2.5   Proposals for change

As part of its wider proposals on civil partnership, the Government proposed the extension of benefits and tax credits to civil partners, and 'equalisation' of the rights and liabilities of civil partners and same-sex couples (Women and Equality Unit (WEU) *Civil Partnership: A framework for the legal recognition of same-sex couples* (June 2003), paras.7.19–7.29; 8.4–8.8; and 9.9–9.10)

In summary, the Government proposed that:

1. Civil partners should have access to contributory, non-contributory and other benefits on the same basis as married couples.
2. Civil partners should be treated as a single family unit for the purposes of means-tested benefits and tax credits.
3. Unregistered cohabiting same-sex couples should be assessed (and generally treated) as a single family unit in the same way as unmarried cohabiting opposite-sex couples.

The changes in (3) were controversial. Baroness Hale, for example, queried whether, once civil partnership became available to same-sex couples, 'those who do not enter it should, like opposite-sex couples, be treated as if they were married for benefit purposes' ('Unmarried couples and the law' [2004] Fam Law 419, at 424). This was the subject of consultation before it went ahead, and the results were published in DTI/WEU *Responses to Civil Partnership: A Framework for the Legal Recognition of Same-Sex Couples* (November 2003). These appeared to show that a majority of respondents accepted this change (see para.4.7) – including some (but not all) respondent organisations in the gay and lesbian community. However, it is not clear from the summary of responses whether all respondents appreciated how, specifically (or how much) the change would affect them.

10.3   CHANGES TO 'COUPLE' STATUS

Before considering the main changes to social security, tax credits and child support, it is important to note how the CPA 2004 has rationalised the four main types of domestic partnership in social welfare and family law, and replaced definitions of 'married couple' or 'unmarried couple' with a new, pervasive definition of 'couple'.

10.3.1   The new definition of 'couple'

The new definition of 'couple' in s.137(1) of the Social Security Contributions and Benefits Act 1992 (SSCBA 1992) (with emphasis added) is:

(a) a man and woman who are married to each other **and are members of the same household**;

(b) a man and woman who are not married to each other **but are living together as husband and wife** otherwise than in prescribed circumstances;

(c) two people of the same sex who are civil partners of each other **and are members of the same household**;

(d) two people of the same sex who are not civil partners of each other **but are living together as if they were civil partners** otherwise than in prescribed circumstances.

This is then mirrored in changes to other social security legislation, including the Social Security Administration Act 1992 (SSAA 1992), s.2AA, and a large number of social security regulations, as provided in the Civil Partnership (Pensions, Social Security and Child Support) (Consequential, etc. Provisions) Order 2005, SI 2005/2877, Sched.3. Further consequential changes were made by the Social Security (Civil Partnership) (Consequential Amendments) Regulations 2005, SI 2005/2878.

One of the consequences of the new definition would seem to be that same-sex partners can register as civil partners but at that stage still not be a 'couple' – at least until they start to share the same household. Such a civil partner would still be treated, for benefits and tax credits purposes, as a 'single' claimant. As a further corollary of the definition in s.137(1)(c), civil partners who have been a couple can cease to be such when one of them moves out of that household and starts to live in a separate household on a permanent basis. Similarly, partners in a same-sex, unregistered relationship do not become a 'couple' until they are, in law, 'living together'. If they have been 'living together', and cease to do so, then they will no longer be parties in a 'couple'. This clearly has important implications for the take-up of benefits and tax credits, and legal liabilities that are linked to 'couple' status – and these are explored further in the discussion of 'exiting' options in **10.4.6** and **10.9** below.

10.3.2   Treatment of unregistered same-sex couples

To ensure consistency of treatment between unregistered same-sex couples and unmarried couples, and to honour the commitment made during consultations that the extension of the cohabitation rule to same-sex partners would be managed 'sensitively' (*Responses to Civil Partnership*, comments on responses in paras.4.7 and 4.8), the CPA 2004 inserted sub-s.137(1A) into SSCBA 1992 as follows:

> For the purposes of this Part, two people of the same sex are to be regarded as living together as if they were civil partners if, but only if, they would be regarded as living together as husband and wife were they instead two people of the same sex.

Elsewhere in the CPA 2004 'living together as civil partners' or 'living together as if they were civil partners' is not defined. This is likely to create real problems because a civil partnership is only defined through the registration process, which is the very thing missing when a same-sex couple live together without registering a civil partnership (see **1.4.8**). In the context of social security, this definition provides an important safeguard, especially given the potentially serious consequences that can flow from an adverse 'cohabitation' decision (see **10.9.7** below).

10.4   MEANS-TESTED BENEFITS

The relevant amendments which make the changes referred to below can be found in Sched.24 to, and Parts 3, 4, and 7 of the CPA 2004, and in the Civil Partnership (Pensions, Social Security and Child Support) (Consequential, etc. Provisions) Order 2005, SI 2005/2877.

10.4.1   Changes from 5 December 2005

On 5 December 2005 most features of the means-tested benefits system were extended to same-sex couples in the same way as for those in an opposite-sex relationship. Specifically:

- civil partners: the same claims and awards arrangements that apply to married couples have applied since 5 December 2005; and
- unregistered same-sex couples: the same claims and awards arrangements apply to them as they do to opposite-sex unmarried couples.

Since 5 December 2005, if two people are living together as a same-sex couple (whether as civil partners or not) benefits claims and awards must be made on the basis of them being a couple and not two single people. Ongoing rights, liabilities and procedures (including rules on reporting 'changes in circumstances' that might affect continuing eligibility) operate as they do for spouses and cohabiting opposite-sex couples. If a member of a same-sex couple on 5 December 2005 was already claiming one or more of the following benefits:

- Income Support (IS);
- income-based Jobseeker's Allowance (JSA (IB));
- Housing Benefit (HB);
- Council Tax Benefit (CTB);
- Pension Credit (PC);
- Working Tax Credit (WTC);
- Child Tax Credit (CTC).

that person will normally have been expected to claim again, but as part of a couple. DWP guidance before 5 December 2005 made it clear that such claimants should seek advice from the office dealing with their claim 'as soon as they can, to see how their claim/application could be affected' (e.g. DWP *Touchbase*, September 2005, 40th Edn, p.15). As far as HB and CTB are concerned, advice from local authorities has been similar to that given by the Department for Work and Pensions (DWP). Specific guidance on the 'living together' rules, and their application to same-sex partners, is also available in HB/CTB A16 (2005) and subsequent 'guidance'.

10.4.2   Partners in 'remunerative work'

Changes made by Sched.24, paras.55–63 mean that from 5 December 2005 IS or JSA (IB) of civil partners or same-sex cohabitants can not normally be paid:

- if the claimant is working in 'remunerative work' (defined as 16 hours per week paid employment); or
- if the claimant's cohabiting partner is working over 24 hours a week.

In some cases the system will treat the claimant as engaged in 'remunerative work', and therefore ineligible for either IS or JSA (IB), for example where an average of 16 working hours per week is produced by reference to the claimant's working hours within their appropriate 'cycle of work' (*Banks* v. *Chief Adjudication Officer* [2001] 4 All ER 62, HL). In practice this is a major factor that prevents a lot of people in part-time work accessing means-tested benefits. However, if the employed same-sex partner works consistently above these thresholds a joint claim for WTC is possible (see **10.7**).

10.4.3   Means-tested benefits: aggregation of resources

A further consequence of the changes made from 5 December 2005 is that civil partners and same-sex couples are subject to the full financial effects of the cohabitation rule, i.e.:

- Capital of the partners is aggregated for the purpose of permitted capital thresholds. For example, this means that since April 2006 if the combined capital of the couple exceeds £16,000, a claim cannot be made for IS, JSA

(IB), HB, or CTB. If capital of this amount is acquired then eligibility will cease for any award of these benefits unless it can be 'disregarded', or the amount falls below that threshold.

- Income of the cohabitants is aggregated: this includes any 'tariff income'. Following changes that came into effect in April 2006, £1 of notional income is attributed to claimants for every slice of £250 above £6,000 and below £16,000 capital (or part thereof), for the purpose of assessing 'income' when claiming IS, JSA (IB), HB and CTB.

This is the result of SSCBA 1992, s.136, which stipulates that if a claimant of an income-related benefit is a member of a family, then subject to exceptions and 'disregards' the income and capital of any member of that family is to be treated as the income and capital of that claimant. Regulation 23 of the Income Support (General) Regulations 1987, SI 1987/1967, contains the aggregation requirement whereby the income and capital of a 'partner' is to be treated as the claimant's, at least while the partner is a member of the same household as the claimant (in the circumstances described in reg.16).

There are a number of other consequences which can impact negatively on couples when they claim means-tested benefits. In the case of HB and CTB, for example, the resources of parties who are in a same-sex 'couple' relation-ship are aggregated and treated as available to them both. Council tax liability became a shared responsibility for civil partners and same-sex couples on 5 December 2005 – and CTB claims and awards must now be dealt with jointly. The effect of this is that enforcement action may be taken against both partners, debts can be pursued against survivors after one of the couple has died, and so forth. Up-dating information about HB and CTB as it affects same-sex couples is available in a DWP update circular (see **www.dwp.gov.uk/ hbctb**).

10.4.4 Income Support Mortgage Interest Assistance (ISMI)

Conditions which regulate access to Income Support Mortgage Interest Assistance (ISMI) – as it is paid to IS and JSA (IB) claimants – apply to civil partners and same-sex partners living together. Consequently an IS or JSA (IB) claimant receiving ISMI support since 5 December 2005 is generally ineligible for IS or JSA if the same-sex partner is working, has too much capital, etc. Any assistance being paid through the ISMI scheme for mort-gage interest payments (under the Income Support (General) Regulations, Sched.3) will also end.

On a more positive note, civil partners or former same-sex cohabitants receiving IS or JSA (IB) coming into the scheme since 5 December 2005 onwards may be assisted in various ways, for example:

1. If the partner is aged over 60, mortgage interest payments can be paid from the start of the claim (Income Support (General) Regulations 1987, SI 1987/1967, Sched.3, para.9).
2. Even if the claimant's mortgage was taken out after 1 October 1995 (so that interest payments are 'new' housing costs under the Income Support (General) Regulations 1987, Sched.3, para.8), the claimant might be assisted by exceptions to the normal 'waiting period' of 39 weeks before assistance can be received. An example is where the claimant has been 'abandoned' by a same-sex partner, leaving the claimant in the same household while responsible for a child or young person under the age of 16. Specifically, the waiting period is then reduced to:

    –   no support in the eight weeks from the date of claim;
    –   50 per cent of assessed costs for the next 18 weeks; and
    –   100 per cent after a total waiting period of 26 weeks.

ISMI costs can also be paid on this preferential basis in other cases, for example:

1. After 'constructive abandonment', i.e. if the claimant has had to leave the household as a result of the partner's unreasonable conduct (*Secretary of State for Work and Pensions* v. *W* [2005] EWCA Civ 570).
2. After the other civil partner or cohabitant has gone into prison on remand.
3. Where the claimant could not obtain a mortgage protection policy (under which mortgage costs are payable) because the claimant is HIV positive (Commissioner's Case CJSA/679/2004).

10.4.5   Means-tested benefits: the financial impact

Clients may require advice on the benefits and tax credits implications of starting (or continuing) to cohabit with a same-sex partner, or registering as a civil partner under the CPA 2004. This will usually require a referral for specialist advice. The following worked example illustrates how benefits could be affected. It underlines how 'living together' with a same-sex partner will in many cases mean claimants have become financially worse off since 5 December 2005.

Conversely, a person who ceases living together with a same-sex partner is usually financially better off if they revert to the status, in law, of a single claimant.

Example 10.1

Two women, Kalvinder and Jane live together as a couple in Jane's house, which is mortgaged. Jane's average weekly mortgage payment is £40. Council tax is £10 per week. Kalvinder is working and earns £28,000 a year. Jane is not working and receives Disability Living Allowance (DLA) Care Component at the lowest rate (£16.05). Kalvinder has savings of £10,000. Jane has capital of £2,000.

Before 5 December 2005 Jane could claim Income Support (IS). She was treated as a single person for the purpose of her claim for IS and CTB. In assessing Jane's IS:

- Kalvinder's earnings and income were disregarded, as they were not a 'couple';
- their capital was not aggregated, as they were not a 'couple';
- Jane's capital was below the £8,000 capital limit for IS (as it was at that time);
- Kalvinder's employment did not prevent Jane claiming IS;
- Jane had nil 'income', and so there was nothing to deduct from her 'applicable amount' when assessing her IS.

At 2005/06 rates, IS of £120.15 was payable. Jane's applicable amount was:

Personal Allowance	£56.20
Disability Premium	£23.95
ISMI Assistance	£40.00

The Income Support Mortgage Interest Scheme (ISMI) assists claimants like Jane by enabling them to include in their 'applicable amount' an amount representing the average weekly amount of interest paid on their mortgage. In this example, £40 was the product of dividing the outstanding mortgage by 52, and multiplying it by the appropriate standard interest rate for ISMI. This part of the IS is normally paid directly to the claimant's lender if it is in the 'mortgage direct' scheme).

Jane's income was nil because she had no earnings or other income, and no benefits which count as income (DLA is disregarded). So she had no weekly income to deduct from her weekly applicable amount. As an IS recipient she also received full CTB to meet the council tax liability (assessed and paid separately by the local authority).

Post-5 December 2005 and civil partnership

From 5 December 2005 the position changed significantly. Jane and Kalvinder were, in law, 'living together', and were therefore a 'couple' within the new SSCBA 1992, s.137(1)(d). The position would have been the same if they had registered as civil partners. This is how the benefits were affected:

- Jane became ineligible for IS as Kalvinder, her cohabitant, was in 'remunerative work', working above the threshold of weekly working hours permitted for the partner of an IS claimant.
- Jane ceased to be eligible for full CTB ('maximum CTB') automatically on the back of her IS. As a fully means-tested benefit eligibility after 5 December 2005 depended on a means-test, and required Kalvinder's earnings to be taken into account. This meant Jane could not get CTB because Kalvinder's income was too high.
- They could not claim IS or JSA (IB) as a couple: Kalvinder was in remunerative work above the 24-hour limit for a partner; and in any case their combined income was too high.
- Eligibility for WTC is possible, but will depend on the precise level of Kalvinder's earnings, and a claim would not be possible if those earnings are too high (although that position could change, for example if her hours reduced and her earnings fell).

10.4.6   Cessation of 'living together'

It has already been noted (**10.4.3** above) that the income and capital resources of civil partners are aggregated. This continues during any temporary periods during which one of the partners is away from the household. While they are treated, in law, as occupying the same household, the aggregation rule (and other barriers to accessing benefits) will apply. This includes the bar that operates if one of them is in 'remunerative work'. Aggregation and the bars to claiming benefits will continue while unregistered partners go on 'living together'. However, existing legislation that provides for cessation of occupation of the same household or the ending of 'living together', now extends to same-sex couples. Accordingly, there is scope for same-sex 'couple' status to be brought to an end using that legislation. This can be achieved in a number of ways. In particular, decision-makers should not treat people as a 'couple' if they have been:

- civil partners, but then make changes in their living arrangements which mean that they should no longer be treated as 'members of the same household' within the purposes of the definition in SSCBA 1992, s.137(1)(c);
- unregistered same-sex partners who have become a 'couple' for the purpose of the definition in SSCBA 1992, s.137(1)(d) as they have the necessary characteristics of 'living together', in law, but they have ceased to 'live together'.

For guidance on how DWP decision-makers apply the rules when 'same household' and 'living together' arrangements come to an end, or change, reference may be made to the DWP's *Decision Maker's Guide* (*DMG*), Vol.3, ch.11 (available on the DWP's website, **www.dwp.gov.uk**). Among other things, para.11071 states that 'living together as civil partners' (LTACP) status ends when there is a 'permanent separation' of the couple; and that decision-makers should accept evidence that one of the couple has left permanently 'unless there are reasons for doubt'.

'Exiting' options

It is important, of course, to be aware of options that facilitate coming out of arrangements that constitute an occupation of the 'same household' or 'living together'. There can be good financial and other reasons why a party to a same-sex couple relationship may need to come out of 'couple' status – and do so as quickly as possible. In particular, a partner will want to reassert some financial independence of the other party, assisted by the state benefit and tax credits systems; and do so by establishing a right to get such support as an individual. For a civil partner, that necessitates demonstrating that he or she is no longer sharing the same household – at least pending a formal separation, or dissolution of the civil partnership. For an unregistered cohabitant, this could be achieved by simply leaving a shared household, and ending aspects of a shared lifestyle that have had the characteristics of 'living together'. Those exiting the 'couple' relationship would then no longer be subject to requirements to make joint claims or other legal bars on claiming as an individual. It may be necessary to show that the actions taken indicate the change is 'permanent'. Existing legal rules which apply to unmarried couples can assist this 'exiting' process. For example they will help partners who have already been living away from the household on a temporary basis, but then put it beyond doubt that they will not be returning to that household. A key provision here is the Income Support (General) Regulations 1987, reg.16(2). This identifies a period of absence which is expected to be longer than 52 weeks. If it is reasonably expected that absence will last for more than that period, this will sustain a conclusion that 'living together' has ended. Claimants would then be able to make claims for benefits as individuals. For a civil partner, the clearest way to ensure that 'couple' status, in law, has ended for benefits and tax credits purposes is to obtain a separation or a dissolution order. Until that can be done, living apart in a new household or, if a new relationship has commenced, in the household of the new partner would normally be necessary.

Example 10.2

Jane and Kalvinder (from **example 10.1**) have become civil partners. Their relationship has now deteriorated. Jane wishes to end the relationship, start a part-time job, and claim IS to assist her (but with the possibility, in the longer term, of increasing her hours above 16 a week, assisted by a switch to tax credits). To achieve this she could obtain a dissolution or a separation order. Until then she should simply leave the household, making it clear that shared occupation of the household has now permanently ceased, and indicating that there is no intention to resume the shared occupation.

Assuming Jane is treated as no longer in a 'couple' relationship with Kalvinder, if her average weekly working hours are kept below 16 she could again claim:

- IS, including Income Support Mortgage Interest Assistance, as part of her 'applicable amount';
- CTB (for which she would, again, be eligible in full).

This is also facilitated by the fact that Jane's claim is no longer barred:

- as a result of living together with a person in remunerative work; or
- through capital being aggregated (so the IS capital limit is not exceeded).

If she works above the 16 hours per week threshold she could claim tax credits.

Separate households in the same property?

In some cases agencies like the DWP will be prepared to accept that two people are no longer a 'couple' even if the former partners continue to occupy the same property if there is evidence that supports the creation of a new, secondary household within that property, or in other exceptional circumstances: for example, when a cohabitee has been asked to leave but refuses to do so (see **10.9.3** below). However, in the case of HM Revenue and Customs (HMRC), who administer tax credits (see **10.7**), decision-makers are generally more reluctant to accept that shared occupation of a household has ended unless they are satisfied that there is clear evidence to support this. Indeed, the legislation requires that the partners must not only be 'separated', but separated in circumstances in which they are 'likely to remain separated permanently', as indicated in *DMG* or, for tax credits purposes, in the Tax Credits Act 2002 (TCA 2002), s.3(3) and (5A). This can sometimes be problematic, for example when after separation a claimant tries to make a new claim as an individual, and decision-makers do not accept that parties have separated. In Commissioner's Case CTC 3864/2004 (17 February 2005) it was noted that the legislation provides no guidance as to when a couple is to be treated as living together, and unlike for benefits where the issue is one of mixed facts and law, the test is 'essentially a question of fact looking at the totality of the evidence'. On that basis the Commissioner allowed an appeal against a decision that the claimant's husband (from whom she had separated, but who had been staying in the same household temporarily) could only be made jointly. For a more detailed account of means-testing procedures and processes benefits, and passported benefits, assistance with housing costs, etc., available to couples see specialist benefits texts such as CPAG *Welfare Benefits and Tax Credits Handbook*, Part 2; or Keith Puttick *Welfare Benefits Law and Practice*, 9th Edn (EMIS, 2006), ch.9 (see also **10.9**).

10.4.7   Jobseeker's Allowance (Sched.24, paras.118–125)

Most of the changes already described in relation to IS and income-related benefits also apply to civil partners and unregistered same-sex cohabitants claiming JSA (IB) claimed and paid under the Jobseeker's Act 1995 and the Jobseeker's Allowance Regulations 1996, SI 1996/207 to jobseekers required to:

- be 'available for employment';
- be 'actively seeking employment';
- enter in to a 'jobseeker's agreement'; and
- comply with jobseeking directions.

The effects of 'living together' are similar to the position discussed above. For example, the circumstances in which claimants are to be treated as being in the same household as a partner (or child for which they or partners are responsible), and are therefore subject to aggregation of resources (which are in the Jobseeker's Allowance Regulations, reg.78) are similar to the Income Support (General) Regulations 1987, reg.16. With the introduction of civil partnership, changes were made, including the following.

1. Joint claims for couples: if the claimant or partner was born after 28 October 1957, is 18 and over, and neither of them is responsible for children, they will usually be subject to joint-claim procedures. Sched.1, para.9C(1) to the Jobseeker's Act 1995 authorises regulations under which civil partners or same-sex cohabitants who were not previously treated as a 'joint-claim couple' are to be treated as such. Both partners will, in most cases, be subject to requirements on jobseeking, availability for work, compliance with job-seeking directions, etc.
2. Jobseeker's Allowance and maintenance: the powers of a court in the Jobseeker's Act 1995, s.23 to make a recovery order to enforce the 'liability to maintain' when JSA is awarded extends to civil partners who are liable to pay maintenance.

10.5 NON-MEANS-TESTED BENEFITS

10.5.1 Incapacity Benefit (paras.14 and 15 of Sched.24)

Sections 30A–30E of SSCBA 1992 set out the NIC and other conditions for receiving Incapacity Benefit (IB). In most cases, IB is contributory, and paid to a claimant who:

*   is 'incapable of work' under the medical tests for incapacity (unless exempt); and
*   has paid sufficient NICs (unless the incapacity was caused by an industrial accident or disease, in which case it is non-contributory).

A key part of the scheme only used to assist claims by former spouses, i.e. widows and widowers (who can use the NIC record of a deceased or divorced spouse). The changes mean that these important rights now extend to civil partners (SSCBA 1992, ss.30A and 30B).

Claimants are also assisted by a 'disregard' of increases paid with state retirement pension.

10.5.2 Bereavement benefits (Sched.24, paras.16–22)

Until recently, only widows could claim bereavement benefits. This was extended to widowers after the landmark test case of *Willis* v. *United Kingdom* [2002] FLR 582, ECHR. The CPA 2004 extends the scheme to civil partners, so that the benefits are accessible if:

- NIC conditions have been met, or the deceased died as a result of an industrial accident, or from a prescribed industrial disease (details are in SSCBA 1992, Sched.3, in particular paras.4 and 5);
- the other qualifying conditions for the particular bereavement benefit have been met.

The benefits are as follows:

1. Bereavement Payment: £2,000, paid as a lump sum following the bereavement.
2. Bereavement Allowance: a weekly amount, paid for a maximum of 52 weeks (SSCBA 1992, s.39B) at the same rate as a full Category A pension to claimants after their spouses or civil partners have died, and who:

   - are over the age of 45;
   - are under pensionable age;
   - do not have a dependent child or children.

   If eligible, the claimant can thereafter claim IS under the IS 'Bereavement Category'.
3. Widowed Parent's Allowance (WPA): a weekly amount, paid to a widow, widower, or surviving civil partner responsible for a qualifying child. It is paid at the same rate as full Category A state retirement pension, with additions for the child or children. Conditions for receipt of WPA by a civil partner are complex (SSCBA 1992, s.39A). Apart from the need to be 'responsible' for a qualifying child, the key requirements for WPA are that the claimant:

   - has a civil partner who dies;
   - is under pensionable age at the time of that death; and
   - has not married or entered into a new civil partnership with someone else.

As well as satisfying the NIC conditions for the benefit (in SSCBA 1992, Sched.3, Part 1, para.5) the surviving spouse or civil partner must be entitled to Child Benefit in respect of a child or qualifying young person. Case law highlights the difficulties in satisfying WPA conditions, including requirements linked to residence with the deceased. This may prove to be a contentious issue in practice: for example in the case of a claim by a surviving civil partner who, at the time of the civil partner's death, is pregnant following artificial insemination. Specifically, she can make a claim if she is pregnant as the result of being:

- artificially inseminated before that time with the semen of some person; or
- as a result of the placing in her before that time of an embryo, of an egg in the process of fertilisation, or of sperm and eggs.

However, she must normally have been living with the deceased civil partner immediately before the time of death. The other conditions in s.39A(3) relating to the child or qualifying young person must also be satisfied.

The changes extending these benefits to civil partners are accompanied by similar restrictions to those applicable to surviving spouses. In particular:

- civil partners will not be eligible, or will cease to be eligible, if they marry or enter into a new civil partnership;
- entitlement is suspended if the claimant lives with another person as husband and wife, or as if they are civil partners.

In the case of Bereavement Payment, the benefit is not payable if the surviving civil partner was cohabiting with someone else (of either sex) at the time of the deceased's death.

10.5.3   State retirement pension benefits (Sched.24, paras.23–51)

In some cases a claimant's bereavement benefits will act as a passport into the state pension benefits rights (including Category B benefits) described in **Chapter 9** (see **9.2**). Civil partners are able to use their former partner's NICs. This facility will be available:

- after annulment or dissolution of a civil partnership as a 'top-up' to improve their own NIC record, and thereby facilitate access to contributory benefits;
- after the partner has died (the position in this respect is aligned to that of widowers).

In addition to the changes made by CPA 2004, Sched.24, reg.2 of the Social Security (Civil Partnership) (Consequential Amendments) Regulations 2005, SI 2005/2878 amends the Social Security (Widow's Benefit and Retirement Pensions) Regulations 1979, SI 1979/642, to clarify when a former civil partner can use the NICs of the other party to the civil partnership to increase their Category A retirement pension. Regulation 2 also modifies the provisions relating to the 'days of deferral' which are to be treated as days on which increments can be earned as the scheme applies to civil partners.

Passported benefits

Despite the improvements made by the CPA 2004, the position of civil partners, and widowers who are eligible for support since 9 April 2001, is still not as favourable as that of many other claimants, and in particular widows receiving widows' benefits under the pre-9 April 2001 regime. For example, they are not eligible for passported benefits such as the State Earnings-

Related Pension Scheme (SERPS) pension; and cannot access Incapacity Benefit based on their deceased spouses' NICs.

10.5.4 The need for a 'claim'

Like spouses, civil partners must formally claim bereavement benefits or any linked state pension rights, including any benefit assisted by a former partner's NIC record, such as a pension paid at a more advantageous rate (a so-called benefit 'switch'). They should do this promptly given the tough restrictions on backdating (*Secretary of State for Work and Pensions* v. *Nelligan* [2003] 1 WLR 894).

10.6 PENSION CREDITS (SCHED.24, PARAS.140–143)

If same-sex partners are a 'couple' within the new definition in s.17(1) of the State Pension Credit Act 2002 (which is similar to that in the SSCBA 1992), Pension Credit must be claimed, assessed and paid on that basis. Otherwise, those living on their own claim as an individual. The age of the partner is immaterial for the benefit. The benefit assists pensioners with no state or occupational pension income, or if income from these (or other sources) is below prescribed thresholds. There are two main benefits, Guarantee Credit and Savings Credit. Guarantee Credit assures claimants of a minimum guaranteed income each week. Savings Credit provides modest supplements to income from retirement pensions and savings. The key benefit (under the State Pension Credit Act 2002, s.2) is the Guarantee Credit. For this purpose the claimant's 'appropriate minimum guarantee' consists of a standard minimum guarantee. There is also scope for additional amounts for:

- mortgage interest costs (similar to ISMI, see **10.4.4**);
- carers; and
- those with a severe disability (or who have a partner with a severe disability) subject to conditions being met.

For a Guarantee Credit claimants must be over the age of 60 (this age will rise progressively to 65 between 2010 and 2020 under the Pensions Act 1995). For Savings Credit, claimants must be over 65. A claimant with a same-sex partner must also claim for the partner. For a single claimant, the benefit brings the claimant's income up to a prescribed level (£114.06 at 2006/07 rates). For a 'couple' there is a couple rate (£174.05 in 2006/07). In the case of a polygamous marriage, further support is available for additional spouses, but of course by definition a civil partnership, even if registered overseas, can only ever involve two people (see also **1.3**).

The new definition of 'couple' means eligibility, and the award itself is assessed as if the parties are a couple. In particular, capital and income is aggregated under the aggregation requirement in the State Pension Credit Act 2002, s.5 – at least while the claimant lives in the same household as the civil partner. Guarantee Credit acts as a passport to other benefits, including maximum HB and CTB.

10.7   TAX CREDITS

10.7.1   Working Tax Credit and Child Tax Credit (Sched.24, paras.144–146)

Working Tax Credit (WTC) and Child Tax Credit (CTC) are major income-related benefits claimed by a sizeable proportion of the working population; and WTC, especially if paid in combination with CTC, can in some cases deliver at least twice as much income than the claimant receives in wages or salary. Since 5 December 2005 civil partners and same-sex cohabitants can only claim and receive WTC or CTC jointly unless HMRC determines they are not a 'couple': or that, having been a couple, they have separated, and are likely to remain separated permanently (TCA 2002, s.3(3), (5A)(a)). Since 5 December 2005 the definition of a 'couple' in TCA 2002, s.3(5A) includes:

(c) two people of the same sex who are civil partners of each other and are neither –

  (i)   separated under a court order, nor
  (ii) separated in circumstances in which the separation is likely to be permanent, or

(d) two people of the same sex who are not civil partners of each other but are living together as if they were civil partners.

Guidance on the operation of this part of the scheme is in the HMRC's Tax Credits Technical Manual (see **www.hmrc.gov.uk**). Applying this requirement is likely to be problematic in some cases (see **10.4.6**). As with IS and JSA (IB), the test for determining if unregistered same-sex partners are 'living together as if they were civil partners' is linked to the current test for deciding if an opposite-sex couple are living together as husband and wife (TCA 2002, s.48(2)).

10.7.2   Same-sex partners: claims, awards and notification

In general terms, the rights and responsibilities of tax credit claimants who are civil partners or same-sex, unregistered partners are aligned with those of married and opposite-sex unmarried couples, respectively. This is facilitated by the Civil Partnership Act 2004 (Tax Credits, etc.) (Consequential Amendments) Order 2005, SI 2005/2919, Part 2, which introduces definitions of 'civil partner', 'couple', etc., into the secondary legislation dealing with tax credits claims, assessment procedures and awards. Regulations dealing with tax credit claims may be made under TCA 2002, s.4 for civil partners and same-sex cohabitants to align their position with that of married couples and unmarried opposite-sex couples. A number of further points are worth noting:

- One partner can be treated as acting on behalf of the other partner when making a joint claim, e.g. following an end-of-year 'renewal' notice to renew a tax credit award (Tax Credits (Claims and Notifications) Regulations 2002, SI 2002/2014).
- Awards are to be made to the claimant or person nominated by a jointly claiming couple as the recipient except when regulations provide otherwise (TCA 2002, s.24). Otherwise, HMRC can determine to whom payments should be made in the case of civil partners' and same-sex couples' claims (Tax Credits (Payments by the Board) Regulations 2002, SI 2002/2173).
- Penalties for not providing information including information to update HMRC on changes of circumstances, renewal, etc. can be imposed on the civil partner or same-sex cohabitant (TCA 2002, s.32).

The Tax Credits Notification of Changes of Circumstances (Civil Partnership) (Transitional Provisions) Order 2005, SI 2005/828, provides that the coming into force of the CPA 2004 was a 'change of circumstances'. So claimants and their partners have been under a duty since 5 December 2005 to inform HMRC that they are living in a same-sex relationship. This is potentially problematic in terms of rights under the European Convention on Human Rights. Whereas people are generally deemed to know the law, from 5 December 2005 there was no actual 'change in the circumstances' for tax credit claimants who at that point were already in a same-sex relationship that had the characteristics of a 'couple' – but who might not have been aware of the change in law. Depending on how HMRC implements the law and 'guidance' there is the potential for 'overpayments' and claimants could be liable to pay back large amounts of overpaid tax credits and face other sanctions. However, such changes must be managed in a way that avoids 'interference' with what can now be characterised in appropriate cases as 'possessions' (see *Stec and Others* v. *United Kingdom*, (2005) 41 EHRR SE18). For further information about WTC and CTC, illustrating how the system works, for example when parties are treated as cohabitants (or cease to be cohabitants), or when income rises or falls during award periods, see the worked examples in Keith Puttick *Welfare Benefits Law and Practice*, 9th Edn (EMIS, 2006), ch.9).

10.8   CHILDREN AND CHILD SUPPORT

10.8.1   Child Benefit (Sched.24, paras.47–48)

Child Benefit is a weekly benefit paid under SSCBA 1992, ss. 141–147 and the Child Benefit (General) Regulations 2003, SI 2003/493, and it is payable to a person who is responsible for a child or qualifying young person. The changes have aligned the position of civil partners and unregistered couples with that of married and unmarried couples. In particular, regulations can be made so that financial contributions made or expenditure incurred by one civil partner in supporting a child can be treated as made (or incurred) by the other civil partner while they are living together. Under s.143(1)(a) a person is treated as 'responsible' for a child in any week if:

(a)   that person has the child or young person living with him or her in that week; or
(b)   that person is contributing to the cost of providing for the child at a weekly rate which is not less than the weekly rate of Child Benefit.

There can be competing claims for the benefit whether or not the partners are separated, but it is usually in the post-separation context that disputes can be particularly problematic (as is the case in Child Tax Credit cases when it is not clear which former partner has responsibility, or it is necessary to determine who has the 'main' responsibility). A former partner qualifying for Child Benefit under head (a) is in a stronger position than a partner or other person relying on (b), even if that partner relying on (a) is not the parent (which under SSCBA 1992, s.147(3) includes a step-parent or adoptive parent).

Despite what appears to be a detailed and comprehensive scheme, catering for a variety of situations, there is plenty of scope for dispute – particularly if a child resides in two households following separation, and both former partners appear to be equally 'responsible'. The benefit can normally only be paid to one claimant (s.144(3); and *R* v. *Swale BC, ex parte Marchant* [2000] 1 FLR 246, CA). The issue of contribution to the maintenance of the child or young person can be important in such cases, although other criteria are important, too, including the greater financial needs of a parent at particular times such as school holidays. In *R (Chester)* v. *Secretary of State for Work and Pensions* (2001) *Welfare Benefits* Vol.9, Issue 1, p. 2, the 'right to family life' in Art.8 of the European Convention on Human Rights assisted a parent who had increased financial needs at particular times like holidays to over-turn a decision that had awarded the benefit to the other parent. This was in spite of the fact that the other parent provided most of the overall 'care time' and the child generally spent more time in the other parent's household.

If one partner in a couple has been receiving Child Benefit, the partners can jointly elect for the other to receive it instead. Otherwise, it is a matter for the Secretary of State, in his discretion, to determine. Decision-makers are also assisted by the other rules on 'priority' in SSCBA 1992, s.144(3) and Sched.10. The discretion of HMRC when resolving disputes is wide, as Richards J considered in *R (on the application of Ford)* v. *Revenue & Customs Commissioners* [2005] EWHC 1109. In that case, where there were two children, he held that there was nothing to prevent HMRC from making one award of Child Benefit to one parent and the other to the other parent if the circumstances merited this. It would seem that this can be done even if one of the parents is living on means-tested state benefits and the other is working (and is less 'in need' of the benefit). This appears to be inconsistent with approaches adopted in other cases, like *Chester* (above) where financial need was a relevant factor that engaged the right to family life of the parent on benefits under Art.8 of the European Convention on Human Rights. The courts have also, at the same time, been unwilling to entertain a claim that the Child Benefit scheme is 'discriminatory' in the way it operates. For example, see *R (on the application of Barber)* v. *Secretary of State for Work and Pensions* [2002] 2 FLR 1181.

Child Benefit can be an important passport to other social security benefits and community care services, as some of those benefits and services can be valuable disputes can be hard-fought. This is one of the factors that the courts can take into account in trying to protect the position of a 'substantial minority carer' who is seeking to access child-related financial support such as the additions paid with Jobseeker's Allowance, as held by the Court of Appeal in *Hockenjos* v. *Secretary of State for Social Security* [2005] 1 FLR 1009.

10.8.2 Child support (Sched.24, paras.1–6 and 126–127)

The Act made a number of important changes to the child support scheme in the Child Support Acts 1991 and 1995, the Child Support, Pensions and Social Security Act 2000, and regulations (see Keith Puttick *Child Support Law: Parents, the CSA and the Courts* (EMIS, 2003)). Changes have also been made to secondary legislation dealing with the assessment and enforcement of child support by the Civil Partnership (Pensions, Social Security and Child Support) (Consequential, etc. Provisions) Order 2005, SI 2005/2877, Sched.4. These ensure that civil partners and unregistered same-sex partners (whether they are the parent with care or the non-resident parent) are treated in the same way as spouses and unmarried opposite-sex partners. A 'parent' in this context means any person who is in law the mother or father of a child, and this includes an adoptive parent but excludes a step-parent (Child Support Act 1991, s.54 and Commissioner's Case CCS/3128/95).

Such equalisation of treatment is reflected, for example, in changes to the provisions on aggregation of income of the non-resident parent and their civil partner or same-sex cohabitant, when assessing disposable income for the purpose of that parent's 'protected income'. The requirement that aggregation is only required when the cohabitant is living together with an adult of the opposite sex is replaced (Sched.24, para.4). Aggregation is also required when the cohabitant is of the same sex (new Sched.1, para.6(5)(b) to the Child Support Act 1991, as originally enacted). Other key changes are assisted by re-defining 'couple' in the Child Support Act 1991, Sched.1, using the same new definition as in social security and tax credits legislation (see **10.3**).

As with social security, the Child Support Agency (CSA) system sometimes revealed significant discrimination against parties to same-sex couple relationships. For example, it treated non-resident parents living in a same-sex relationship less favourably when their net weekly income was being assessed for the purposes of an assessment or calculation, notably in not permitting reductions for other children living in the same household. This was highlighted in the case of *M* v. *Secretary of State for Work and Pensions*; *Langley* v. *Bradford Metropolitan District Council* [2005] 1 FLR 498, CA which showed that a non-resident parent in a same-sex relationship who was assessed for child support was worse off under the scheme than one in an opposite-sex relationship. In M's case she was living in a same-sex relationship with another woman (also a non-resident parent). M's children lived with her for two and a half days a week, and the rest of the week with their father. Her maintenance liability had been assessed at about £47 per week. Had she been assessed as a member of an opposite-sex couple in a comparable position her liability would have been approximately £14 a week.

To avoid the effects of such discrimination the Commissioner, on appeal, decided that in assessing M's child support liability the concept of 'family' and 'partner' in the Child Support (Maintenance Assessments and Special Cases) Regulations 1992, SI 1992/1815, reg.1(2) had to be interpreted by reference to the requirements of the Human Rights Act 1998, and in particular the right to family life in Art.8 and the non-discrimination provision in Art.14 of the European Convention on Human Rights. Without that interpretation, he said, the 1992 regulations would give a non-resident parent who was a member of an opposite-sex couple an advantage in the assessment of liability to pay child support that was not available to a party to a same-sex couple. This approach was assisted by the House of Lords decision in *Ghaidan* v. *Godin-Mendoza* [2004] 2 FLR 600. The argument that M, a party to a same-sex couple, could not be assisted by Art.8 because same-sex relationships did not come within the Convention concept of 'family life' failed in the Court of Appeal. An alternative argument raised by the Secretary of State also failed. This was that, even if Art.8 was engaged, there was no sufficient analogy between same-sex and opposite-sex couples for the purposes of the child support scheme to attract any Convention rights, including any protection under Art.14 in relation to 'discrimination', or that even if such rights did apply they could be 'justified'. Despite what appeared to most commentators as clear institutionalised discrimination against lesbian and gay parents in the way the child support system was being run, the DWP maintained that the Commissioner and court had misdirected themselves. The DWP succeeded when the Lords, in *Secretary of State for Work and Pensions* v. *M* [2006] UKHL 11 (Baroness Hale dissenting) not only allowed the Government's appeal, but also held that this part of the child support scheme did not even fall within the ambit of Art.8 requirements on 'respect for family life'. Lord Bingham, agreeing with the dissenting judge in the Court of Appeal (Kennedy LJ), observed:

> I do not think the enhanced contribution required of Ms M. impairs in any material way her family life with her children and former husband, or her family life with her children and her current partner, or her private life. No doubt Ms M. has less money to spend than if she were required to contribute less (or would do so, but for the discretionary adjustment to which my noble and learned friend refers in para. 46 of his opinion). But this does not impair the love, trust, confidence, mutual dependence and unconstrained social intercourse which are the essence of family life, nor does it invade the sphere of personal and sexual autonomy which are the essence of private life.

Nor did he think Art.1 of the First Protocol to the Convention (interference in possessions) was engaged:

> I regard the application of a rule governing a non-resident parent's liability to contribute to the costs incurred by the parent with care, even if it results in the non-resident parent paying more than she would under a different rule, as altogether remote from the sort of abuse at which [Art.1 of the First Protocol] is directed.

Given that as from 5 December 2005 the CPA 2004 remedied the inconsistency of treatment causing the litigation, the decision has no prospective effect. However, it affected the scope for retrospective adjustments to assessments, and claims for compensation by non-resident parents in same-sex relationships, who in some cases will have paid significantly more maintenance than other parents in opposite-sex relationships. Where discernible, the majority of the House seems to have based their reasoning, in part, on the facts that the alleged discrimination took place in 2001/02 and that at that time the same-sex relationship was not 'family life' or that the treatment was not a violation of that family life. However, this leaves it open that any such treatment now, after the introduction of civil partnership, would be a breach of the Human Rights Act 1998. Lord Mance said so explicitly at para.152 of his speech:

> I have little doubt that the Strasbourg Court would see the position now as having changed very considerably, and that, if such an issue were to come before it in

respect of the position in 2006, Mrs M's same-sex relationship could very well be regarded, in both Strasbourg and the United Kingdom, as involving family life for the purposes of article 8.

Even when Convention Articles *are* engaged in cases where it can be shown that there has been discrimination and less favourable treatment (which *M* shows is not always easy to do), there are other reasons why the courts have difficulties in deploying Convention Articles in such cases. In particular, the statutory defences in the Human Rights Act 1998, s.6(2) can, and do, assist agencies like the DWP. In effect, these can immunise discriminatory legislation, and operating procedures, from the intervention of the courts. This has been illustrated, for example, in *R (Hooper and Others)* v. *Secretary of State for Work and Pensions* [2005] 1 WLR 1681, HL. In that case, despite the apparent application of the Human Rights Act 1998, s.6(1) to the case (which was concerned with discrimination in pensions), s.6(2) then protected the DWP's position on the basis that primary legislation prevented the agency acting in any other way than it did.

10.8.3 Changes to the CSA system

There are several further specific changes.

- There is a new definition of a 'couple' in the Child Support Act 1991, Sched.1, para.10C(5) similar to that for social security.
- Income provisions in the maintenance assessments scheme in the Child Support Act 1991, Sched.1, as originally enacted in the old CSA regime, are extended to include parents living together in the same household with another person who is their civil partner or same-sex cohabitant.
- Young people will no longer receive CSA maintenance if they become civil partners (Child Support Act 1991, s.55): although they do not lose that right just by cohabiting with a same-sex partner (s.55(2)).
- The court retains jurisdiction to make financial orders under CPA 2004, Scheds.5, 6 and 7 in the same way that it retains such jurisdiction under the relevant legislation for spouses and former spouses (Child Support Act 1991, s.8(11)(ea)).

10.9 COHABITATION AND 'LIVING TOGETHER' RULES

10.9.1 Introduction

It will be readily apparent from the preceding sections that parties' entitlements, rights and liabilities, and the value of their benefits depend on whether they are, in law, a 'couple' within the new definition in the Social Security

Contributions and Benefits Act 1992, s.137(1) or the other Acts referred to above.

In the case of civil partners, 'couple' status requires that the parties are 'members of the same household'. This follows from the definition in SSCBA 1992, s.137(1)(c), which stipulates 'two people of the same sex who are civil partners of each other and are members of the same household'. Before two people of the same sex who are not civil partners can be treated as a 'couple' they must be must be 'living together' as if they were civil partners 'other than in prescribed circumstances'. The reference to 'prescribed circumstances' indicates that the Government has the power to make regulations, to issue guidance and identify specific circumstances in which there will not be couple status. At the time of writing no regulations had been made. The Tax Credits Act 2002, s.3(5A) provides a similar definition, but with the differences already noted in the discussion in **10.7.1** above.

10.9.2 Cohabitation and existing case law

The existing case law principles on 'living together' (sometimes still called co-habitation), have not been changed by the introduction of civil partnership. However, the DWP and other agencies have been reforming the procedures they adopt, updating forms and carrying out staff training. They have also updated 'guidance' in the *DMG* to reflect the changes made by the Act, and to try to ensure staff apply the rules fairly. In the course of consultations, and after seminars with key interest groups that included the Lesbian and Gay Lawyers Association, Stonewall, the Social Security Advisory Committee, the Local Government Association and Citizens Advice, the Government confirmed that the cohabitation rule would be reformed. A minister in the DWP, Baroness Hollis, said:

> We considered whether the existing test for living together as husband and wife for cohabiting unmarried opposite-sex couples was still appropriate in its language and, if so, whether it could be applied to same-sex relationships. What we came up with as a result was a need to readdress that test across the board . . . we are getting a new framework in which we can train our staff to act appropriately, sensitively, discreetly but even-handedly with opposite-sex and same-sex couples in future.
>
> (HL Grand Committee, *Hansard*, Col.GC 466, 25 May 2004)

In the meantime the main principles developed within existing case law will continue to be relevant, especially when determining if partners are sharing the same household and 'living together'. What follows is a summary of the principles and main cases that inform those concepts.

10.9.3 Members of the same household

The use of the phrase 'members of the same household' in the new definitions indicates that the test for determining whether civil partners are a 'couple' has been aligned to existing law and case law on the point, as it has been developed and applied to married couples. 'Household' is not defined in the legislation, and so the courts and tribunals use a 'normal everyday meaning' (*DMG*, para.11016). A key consideration is that the parties can be treated as sharing the 'same household' even though they have periods of temporary separation (*Santos* v. *Santos* [1972] All ER 246). Sharing the 'same household' is generally not possible if one of the parties lives in another household. However, it is not sufficient simply to have another property (for example a rented flat) if, in fact, that accommodation is seldom used (*DMG*, para.11020). A further consideration is that a person cannot be a member of more than one household at the same time, and so cannot be a member of more than one 'couple' relationship at the same time (*DMG*, para.11020 and Commissioner's Case R(SB) 8/85). Nor can a person be in a couple where the relationship is illegal (as it would be, for example, if the other person was under age) or where the parties are living in the 'prohibited degrees of relationship' for marriage or civil partnership (*DMG*, para.11032 and Sched.2 to chapter 11; but see **3.3.1**). Similarly, there cannot be 'living together' in the context of 'multiple relationships', for example where a third person lives in the same household as a couple who are civil partners. In general social security law does not recognise multiple relationships in the same way as it recognises polygamous marriages and this is reflected in the *DMG* (at para.11033).

Whether parties are living in the same household or not is generally a question of fact, based on the best up-to-date evidence available to decision-makers, tribunals and courts. The practical importance of this approach is that a civil partner can bring 'couple' status to an end by simply leaving the household. The change in status is then put beyond doubt if that person occupies a separate household with the requisite intention to do so on more than just a temporary basis. In principle, it is also possible for couple status to end with the formation of a new, separate household within the same property (if that is viable in practical terms, see **10.4.6**). Another possibility is that although the relationship has ended, one of the parties (or both parties) are unable, or unwilling, to leave the accommodation they have been in. The question of whether there can from that point still be a shared household, and 'couple' status, is a difficult one. However, guidance in the *DMG* recognises that civil partners who 'separate' but refuse to leave the home are 'not necessarily' to be treated as living in the same household (*DMG*, Vol.3, ch.11, para.11018). In practice the criteria used by decision-makers in all the welfare agencies tend to show that it is harder for married couples, and now civil partners, to show that 'couple' status has ended – at least while they continue to share the same accommodation. This is illustrated, particularly, by the way decision-makers tend to impute couple status more readily to married parties when a party returns to the household following a period when they have been living apart.

Unregistered same-sex couples

The requirement here is that 'couple' status requires that the partners are 'living together'. That test is specifically made dependent on whether the partners would be regarded as 'living together as husband and wife' if they were an opposite-sex couple (see **10.4.6**). The two main requirements that must be satisfied before two people can be treated as 'living together' are that they must:

- be members of the same household; and
- the relationship has the characteristics of a couple 'living together as husband and wife' (LTHAW).

The reasons for the shared occupation of the household must be carefully considered. What may look like LTHAW may, in fact, be something else (Commissioner's Case R(G) 1/79). Thus, if two elderly or disabled people live in the same household for companionship or because one provides care for the other and that is the main reason for them sharing the accommodation, their status will not be LTHAW nor, therefore, living together as if they were civil partners (Commissioner's Case R (SB) 35/85 and *DMG*, para.11019).

Similar considerations apply to tax credits as a result of the definition of 'couple' in TCA 2002, s.3(5A), although there is a notable difference in the wording in relation to the ending of couple status. Specifically, HMRC looks to either separation through a court order or separation in 'circumstances in which the separation is likely to be permanent' (TCA 2002, s.3(5A(c); see also **10.4.6**). This was also an issue in Commissioner's Case CTC 4025/03. In this case a woman with five children married and the husband joined the household. The relationship broke down, and he left the household, but stayed in contact and continued to pay the mortgage. A decision by HMRC that cohabitation continued was upheld on appeal. HMRC expects to be notified of such changes (Tax Credits Technical Manual, at TCTM/05001; see **www.hmrc.gov.uk/manuals/index.htm**). If HMRC then decides that the separation is 'in circumstances in which the separation is likely to be permanent' (TCA 2002, s.3(5)(b)) a new claim for tax credits may be required (which is assessed as a claim by a single claimant, and without taking into account the presence and income of the former cohabitant).

10.9.4 *Crake* and 'cohabitation'

In the leading case of *Crake* v. *Supplementary Benefits Commission* [1981] FLR 264, Woolf J described the six aspects of the cohabitation used by Adjudication Officers and tribunals as 'admirable signposts':

1. membership of the same household;
2. the stability of the relationship;
3. the financial support given by the parties to each other;
4. whether there is a sexual relationship or not (although the absence of such a relationship is not necessarily decisive either way);
5. care of children; and
6. the extent to which the parties behave as a couple publicly, for example with family and friends.

In later cases like *Re J (Income Support: Cohabitation)* [1995] 1 FLR 660, in which a Commissioner had to decide if a woman lived with a disabled claimant as his carer or as a cohabitant in a relationship akin to 'husband and wife', it was held that it was inappropriate to try to resolve the issue by reference to any specific criteria. However, matters such as whether or not the parties supported each other financially were not necessarily decisive in determining such status. *Kimber* v. *Kimber* [2000] 1 FLR 383 provides a useful analysis of the leading cases and principles, although the judge in that case observed that it would be 'foolhardy to attempt to reduce to a judicial soundbite a comprehensive list of criteria', adding that 'the authorities are replete with warnings of the dangers of doing so'. The following factors were considered important in deciding that there was cohabitation in the context of a maintenance agreement that provided for payments to continue to the wife until remarriage or cohabitation for more than three months:

- living together in the same 'household' (i.e. under the same roof, apart from illness, holidays, work and other periodical absences);
- sharing of daily tasks and duties;
- stability and permanence in the relationship (i.e. not a temporary relationship such as a temporary infatuation or 'passing relationship' such as a holiday romance);
- if a sexual relationship is ongoing;
- the financial affairs of the parties to the relationship as a potential 'couple';
- evidence of an assumption of responsibility by the alleged cohabitant for the wife's child, and the 'bond' that had formed between them;
- sufficient evidence of cohabitation in terms of what a reasonable person with 'normal perceptions' would perceive.

The necessity for a degree of 'stability and permanence' in a same-sex relationship has parallels with the tough approach that seems to be adopted in cases where a surviving partner is trying to establish a right of succession to an assured tenancy under the Housing Act 1988, s.17. In such cases it has been held that a survivor cannot assert rights comparable to those of a 'spouse' for the purposes of s.17(4), and thus resist a landlord's claim for possession, without demonstrating that the relationship is sufficiently 'permanent' (*Nutting* v. *Southern Housing Group Ltd* [2005] 1 FLR 1066). Guidance in the *DMG* urges decision-makers to consider 'all relevant factors in a relationship' and says 'the significance of each factor can only be determined in the context of all of the factors with none being decisive' (para.11045). It refers to other potential factors and indicators and says that the characteristics of husband and wife may include mutual love, faithfulness, public acknowledgment, sexual relations, shared surname, children, endurance, stability, interdependence, and devotion'. It also provides a helpful commentary on the key factors and the case law. In addition to the leading cases referred to, important principles have been developed by the Social Security Commissioners. Their decisions are binding on decision-makers. Accordingly, the *DMG*, which has been updated to coincide with entry into operation of the CPA 2004, refers to leading decisions on key points.

10.9.5   Application to same-sex relationships

It remains to be seen how the criteria referred to in cases like *Crake* (above) and *Kimber* (above), subsequent Commissioners' decisions and the updated *DMG* will impact decision-making processes affecting same-sex relationships and the issue of whether parties are 'living together'. It is not unusual for decision-makers (and tribunals) to apply the existing test incorrectly. In an area where the success rate of appellants runs at over 52 per cent (DWP *Statistical Summary*, March 2005) the chances of a successful appeal are likely to be very good. This is one of the reasons why the Government has reviewed the operation of the 'living together' regime. The reasons why it is proving so difficult to apply the rules are worth considering. First, there must be sufficient evidence to sustain a finding that the parties occupy the same household, and do so with a sufficient degree of continuity. This may be difficult to show for a range of possible reasons, not least because one of the partners may also occupy separate accommodation (Commissioner's Case R(SB) 8/85) and only spend occasional periods in the same accommodation as their partner. Second, there must be a finding, sustained by the available evidence, that the relationship has characteristics which are analogous to living together as 'husband and wife'. This was already exceedingly problematic before 5 December 2005 and in practice very difficult for decision-makers and presenting officers at tribunals to show in the application of the case law to opposite-sex relationships. In the context of same-sex relationships it is already proving problematic, even after the DWP and HMRC have updated guidance on the application of the scheme to same-sex couples.

At the heart of the problem is the need, in law, before a 'living together' determination can be made for it to be shown that there is 'stability' and a degree of 'permanence' in the relationship. This may not always be the case. The relationship may not, for example, be 'exclusive'. This is not, in itself, likely to be decisive, given that even in long-term relationships the parties may engage in other relationships without necessarily interrupting the continuity of the main relationship. However, it is obviously a factor that must be carefully addressed in deciding if the relationship is 'stable' or 'permanent'. Furthermore, the last criterion referred to in *Kimber*, i.e. that there should be sufficient evidence of cohabitation in terms of what a reasonable person with 'normal perceptions' would consider, is undoubtedly problematic – especially in the context of same-sex relationships where decision-makers, tribunals and the courts will in many cases lack the experience to make such judgments. In addition, same-sex couples may in fact expressly claim to neighbours and colleagues that they are not a couple because they want to avoid exposing themselves to harassment or abuse. This is unlikely to be the case for opposite-sex couples and so applying the case law in the same way will not do justice to the facts and circumstances of every same-sex couple.

10.9.6 Providing information about 'changes in circumstances'

When benefits claims are made, claimants are required to furnish information about their circumstances (Social Security (Claims and Payments) Regulations 1987, SI 1987/1968, reg.7(1)). At that point, if there is another adult member of the household it may be necessary for that person to explain, or at least give an indication of, the nature of their relationship with the claimant. If this is not done, and an agency later becomes aware of the presence of another adult in the household through other means (such as cross-matching data from other agencies or from a 'fraud hotline'), there is a risk that this could lead to 'an adverse inference' being drawn by decision-makers (as indicated by Commissioner Goodman in Case *75/95 (at para.11). Once an award has been made, if another adult joins the household, this fact should be reported – if necessary accompanied with a statement or supporting evidence to indicate that the claimant and other adult are not living together as a 'couple'. Undoubtedly, this is likely to be a procedure which will cause concern, especially as it could be seen as a form of imposed 'outing'. However, if there is an explanation for that person's presence then it should, arguably, be provided at that point, if only to avoid misunderstandings later. The key point is that the mere presence of another adult in the household is not in itself, in law, 'living together' (as indicated by Woolf J. in *Crake*, above). The evidence might indicate, for example, that one of them is just a lodger or at least the authorities cannot show that he is more than that (Commissioner's Case R(G) 3/71). Potential indications of cohabitation must be considered fairly and objectively by decision-makers, and in accordance with relevant cohabitation criteria, as made clear in leading Commissioners' cases, for example Commissioners' Cases R(SB) 17/81; R(SB) 35/85; and CIS/317/1994. In particular, the claimant's sexual orientation is not a criterion.

'Reporting' procedures

Claimants are advised of the specific reporting actions needed, and these can vary between different types of benefit or tax credit. In general terms, notifications by civil partners and same-sex couples since 5 December 2005 onwards should be made:

- in the 'prescribed manner';
- to a prescribed office or person; and
- promptly and normally in writing (SI 2001/3252) although there has been some relaxation since April 2004, for example permitting telephone notifications in some cases.

Needless to say, it is prudent to retain a copy of any notification of changes.

There are many kinds of 'changes' which are reportable, but in the context of same-sex relationships examples of reportable changes include:

1. Adults joining the household. In relation to tax credits, the Tax Credits Technical Manual (at TCTM/05001) makes it clear that when people 'begin living together as a couple', this must be reported. Clearly there will be situations in which the claimant may consider the change is not reportable (for example if the other adult is a tenant or carer). If there is any doubt as to the status of the relationship and whether it amounts to 'couple' status, it is prudent to seek specialist legal advice.
2. The claimant or partner acquiring new capital or income resources, including a house in which the claimant does not live as his or her main residence and which cannot otherwise be 'disregarded' (*Wilkinson* v. *Chief Adjudication Officer* [2000] 2 FCR 82, CA).
3. The claimant (or partner) entering new employment or increasing working hours above the permitted threshold; normally this is 16 hours per week for IS or JSA (IB) (24 hours for the civil partner or cohabitant).
4. Continuing to receive local authority benefits like HB or CTB after the partner who made the claim has left the household for which the award was made.

10.9.7   Same-sex relationships: recovery and criminal liability

Undoubtedly there will be situations when a person on benefits enters into a same-sex 'couple' relationship, but fails to report that change. The law, to date, has not been generous in taking oversights into account and allowing them to be a ground on which to avoid civil or criminal liability even when they are innocent. Specifically, reporting failures may lead to:

- civil recovery of overpayments; and
- criminal proceedings.

Civil recovery

If the failure to report is the cause of the overpayment, then subject to a tribunal appeal (or an administrative revision or supersession of the decision) there may be civil recovery from the claimant, even if the failure to disclose is wholly innocent (SSAA 1992, s.71(1); *Jones* v. *Chief Adjudication Officer* [1994] 1 WLR 62 at p.65B, CA).

This has been made even easier for the authorities following two leading cases in 2005. In the House of Lords in *Hinchy* v. *Secretary of State for Work and Pensions* [2005] 1 WLR 967 Lord Hoffman, in the leading speech, made it clear that it is the claimant who is best placed to know about changes in his or her circumstances. Consequently the claimant has the principal responsibility for reporting changes so that overpayments can be avoided. In *B* v. *Secretary of State for Work and Pensions* [2005] 1 WLR 3796, the Court of Appeal upheld the decision of the tribunal that there is no precondition to recovery that reporting (or 'disclosure') be shown to be 'reasonably expected'. These two leading cases are likely to prove particularly significant for those who fail to report their same-sex 'couple' status; and if anything the system has become considerably tougher on failures to report such status, or changes. In *B* the Court of Appeal held that although the claimant had learning disabilities and these prevented her from realising the significance of leaving the household to be taken into care (making her ineligible for benefits), this did not relieve her of the duty to report the change, and her liability to repay the overpaid benefit. However, given that the Secretary of State had a discretion whether or not to pursue recovery of overpayments, Stephen Sedley LJ emphasised the need for that discretion to be used reasonably. Officials had to decide:

> whether it was right to take advantage of his entitlement to recover overpaid sums which in all probability will have been spent in cases like the present, by people who did not realise that they were being overpaid.

A change made to SSAA 1992, s.71(9) by CPA 2004, Sched.24, para.58(2) means that an overpayment made to a civil partner can be recovered from the benefits paid to that person's partner, aligning the position with opposite-sex cohabitants. This also applies to recovery under SSAA 1992, s.78 of Social Fund payments.

Criminal liability

The authorities may decide to go further, and initiate criminal proceedings. In particular, SSAA 1992, s.111A(1A) makes it an offence not to make a prompt notification of a change of circumstances affecting entitlement to a benefit if that change is not excluded from the notification requirement by regulations and the claimant knows that the change would affect entitlement (although cases like *Harrison* v. *Department of Social Security* [1997] COD 220 show that a degree of dishonesty is required to maintain a successful prosecution).

10.9.8 Procedures to ascertain 'living together'

A number of procedures are used if the authorities believe a claimant is cohabiting, and wish to undertake further enquiries before making a decision. These include:

- 'gateway intervention reports' (for example JCP7 04/05, which is used to obtain information about claimants' living arrangements, headed 'Information about Where You Live and the People who Live with You');
- home visits in the course of which information can be obtained and informal interviews conducted (within the limits in the *Fraud Investigators' Guidelines*); and
- more formal face-to-face interviews under caution (IUCs), which are more closely regulated by the:

  - Fraud Investigators' Guidelines,
  - Police and Criminal Evidence Act 1984 and Codes of Practice under that Act and
  - the Human Rights Act 1998 and the right to a fair trial under Art.6 of the European Convention on Human Rights (which guarantees minimum standards of protection at pre-trial stages, including in interviews and other evidence-gathering procedures).

  The interviews are very structured, and tape-recorded. The interviewee is cautioned, and made aware that he or she can be accompanied by a legal representative (a key requirement now for Art.6 purposes).

There are a variety of forms used by agencies like the DWP when conducting enquiries and interviews. 'Living together' enquiries will generally use Form CP2 (LT) 04/05 *Living Together as Husband and Wife*. This has been rebadged as 'LTAHW/CP' and adapted by the DWP for same-sex 'living together' cases so that it is 'gender neutral'. If possible, interviewers will try to ensure the person living in the same household attends and is given the opportunity to answer questions to assist the enquiry. The enquiry will usually focus on key questions such as:

- the date when sharing of the accommodation began;
- whether (and why) the accommodation is being shared;
- the nature of the relationship;
- whether there is another address either party regards as 'home';
- the parties' financial arrangements;
- the extent of financial and other integration of the relationship; and
- whether other people (friends, relatives, etc.) see the parties as a 'couple'.

The interviewee (and 'other person', if in attendance) will generally be asked to sign a declaration at the end of the report that answers given are 'correct and complete as far as I know and believe'.

10.9.9 Post-5 December 2005: sanctions against same-sex couples?

The Government undertook to handle key changes like the extension of the 'living together' rules to same-sex couples 'sensitively' (DTI/WEU *Responses to Civil Partnership – A Framework for the Legal Recognition of Same-Sex Couples* (November 2003), para.4). So it remains to be seen how potential civil and criminal sanctions will be handled in cases when there are reporting and other failures, especially if it is clear that they are wholly innocent. It is unclear how this commitment might translate in practice, but the DWP Minister, Baroness Hollis, stated in the House of Lords that:

> We will do our best to ensure that all couples, whether of the same sex or of the opposite sex, let alone civil partners, understand the implications of how social security legislation will affect them once this Bill comes into force in a year or so. Equally, we will seek to avoid asking for repayments from someone who has inadvertently made a mistake and failed to appreciate that, although they have not entered into a civil partnership, nonetheless they are affected because they now form a same-sex couple.
>
> HL Grand Committee, 5 May 2004 at GC490

A more detailed discussion of civil recovery, action by HMRC in tax credits cases and criminal proceedings is outside the scope of this work. Reference may be made to texts such as CPAG *Welfare Benefits and Tax Credits Handbook*, Part 2; or Keith Puttick *Welfare Benefits Law and Practice*, 9th Edn (EMIS, 2006), ch.9.

10.10 SUMMARY OF MAIN POINTS

In summary, the following changes have been made by the CPA 2004.

1. Civil partners and unregistered same-sex partners are now within a new definition of 'couple' for the purpose of determining rights and respon-

sibilities in relation to take-up and payment of contributory and non-contributory benefits and tax credits, and for child support purposes.

The general principle is that 'couple' status means that they are to be treated as a single unit rather than as two separate individuals. This means that claims must normally be made jointly, and resources aggregated. These and other requirements continue while they are 'members of the same household'.

2. Civil partners are subject to the same legal responsibilities as well as rights in relation to other aspects of benefits and tax credits take-up, including the duty to disclose their status, and any 'changes in circumstances' affecting their eligibility to benefits or tax credits.

3. While they are 'living together' and therefore are within the new definition of a 'couple', unregistered same-sex partners must claim jointly and be paid any benefits or tax credits to which they are entitled as a couple rather than as individuals, at least while they continue to 'live together'. Their legal rights and responsibilities, including the duty to disclose their status, 'changes in circumstances', etc. are aligned with those of an unmarried opposite-sex couple.

4. Pending future reform of the law relating to 'living together', the DWP, HMRC, local authorities and other welfare agencies will apply the existing law in determining whether civil partners are 'members of the same household', and unregistered same-sex partners are 'living together'. The administrative procedures used by the DWP and other agencies for determining if 'couple' status exists (or has ended) have been modified and are periodically revised.

CHAPTER 11

Immigration

Barry O'Leary

11.1 INTRODUCTION

11.1.1 Overview

The Civil Partnership Act 2004 is without doubt an extremely important step forward for people who wish to come to or stay in the UK to be with their same-sex partner. For those who wish to take on the rights and responsibilities of civil partnership, the CPA 2004 and the associated secondary legislation will ensure that many of the difficulties previously encountered by same-sex bi-national couples are avoided.

This chapter does not aim to be an exhaustive discussion of immigration law as it relates to same-sex couples. Its purpose is to highlight the most important aspects of the impact of the CPA 2004 on immigration law. It deals with:

- the provisions for same-sex partners before the CPA 2004 came into force and the continuing relevance of the 'unmarried or same-sex partner rules' for same-sex bi-national couples (see **11.1.2**, **11.5** and **11.8.1**);
- applications from inside or outside the UK for those who have registered as civil partners of British citizens and people with permanent residence (see **11.2.1**);
- the situation for those who are currently outside the UK and who wish to enter into a civil partnership with British citizens and people with permanent residence (see **11.2.2**);
- the effect of the CPA 2004's recognition of overseas regimes (see **11.2.3**);
- the position for the partners of EEA nationals and those with limited leave to remain in the UK (see **11.3**);
- immigration control and the restrictions on the formation of civil partnerships (see **11.4**) – important points which must be borne in mind by advisers given the widely held perception amongst clients that the CPA 2004 will provide a very simple solution for all couples, when this is not in fact the case;
- civil partnership visit visas (see **11.6**);
- naturalisation as a British citizen (see **11.7**);

- a comparison of civil partners and unregistered same-sex partners (**11.8.1**);
- the effects of an applicant's past immigration history and the special circumstances of civil partners making applications to come to the UK from abroad (**11.8.2** and **11.8.3**).

11.1.2   The changing law

The Civil Partnership Act 2004 is the culmination of the struggle for immigration rights by same-sex bi-national couples who have frequently faced more difficulties in staying together in one of their countries than their heterosexual counterparts, who can usually marry and base an application for the right to enter or remain in either country on the marriage. The fight for immigration rights in this context was led by the Stonewall Immigration Group (SIG), now known as the UK Lesbian and Gay Immigration Group (UKLGIG). Until 1997 there was no provision at all for leave to be granted to enter or remain in the UK on the basis of a same-sex relationship. A number of brave couples, with the support of SIG, made applications to the Home Office for leave to remain. SIG lobbied the Labour party who were then in opposition and managed to obtain a promise that when the party entered government provision would be made for such bi-national couples.

Labour won the general election in May 1997 and a concession for cohabiting same-sex couples was introduced in October 1997. Although this was undoubtedly an achievement, the requirement that a couple had already lived together in a relationship akin to marriage for four years was onerous. Following further lobbying the period was reduced to two years in 1999 and in October 2000 the provisions ceased to be merely a concession and became part of the Immigration Rules. These rules (often referred to as the 'unmarried partner rules') are available to cohabiting same-sex and opposite-sex couples (now the 'unmarried or same-sex partner rules' rr.295AA–295O, see **11.5**).

Before the CPA 2004 came into force the unmarried partners rules were the only provision on which an individual could rely when making an application on the basis of a same-sex relationship (unless a claim could be sustained under Art.8 of the European Convention on Human Rights)**.** The CPA 2004 undoubtedly makes it easier for many who, while in a committed relationship, may have difficulty meeting the two-year cohabitation requirement. The unmarried or same-sex partner rules remain in place for those who cannot or choose not to register their relationship.

Few specific references to immigration matters are to be found in the CPA 2004. Instead, the Immigration Rules were amended to include civil partners, proposed civil partners and so on. These rules can be found online on the Immigration and Nationality Directorate (IND) website (**www.ind.homeoffice. gov.uk**).

Most of the discussion in this chapter will centre on the civil partners of British citizens and the civil partners of individuals with indefinite leave to remain in the UK (also known as permanent residence or settlement) who are treated equally under the Immigration Rules, although there are differences in connection with naturalisation. However, as with the immigration rules relating to spouses and unmarried partners, not only the partners of British citizens and persons with permanent residence benefit from the changes. The CPA 2004 will also assist the civil partners of EEA and Swiss nationals (see **11.3.2**) and the civil partners of individuals with certain limited leave to remain (see **11.3.1**).

11.2 PARTNERS OF BRITISH CITIZENS AND PEOPLE WITH PERMANENT RESIDENCE

11.2.1 Civil partners

The amended Immigration Rules treat civil partners in the same way as spouses (rr.277 and 278 of Part 8 of the Rules). The civil partner of a British citizen or a person with indefinite leave to remain (permanent residence) can make an application for leave (permission) to enter or remain in the UK on the basis of that civil partnership. The requirements for such an application mirror those for a spouse who applies on the basis of a marriage.

At the time of writing the amendments to the Immigration Rules seem to leave some editorial tidying up as the insertion of 'or civil partner', etc. is inconsistent. However, the experience of immigration practitioners is that these inconsistencies are not creating practical difficulties, although they must of course be put right. Thus the requirements for leave to remain in the UK (applications from within the UK) as a civil partner are as follows:

Requirements for an extension of stay as the spouse or civil partner of a person present and settled in the United Kingdom

284. The requirements for an extension of stay as the spouse of a person present and settled in the United Kingdom are that:

  (i)   the applicant has limited leave to enter or remain in the United Kingdom which was given in accordance with any of the provisions of these Rules, other than where as a result of that leave he would not have been in the United Kingdom beyond 6 months from the date on which he was admitted to the United Kingdom on this occasion in accordance with these Rules, unless the leave in question is limited leave to enter as a fiancé or proposed civil partner; and

  (ii) is married to or the civil partner of a person present and settled in the United Kingdom; and

  (iii) the parties to the marriage have met; and

    (iv)   the applicant has not remained in breach of the immigration laws; and

    (v)   the marriage has not taken place after a decision has been made to deport the applicant or he has been recommended for deportation or been given notice under Section 6(2) of the Immigration Act 1971; and

    (vi)   each of the parties intends to live permanently with the other as his or her spouse and the marriage is subsisting; and

    (vii) there will be adequate accommodation for the parties and any dependants without recourse to public funds in accommodation which they own or occupy exclusively; and

    (viii) the parties will be able to maintain themselves and any dependants adequately without recourse to public funds.

The requirements relating to leave to enter (applications from outside the UK) are the same, but without points (i), (iv) and (v) and with the requirement that the applicant holds a valid entry clearance (a visa) in this category.

On a successful application the civil partner will be granted leave for a probationary period of two years. During this two-year period there will be no restrictions on the civil partner's right to work, but there will be a prohibition on 'recourse to public funds'. The list of 'public funds' can be found at Chapter 1, Section 7 of the Immigration Directorate Instructions on the IND website (**www.ind.homeoffice.gov.uk**) and this can be used to assess whether a client has relied on public funds. Briefly, the list of public funds for immigration purposes covers all non-contributory benefits, tax credits, and housing and homelessness assistance.

If at the end of the two-year period the civil partner has remained living with his or her partner and has had no recourse to public funds (other than in exceptional circumstances), the civil partner will be granted indefinite leave to remain in the UK (permanent residence). There is also provision to grant indefinite leave to remain to foreign civil partners whose relationship has ended due to bereavement or domestic violence (rr.287(b) and 289A–289C).

Those who have been in a civil partnership outside the UK for four years before the application for indefinite leave to enter are able to do so without the need for a probationary period (rr.281(i)(b) and 282). However, since the requirement is that the applicant formed a civil partnership at least four years ago, it would appear that this provision does not immediately apply to those who have married or registered a partnership overseas before 2005, because all those overseas relationships that were entered into before 5 December 2005 are deemed to have been formed on that date (s.215(3), see also **8.4.3**).

The fact that civil partners are not required to demonstrate prior cohabitation clearly benefits many couples. However, a note of caution needs to be made for those advising prospective civil partners. Many couples may think that the CPA 2004 will be a simple cure for current immigration problems – that it will simply be a question of registering a civil partnership and then making an application on that basis from within the UK. This is, however, not the case. As with the rules relating to spouses, someone who makes an application for leave to remain as a civil partner from within the UK must have leave to be here, which was granted for over six months' duration unless that leave was granted as a proposed civil partner (see **11.2.2**). This leave cannot be leave granted outside the Rules (e.g. discretionary leave to remain). If a civil partner is in the UK without leave, any application for leave on the basis of a civil partnership needs to be made from outside the UK unless there are exceptional circumstances (see **11.8.3**). However, the question of whether an applicant has leave (and whether the applicant can meet requirements (i), (iv) and (v) above) arises on very few occasions as s.249 and Sched.23 mean that those without leave or with leave of short duration simply cannot register a civil partnership in the UK (see **11.3.1**).

11.2.2   Proposed civil partners

The initial consultation paper (WEU *Civil Partnership: A framework for the legal recognition of same-sex couples* (June 2003)) did not deal with those individuals who are not in the UK but who wish to come to the UK in order to enter into a civil partnership and subsequently apply for leave to remain on the basis of that partnership. Following representations on this point by the Lesbian and Gay Lawyers Association (LAGLA) and UKLGIG, the rules for fiancé(e)s have been extended to proposed civil partners (rr.289AA–295). A proposed civil partner, if successful in the application, is granted a six-month visa to enable the individual to enter the UK, register the civil partnership and subsequently apply from within the UK for leave to remain as a civil partner. The requirements for fiancé(e)s and proposed civil partners are set out in r.290:

> **290.** The requirements to be met by a person seeking leave to enter the United Kingdom as a fiancé(e) or proposed civil partner are that:
>
> (i)   the applicant is seeking leave to enter the United Kingdom for marriage or civil partnership to a person present and settled in the United Kingdom or who is on the same occasion being admitted for settlement; and
>
> (ii)   the parties to the proposed marriage or civil partnership have met; and
>
> (iii)   each of the parties intends to live permanently with the other as his or her spouse or civil partner after the marriage or civil partnership; and
>
> (iv)   adequate maintenance and accommodation without recourse to public funds will be available for the applicant until the date of the marriage or civil partnership; and
>
> (v)   there will, after the marriage or civil partnership, be adequate accommodation for the parties and any dependants without recourse to public funds in accommodation which they own or occupy exclusively; and
>
> (vi)   the parties will be able after the marriage or civil partnership to maintain themselves and any dependants adequately without recourse to public funds; and
>
> (vii)   the applicant holds a valid United Kingdom entry clearance for entry in this capacity.

The requirement that an applicant for leave to remain as a civil partner must have been granted more than six months leave to remain (as seen at **11.2.1**) does not apply to those who have been granted leave to enter as proposed civil partners. Although the Immigration Rules do not yet reflect this, it is happening in practice. Also, those who have leave in this category do not need to obtain a certificate of approval (see **11.4**).

It is likely that more proposed civil partners will apply for leave than fiancé(e)s. The reason for this is simply that when two individuals decide that they wish to marry and live in the UK, they can get married abroad in almost every country in the world. This is not the case for same-sex marriage and partnership, which is still only available in a limited number of countries. Many same-sex partners will therefore need to come to the UK as a proposed civil partner in order to have the opportunity to register the civil partnership in the first place. There are two situations where this will not be necessary:

- when the couple are able to enter into an overseas relationship under s.212 (see **11.2.3** and **8.4**) in another country; or
- when the couple are able to register at an overseas diplomatic mission under the provisions under s.210 (see **8.3.1**).

11.2.3 Recognition of overseas regimes

Before the CPA 2004 came into force, the UK would not allow those who had entered into a same-sex marriage abroad to enter the UK as a spouse on the basis of that marriage. This position was challenged by lawyers involved with UKLGIG who stated that there was nothing in the Diplomatic Policy Instructions to prevent a same-sex 'marriage' being a basis for leave to enter or remain as a spouse. The response by the Home Office was simply to change the instructions so that they specifically stated that same-sex marriages would not be recognised. This amendment was made in 2004 at the same time as the Civil Partnership Bill was brought through Parliament, and in apparent contradiction to the work that the Government was doing on civil partnership. However, since the coming into force of the CPA 2004, this position has changed. Provision is now automatically made for those who have entered into an overseas regime recognised under s.212. An overseas relationship is recognised as a civil partnership if it is listed in Sched.20 or meets the conditions set out in s.214 (see **8.4**). If a relationship is recognised as a civil partnership, it can form the basis of an application for leave to enter or remain as a civil partner. This applies to applications by civil partners of British citizens and persons with indefinite leave to remain as well as any of the other categories set out below.

11.3 CIVIL PARTNERS OF OTHERS

11.3.1 Civil partners of those with limited leave to remain

There are a number of categories of people who may come to the UK for a fixed period of time, often to work here (either as employed or self-employed people) or as students. These include work permit holders and highly skilled migrants. These people, of course, often wish to bring their partners.

Unmarried partners can only be brought in certain work-related categories but there are more instances in which a person with limited leave may bring a spouse to the UK, for example students. The initial Government Consultation Paper did not make reference to the civil partners of individuals with limited leave to remain, and in its response LAGLA requested confirmation that the foreign partners of those with limited leave will be given leave to enter and remain as dependants. As a result the existing rules for spouses have been extended to civil partners. This is a great step forward for students because it allows them to bring their same-sex partners for the first time (as civil partners).

There remain practical difficulties in this area for same-sex couples, which spouses do not have. To take advantage of these provisions same-sex partners will have to be registered civil partners, either:

- by registering as civil partners in the UK; or
- by marrying or registering abroad in a regime that allows for recognition as an overseas relationship as defined under s.212 (see **8.4**).

Registering a civil partnership at an overseas post under s.210 is not an option because one partner has to be a British citizen. The options therefore would be as set out below.

1. Register an overseas relationship in their home country (see **8.4**). This will only be possible for a limited number of applicants because so far only a few countries have same-sex partnership regimes and many of these countries are part of the EU, so that these issues do not arise.
2. Register in a third country. The problem is that most countries have restrictions and residence or nationality requirements, although Canada seems to be a notable exception. Nevertheless, the couple would need to go to the expense of time and money to travel abroad for a wedding or registration.
3. Register as civil partners in the UK. The proposed civil partner category that mirrors fiancé(e)s would not be of any help as this is limited to the partners of British citizens, those with indefinite leave to remain or EEA nationals, and is not open to the partners of people with limited leave to remain.
4. In most cases, the only option available will be to enter the UK on a civil partnership visit visa (see **11.6**). This allows any person to enter the UK

for the purpose of entering into a civil partnership. It does not, however, allow for a person in that category to change their status while in the UK to that of civil partner. This means that the partner of the work permit holder, etc. has to enter on a civil partnership visit visa, register the civil partnership, then leave the UK and make a fresh application for leave to enter as a civil partner from abroad. This is an extremely cumbersome, expensive and time-consuming process for the couple involved and could put people off from coming here. This could potentially be detrimental to the UK's desire to attract highly skilled people and students from abroad. In practice, a similar problem does not arise for opposite-sex couples as they are almost always able to marry in their home country.

Representatives of ILPA, LAGLA and UKLGIG suggested possible solutions to the IND, which agreed to consider them. However, IND simply asked for examples to be brought to its attention (which can be done through UKLGIG).

11.3.2 Civil partners of EEA nationals

There has traditionally been some confusion over the exact position of same-sex partners of European Economic Area (EEA) and Swiss nationals who are exercising their right to free movement under the EU and EEA treaties to live in the UK because, while the spouses of EEA nationals fell under explicit provision of EU law, there had (until now) not been any provision for same-sex partners under EU law. It was, however, clearly established that the unmarried partners of EEA nationals should be treated in the same way as partners of British citizens under the prohibition on discrimination on grounds of nationality in EU law. The only difference is that the partners of EEA nationals need to have been in the UK for a longer period than partners of British citizens or settled persons before permanent residence is reached.

Civil partners of EEA nationals will now be treated in the same way as spouses, and other same-sex partners will be treated in the same way as unmarried partners (see European Directorate Instructions on the IND website). The proposed civil partners of EEA nationals who are outside the UK do not face the same potential difficulties as the proposed civil partners of those with limited leave to remain referred to at **11.3.1**. This is because r.290A provides that:

> 290A For the purposes of paragraph 290 and paragraphs 291–295, an EEA national who holds a registration certificate or a document certifying permanent residence issued under the 2006 EEA Regulations [SI 2006/1003] (including an EEA national who holds a residence permit issued under the Immigration (European Economic Area) Regulations 2000 [SI 2000/2326] which is treated as if it were such a certificate or document by virtue of Schedule 4 to the 2006 EEA Regulations) is to be regarded as present and settled in the United Kingdom.

This means that partners of EEA nationals can apply to enter the UK as proposed civil partners once the EEA national has obtained a registration certificate (see **11.2.2**).

The European Economic Area (EEA) includes:

- the 'old' EU countries: Austria, Belgium, Denmark, Finland, France, Germany, Greece, Ireland, Italy, Luxembourg, Portugal, Spain, Sweden, the Netherlands and the UK;
- Malta and Cyprus who joined in 2004, but who were immediately treated in the same way as 'old' EU countries for immigration purposes;
- the other eight EU accession countries that joined in 2004 ('A8'): the Czech Republic, Estonia, Hungary, Latvia, Lithuania, Poland, Slovakia, Slovenia;
- Iceland, Liechtenstein and Norway;
- under r.257, Swiss nationals are treated as EEA nationals for immigration purposes.

Many EU Member States have overseas territories and residents of those territories may also have passports of the motherland. Irish nationals can be treated as holders of indefinite leave to remain or as EEA nationals and care should be taken in choosing which status is preferable. Treating an Irish national as the holder of indefinite leave to remain can mean that the civil partner will be eligible for indefinite leave to remain at an earlier stage.

There is an unresolved issue in this area. A8 nationals cannot obtain registration certificates until they have completed one year on the workers registration scheme or are self-employed. This means that their partners will not be able to enter as proposed civil partners as they will not meet the requirements of r.290A.

In 2004, the EU adopted Directive 2004/58/EC on the rights of citizens of the Union and their family members to move and reside freely within the territory to be implemented by 30 April 2006. The UK therefore introduced the Immigration (European Economic Area) Regulations 2006 (SI 2006/1003). This directive recognises a limited right to free movement for partners who are not heterosexual spouses (including same-sex partners). The final text is somewhat of a compromise but it does mean that for the first time same-sex partners can fall under EU freedom of movement law and the confusion referred to above may become a thing of the past. A good discussion of the directive can be found on the website of the International Lesbian and Gay Association Europe (**www.ilga-europe.org**).

11.4 IMMIGRATION CONTROL

The often-held belief that bi-national couples can simply regularise their immigration status by registering a civil partnership in the UK is false because there are restrictions on the ability to enter into a civil partnership (CPA 2004 s.249 and Sched.23). These were late amendments to the Bill introduced in order to bring the CPA 2004 into line with the measures affecting marriage introduced by the Asylum and Immigration (Treatment of Claimants etc.) Act 2004, ss.19 to 25.

The effect of CPA 2004, s.249 and Sched.23 is that, in order to enter into a civil partnership, an individual needs permission from the Secretary of State for the Home Department unless that individual:

- is a British citizen; or
- has the right to abode; or
- is an EEA national; or
- is not subject to immigration control for another reason; or
- has been granted indefinite leave to remain; or
- is entering into a registration with a former spouse if one of them has changed sex; or
- has been granted leave to enter as a proposed civil partner or a civil partnership visitor.

Permission is given in the form of a certificate of approval. The Home Office guidance can be found at Section 15 of Chapter 1 of the Immigration Directorates Instructions on the IND website (**www.ind.homeoffice.gov.uk**). The guidance states that in order to qualify for the certificate of approval from the Home Office applicants must have been granted leave to enter or leave to remain for more than six months from the date that they were admitted into the UK and three months of that leave must still be outstanding. The guidance does allow for discretion in exceptional circumstances, and these are outlined at Annex NN to Chapter 1. It is envisaged that such circumstances will be rare, but legal advisers will have to be ready to argue for them in situations where the remedies of leaving the country and registering abroad or re-entering as a proposed civil partner are not available.

The options open to those who do not fall into any of the above categories and whose leave is either for six months or less or has less than three months to run are as follows.

1. Leave the UK and return to the country of origin and then apply for leave to enter as a proposed civil partner (see **11.2.2**). It is sometimes possible to ask an overseas post in a third country to deal with an application, but they must be approached on a case-by-case basis as there is no requirement for them to process applications for those who are not resident there.

2. Leave the UK and register abroad as a civil partner (**8.3.1**) or enter into a recognised overseas relationship (**8.4**) and then apply for leave to enter as a civil partner.

3. Obtain extended leave that is valid for more than six months, e.g. under the unmarried and same-sex partner rules, and then apply for a certificate of approval.

For the third option the category chosen should not be one which requires an intention to leave because this may create difficulties over how that extension of visa was obtained and whether a false declaration was made because the applicant never had the intention to leave. This would for example apply to leave as a student below degree level.

The restrictions on marriage may be a breach of human rights because they restrict the right to marry under Art.12 of the European Convention on Human Rights. The restrictions do not apply to marriages in the Church of England or Church in Wales, but they apply to all other civil and religious marriages. Therefore there is discrimination on the basis of religion, which (even if there is no general breach of Art.12) may be a breach of Art.12 in combination with the non-discrimination provisions under Art.14. For same-sex couples there may in addition be a breach of Art.14 in combination with Art.8 (right to private life) because the restrictions apply to all same-sex couples as there is no Church of England option for the registration of civil partnership. Just before going to print, Silber J in *R (on the application of Baiai)* v. *Secretary of State for the Home Department* [2006] EWHC 823 (Admin) found that the restriction on marriage was a breach of Arts.12 and 14. At the time of writing further judgments are awaited in this matter and the Home Office has not changed its practice.

11.5 THE UNMARRIED AND SAME-SEX PARTNER RULES

Although this chapter aims to deal primarily with the impact of the Act, the unmarried and same-sex partner rules remain relevant for same-sex couples because there are situations where these are still a better option. The most obvious example is that where same-sex partners want to live together in the UK, but do not want to take on the rights and responsibilities of civil partnership. Other situations can be envisaged where the unmarried and same-sex partners rules may be preferable and these are discussed at **11.8.1**. It is therefore important that these rules remain in place.

The requirement of these rules which most frequently creates difficulty is that of 'living together in a relationship akin to marriage or civil partnership which has subsisted for two years or more'. The Home Office's interpretation of the phrase can be found at Annex Z, Chapter 8, Section 7 of the Immigration Directorate's Instructions (available at **www.ind.homeoffice.gov.uk**). The Home Office's guidance states that a couple must have lived together for the two years preceding the application, although gaps totalling six months during that period will be allowed if there is good reason. Although this guidance is open to challenge in individual cases and should not be accepted as the only interpretation of the Rules, those who do not have clear two years' cohabitation with not more than six months apart during that time may have their application refused. By contrast, there is no requirement for civil partners to have lived together for the foreign partner to be able to apply for leave to enter or remain in the UK on the basis of the civil partnership (see **11.2.1**).

11.6   CIVIL PARTNERSHIP VISIT VISA

Anyone can apply to come to the UK as a visitor to enter into a civil partnership here. However, they cannot enter on a simple visitor's ('tourist') visa but must obtain a 'civil partnership visit visa' which mirrors the marriage visit visa (rr.56D to 56F).

This category must be distinguished from the proposed civil partner visa. It does not allow the holder of the visa to stay here for any purpose other than the registration and it is not possible to switch from this category into leave to remain as a civil partner even if one partner has leave to remain in another category. As with all visitors' categories, this category requires an intention to leave the UK after the registration. This visa can of course also be used by one partner to enter the UK to register a civil partnership with someone who is here on another basis, such as someone with limited leave to remain (see **11.3.1**).

11.7   NATURALISATION AS A BRITISH CITIZEN

Generally, naturalisation as a British citizen requires five years' lawful residence in the UK, at least one year of which must have been completed as the holder of indefinite leave to remain. The spouses of British citizens, though, can naturalise after three years. Full guidance can be found in the Nationality Instructions on the IND website (**www.ind.homeoffice.gov.uk**). Previously, same-sex partners have always had to follow the five-year lawful residence route. They have not been in a position to naturalise more quickly than this even if their residence in the UK was gained on the basis of a relationship with a British citizen. LAGLA and the UKLGIG, in their responses to the Consultation Paper, asserted that civil partners should also be able to naturalise after three years, giving parity with spouses. The Government agreed with this suggestion and the CPA 2004 provides for this at Sched.27, para.72 which amends s.6(2) of the British Nationality Act 1981. The amendments go further than just allowing naturalisation for civil partners after three years and insert civil partnership in many instances where the British Nationality Act 1981 refers to marriage.

11.8 PRACTICAL POINTS

11.8.1 Civil partner or (unregistered) same-sex partner?

It goes without saying that nobody should enter into a civil partnership purely for immigration reasons. As other chapters in this book illustrate, there are many rights and responsibilities that come with civil partnership and such a serious commitment should only be undertaken by those who wish to take on those rights and responsibilities. However, especially in the early stages of the CPA 2004 it will undoubtedly be the case that there will be committed couples who have decided they want to enter into a civil partnership, but who also meet the requirements of the immigration rules relating to unmarried partners. There is therefore often a choice for an individual as to which category to use. First, the basis of the application will not affect the time at which the foreign partner will be eligible for indefinite leave to remain in the UK (r.287(i)(b)). A same-sex partner who becomes a civil partner can apply for indefinite leave to remain as a civil partner at the end of the two-year probationary period for unmarried and same-sex partners. The change from unmarried partner to civil partner does not affect the probationary period so long as the individual has registered a civil partnership with the same partner and not somebody else. This means that people who have already been granted leave as an unmarried or same-sex partner can remain on that status until they are eligible for indefinite leave to remain even if they become civil partners.

The question arises therefore of whether people who meet the immigration rules for unmarried partners should enter into a civil partnership with the foreign partner and then apply for leave as a civil partner, or whether the foreign partner should apply for leave under the unmarried or same-sex partner rules first before entering into a civil partnership. They will need to consider the following points:

1. It is not possible to switch within the UK from the status of visitor to civil partner (r.284). However, it is possible to switch from the status of visitor to unmarried partner (r.295D(i) does not expressly prohibit this). For this reason, if someone is here as a visitor and meets the unmarried and same-sex partner rules, it may be better to make an application under those rules rather than having to leave the UK to make an application for leave to enter as a proposed civil partner (see also **11.2.2**).
2. Related to the above, anyone who has been granted six months or less leave or who has less than three months remaining on their leave will not be granted a certificate of approval from the Home Office. Therefore they would need to leave the UK and either register their relationship abroad (see **11.4**) or enter the UK as a proposed civil partner (see **11.2.2**). However, if they have been cohabiting with their partner for two years

and can prove this, they can make an application for leave to remain as an unmarried partner and then, once that leave has been granted, apply for a certificate of approval to enter into a civil partnership. As they will have two years' leave to remain at that point, the certificate of approval should be granted.

3. There is also a time factor to be considered. Even if an individual is entitled to a certificate of approval, the time estimates for certificates to be granted will vary. Waiting for a certificate of approval and then entering into a civil partnership before making an application may delay the point at which the foreign partner will ultimately be eligible for indefinite leave to remain. In this situation, the couple may wish to apply for leave on the basis of their unmarried partnership, notwithstanding the fact that they do plan to enter into a civil partnership in the very near future.

4. At the time of writing, though, the Home Office is taking an extremely strict view on the type of documentation required for a successful unmarried partners' application. Depending on the circumstances therefore, this may mean that an application on the basis of a civil partnership is the preferred option.

These are just some of the scenarios which can be envisaged and advisers and clients should always consider which option is the best for any individual couple considering also the factor of legal costs and time delay.

11.8.2   Past immigration history

As set out above (**11.4**), where someone is not allowed to enter into a civil partnership in the UK or to make an application on the basis of a civil partnership because they have breached UK immigration law (e.g. by overstaying), one solution is to leave the UK and make an application to enter as a proposed civil partner or as a civil partner from abroad. This will indeed often be the simplest and quickest solution. However, although the Immigration Rules relating to leave to enter do not specifically refer to past immigration history, there is discretion for applications to be refused on that basis (r.320), although in practice this is rare. Such refusals may be challengeable at appeal on human rights grounds, but applicants need to be warned of the potential problems.

11.8.3   Making applications from abroad

There may be individuals who are not willing to make applications on the basis of their same-sex partnership in their country of origin due to the legal or social position concerning homosexuality in that country. In such cases, consideration will need to be given to whether there are arguments to be made that the case is exceptional and matters should be dealt with in the UK or whether there is a third country to which that individual would be willing and able to travel where the overseas post would be willing to process the application. For instance, would a client returning to a country where homosexual conduct is illegal wish to carry the necessary documentation through immigration control on entering that country?

Advisers can be proud of the near equality that we have achieved in the UK but need to be aware that it is an achievement that is matched in very few countries around the world and clients' concerns must be listened to accordingly.

CHAPTER 12

Housing and tenancies

Anne McMurdie

12.1 INTRODUCTION

Security of the home, whether owned or rented, is of the utmost importance to most people. Although security in the private rented sector has been eroded by successive governments over the past 20 years, there is still valuable protection for public sector and housing association tenants and a small number of private sector tenants. The Civil Partnership Act 2004, s.81 and Sched.8 introduce a series of amendments to the existing legislation which regulate the rights of tenants across different types of tenure. The amendments accord rights to civil partners in line with those of spouses and give rights in some contexts to those who 'live together as if they were civil partners'. The problems with the definition of this term are highlighted elsewhere (**1.4.8**). This chapter will look into the changes made to housing law in the following areas:

- the rights to inherit (succeed to) a tenancy on the death of the tenant, and the right to transfer (assign) tenancies (**12.2**);
- the law of protection from eviction (**12.3**);
- the exercise of the right to buy and the right to enfranchisement or extension of long leases (**12.4**);
- other incidental amendments in different contexts which are dealt with briefly at the end of the chapter (**12.5**).

In all these areas civil partners have been put in the same category as spouses and wherever there is a provision for people 'living together as husband and wife', a provision for people 'living together as if they were civil partners' has been added.

12.2   SUCCESSION AND ASSIGNMENT RIGHTS

12.2.1   Tenancies

The rights of tenants vary depending on what type of landlord they have, and these rights are governed by different Acts.

Secure and introductory tenancies

Most council tenants, and some long-standing housing association tenants, have a secure tenancy. Secure tenants enjoy a high degree of protection from eviction, have rights to transfer their tenancy and for a resident family member to inherit the tenancy on their death. These rights are set out in Part 4 of the Housing Act 1985. Some local authorities have schemes where new tenants are granted an introductory tenancy for an initial 12-month period. Provided the tenancy has not been brought to an end at the end of the period, the tenancy becomes a secure tenancy.

Assured tenancies

Most housing association tenants and some private tenants have an assured tenancy. Assured tenants enjoy a high degree of protection from eviction. They have limited rights for someone else to inherit the tenancy on their death.

Assured shorthold tenancies

Most private sector tenants have an assured shorthold tenancy. These are governed by the Housing Act 1988. Assured shorthold tenants have very limited rights, as the tenancy can be ended when the contractual period comes to an end by the landlord serving the correct notice. Assured shorthold tenants have the same rights as assured tenants in relation to someone inheriting the tenancy on their death.

Demoted tenancies

Local authorities or registered social landlords can apply to the court for an order that a secure tenancy or an assured tenancy becomes a demoted tenancy for one year. Landlords apply for demoted tenancies to take action against tenants who have been involved in anti-social behaviour. Demoted tenants can be evicted much more easily than secure council tenants and lose other rights, such as the right to buy.

Rent Act tenancies

Most private sector tenancies created before January 1989 are governed by the Rent Act 1977. Rent Act tenants have a high degree of protection from eviction, and have the right for a resident family member to inherit the tenancy on their death. The rent the landlord can charge is controlled and the tenant has the right to register a fair rent.

12.2.2   Succession rights

Housing law provides for certain tenancies of residential accommodation to pass to the spouse or family member of the tenant on the death of the tenant. The exact criteria to be met for a succession to take place depend on the type of tenancy. Before the introduction of the CPA 2004, the House of Lords twice considered the definition of the terms 'living together as husband and wife' and 'family member'. These cases extended the class of those who could succeed to a tenancy to include a same-sex partner. *Fitzpatrick* v. *Sterling Housing Association Ltd* [2001] 1 AC 27 was concerned with a Rent Act tenant. The Rent Act 1977 provides that the tenant's spouse (which includes someone living with them as husband and wife) at the time of their death would inherit a Rent Act tenancy. The court decided that a same-sex couple were not living together as husband and wife and so could not be treated as the 'spouse' of the other, as that definition required that the persons are of a different sex. However where there was a stable and permanent relationship between same-sex partners, one partner would be regarded as a family member of the other. The resident family member of a Rent Act tenant can inherit an assured tenancy where there is no spouse to inherit the tenancy at the time of the tenant's death. As they inherit an assured tenancy, rather than a Rent Act tenancy, they will have to pay a market rent, rather than a fair rent.

The House of Lords in *Ghaidan* v. *Godin-Mendoza* [2004] 2 FLR 600 looked at the matter again in the light of the Human Rights Act 1998 having come into force. The majority found that the Human Rights Act 1998 required that the term 'living together as husband and wife' should be read to include same-sex partners.

The CPA 2004 puts the extension of the succession rights to same-sex partners which had already been effected by *Mendoza* on a statutory footing.

12.2.3   Secure, introductory and demoted tenants

Succession

The rights to succeed to a secure tenancy are set out in Part 4 of the Housing Act 1985, in ss.87–89. The Housing Act 1985 is amended by the CPA 2004 to

231

provide that on the death of a periodic secure tenant the tenancy will pass to the tenant's spouse or civil partner if they are living in the accommodation as their only or principal home at the time of the tenant's death.

If there is no spouse or civil partner to take the tenancy, it can pass to a family member who has resided with the tenant for the 12 months preceding the tenant's death. The Housing Act 1985, s.133 defines 'family member' by reference to a fixed list, and this list has been amended by the CPA 2004 to include a civil partner or person living together with the tenant as if they are civil partners. This is designed to put the decision in *Mendoza* (above) on a statutory footing. Those living together as husband and wife have always been treated as family members for the purposes of this Act, and by extending the definition to include those 'living together as if they are civil partners' this is meant to apply to same-sex cohabitants (see also **1.4.8**).

The definition of family member is also amended by the CPA 2004 to the effect that a relationship by civil partnership shall be treated as a relationship by blood, and thus, for example, the sister or niece of the civil partner will be a family member for succession purposes.

The statute only allows for one succession. What is meant by 'succession' is not obvious, as it includes:

- when a joint tenancy becomes a sole tenancy by survivorship;
- when the tenancy was assigned to the tenant by a spouse, civil partner or family member; or
- when the tenancy vests in the tenant following the death of the previous tenant.

However, certain assignments which arise in pursuance of property adjustment orders in family proceedings are not taken to be a succession, and thus a succession following transfer of the tenancy is allowed. This applies to assignments of a tenancy ordered under MCA 1973, ss.23A and 24 (property adjustment orders in connection with family proceedings) and to orders made under the Matrimonial and Family Proceedings Act 1984, s.17(1) (property adjustment order after overseas divorce). Similarly, an assignment pursuant to a property adjustment order in connection with civil partnership proceedings is not treated as a succession.

Orders made under the Family Law Act 1996, Sched.8 where the court has powers to order the transfer of a tenancy to a spouse, civil partner or cohabitant, are not affected by this provision. The mechanism for a transfer under the Family Law Act 1996 is for the tenancy to be vested in the new tenant, rather than for the court to order the tenancy to be assigned. If the tenancy is transferred under the Family Law Act 1996 it will not count as a succession.

Where the tenant dies and no one is entitled to succeed under these rules, the tenancy ceases to be a secure tenancy. This means that the rights which flow from having a secure tenancy, including the right to buy and the right for possession only to be granted by the court on specified grounds, come to an end. The landlord will be able to bring the contractual tenancy to an end by serving a notice to quit. However, where the tenancy passes on the death of the tenant in the course of the administration of the tenant's estate pursuant to a property adjustment order in family proceedings the tenancy will continue to be a secure tenancy. The CPA 2004 has made the equivalent provision for where the tenancy passes pursuant to a property adjustment order in connection with civil partnership proceedings.

Assignment

Sections 90–91 of the Housing Act 1985 deal with the circumstances in which a secure tenancy can be assigned to someone else. In general a secure tenant can assign his or her tenancy by deed, but the assignee will only take a secure tenancy with all of the rights and protections of a secure tenancy if the assignee is someone who would be qualified to succeed to the tenancy if the tenant died immediately before the assignment (see also **12.2.2**). The effect of the CPA 2004 extending the class of people who can succeed to the tenancy thus has the effect of extending the class of those to whom a secure tenancy can be assigned.

Introductory and demoted tenants

Sections 132–134 of the Housing Act 1996 set out the equivalent regime for the assignment of and succession to introductory tenants. Section 143(H)–(K) of the Housing Act 1996 does likewise for demoted tenancies. These mirror the provisions for secure tenants set out above. Both provisions have been amended by the Act so that civil partners and those living together as civil partners have the same rights to inherit and be assigned tenancies as spouses and those living together as husband and wife.

12.2.4   Assured and assured shorthold tenants

The right to succeed to an assured tenancy is set out in Part 1 of the Housing Act 1988. It is much more limited than the succession rights for secure or Rent Act tenancies. Section 17 of the Housing Act 1988 now provides that when a periodic assured tenant dies, the only person who can succeed to the tenancy is the tenant's spouse or civil partner if he or she was occupying the accommodation as his or her only or principal home when the tenant died. The definition includes a person who was living with the tenant as the tenant's wife or husband or as if they were civil partners. For assured periodic tenants, succession takes place irrespective of the tenant's will or intestacy. Where there is no spouse or civil partner (including cohabitant), there is no provision for the tenancy to pass to another family member. There can only be one succession, which includes where a joint tenancy becomes a sole tenancy by survivorship, as well as when the tenancy vests in the tenant following the death of the previous tenant.

Fixed-term contractual assured tenancies or assured shorthold tenancies which are for a fixed term that has not yet expired pass by the will or intestacy of the deceased tenant. The beneficiary will take an assured tenancy for the remainder of the fixed term. At the expiry of the term, the new tenant will become a periodic assured tenant, but will be deemed to be a successor, and therefore no further succession can take place.

12.2.5 Rent Act tenants

The rights to succeed to a Rent Act tenancy are set out in the Rent Act 1977, Sched.1. The Rent Act 1977 is amended by the CPA 2004 to provide that on the death of a Rent Act tenant the tenancy will pass to the tenant's spouse or civil partner if he or she is living in the accommodation as his or her residence at the time of the tenant's death. A person who is living with the original tenant as his or her wife or husband is treated as the spouse of the original tenant. The schedule has now been amended to include civil partners and those living together as if they were civil partners. They succeed to a statutory tenancy and enjoy the benefits of entitlement to a fair rent and limited grounds for eviction.

Where there is no spouse or civil partner to succeed, a family member can succeed to the tenancy if the family member was living with the original tenant at the time of death and for the preceding two years. Unlike the provisions for secure tenants there is no fixed list or definition of 'family member'. It is to be assumed therefore that the relationship by civil partnership shall be treated as a relationship by blood. However, a family member is only entitled to succeed to an assured tenancy, which will have a market rent and wider grounds for possession. In *Mendoza* (above) this was, of course, the issue why Mr Mendoza was not content simply to accept the rights granted to Mr Fitzpatrick in the earlier case.

12.2.6 Agricultural tenants

The CPA 2004 has amended the provisions which regulate the right to succeed to agricultural tenancies so that where a right exists for a spouse or an opposite-sex partner to succeed, this right has been extended to civil partners and those living together as if they were civil partners.

The Housing Act 1988, s.24 and Sched.3 regulate assured agricultural occupancies. One of the criteria to be met to benefit from the protection of the Housing Act 1988 is that the occupier must be a qualifying agricultural worker, as defined by that Act. Where the qualifying occupier dies, that person's widow, widower or surviving civil partner will still retain protection as if he or she were a qualifying agricultural worker, provided that he or she was living with the occupier immediately before their death. The definition includes someone who was living with the previous occupier as his or her wife or husband, or as if they were civil partners.

For protected tenancies regulated by the Rent (Agriculture) Act 1976, ss.3 and 4 of that Act provide for a surviving partner who was living with the original occupier at the time of death to succeed to become either the protected or statutory occupier. A surviving partner now includes a civil partner or a person living with the occupier as if they were civil partners.

The Agricultural Holdings Act 1996 makes provision for the terms of the tenancy of certain agricultural holdings. Sections 36–48 set out the provision which allows for certain close relatives of a deceased tenant to apply to the Agricultural Land Tribunal for a new tenancy. The Agricultural Holdings Act 1996 also allows certain tenants of agricultural holdings on retirement to nominate a successor who is a close family member, who can apply to the Tribunal for a new tenancy (at ss.50–58). The CPA 2004 amends the definitions to place civil partners and the family members in the same position as spouses and family members of the deceased or retiring tenant.

12.3 PROTECTION FROM EVICTION

12.3.1 Agricultural tied accommodation

Section 3 of the Protection from Eviction Act 1977 provides that an occupier of agricultural tied accommodation cannot be evicted without a court order. Where the tenancy of an agricultural employee comes to an end and does not become a statutory tenancy, the court has additional powers set out in s.4 of that Act to postpone the date for possession in certain circumstances for up to six months. This power can be exercised in favour of the tenant under the former tenancy, the tenant's widow or widower or the tenant's surviving spouse or surviving civil partner, if he or she was residing with the deceased at the death. If the former tenant leaves no such widow or widower or surviving civil partner, any member of their family residing with the tenant at the time of death can apply for this protection.

12.3.2 Caravan dwellers

The Caravan Sites Act 1968 provides a degree of protection from eviction and harassment to caravan dwellers. Section 3 creates an offence of unlawful eviction and harassment in relation to the occupier of a caravan on a protected site, or in relation to their widow or widower. This protection is extended by the CPA 2004 to the occupier's surviving civil partner.

12.3.3   Amended grounds for possession

The statutory regimes which regulate residential tenancies all make provision for the grounds on which the court must or may order possession.

A common theme across the tenures in the private sector is the right of a landlord to regain possession when the property is reasonably required for occupation by the landlord or his or her spouse. This is the case for Rent Act tenancies (Rent Act 1977, Sched.15) and assured tenancies (Housing Act 1988, Sched.2). In both cases the definition has been changed by the CPA 2004 to provide that this should include the right to regain possession for occupation by a civil partner. For Rent Act tenancies the ground for possession is also available where the landlord requires possession for a family member to occupy the accommodation, and the CPA 2004 has duly amended the definition of family member to include civil partner and to treat the family members of the civil partner as the family members of the landlord.

The equivalent ground for possession also occurs in:

- Landlord and Tenant Act 1954, Sched.3 which provides security of tenure for residential tenants under long leases at low rents; and
- Local Government and Housing Act 1989, Sched.10 which regulates residential tenancies of 21 years or more.

The ground for possession where the property is reasonably required for occupation by the landlord, spouse or family member has been similarly amended.

For secure tenants and assured tenants of registered social landlords or charities the court has a power to grant possession where there has been domestic violence. Where a couple occupy accommodation together and one or both of them are tenants and one partner has left because of the violence or threats of violence of the other partner, the court can evict the violent partner if the court is satisfied that the partner who has left is unlikely to return. The definition of partner in the Housing Act 1985, Sched.2 and the Housing Act 1988, Sched.2 has been extended by the CPA 2004 to include civil partners and those living together as if they were civil partners.

12.4   RIGHT TO BUY AND OTHER DISPOSALS

12.4.1   Right to buy

The right to buy for secure tenants is set out in Part 5 of the Housing Act 1985. The Civil Partnership Act 2004 makes a number of amendments. First, a secure tenant may exercise the right to buy jointly with up to three other members of his family who reside with him (Housing Act 1985, s.123). The definition of 'family member' is extended by the CPA 2004 to include a civil partner. Secondly, any discount previously given to a person exercising the right to buy, or to their spouse or civil partner, is deducted from the allowable discount on a subsequent right to buy. This applies where the spouse or civil partner is living with the purchaser at the time that they give notice claiming the right to buy.

The Housing Act 1985, Sched.4 sets out the period of residence necessary to qualify for the right to buy and for the discounts. This has been amended by the CPA 2004 to provide that account will be taken of the period of time that a civil partner or deceased civil partner was occupying relevant accommodation, in the same way as for a secure tenant's spouse.

In certain circumstances a secure tenant has the right to buy on rent-to-mortgage terms (Housing Act 1985, s.143). The existing rent payments are turned into mortgage payments of a capital sum borrowed from the landlord. The difference between the sum borrowed and the full purchase value of the property is the landlord's share which is secured by a charge on the property. This is to be repaid on subsequent disposal or death of the owner. Some disposals are exempt; these are set out in the Housing Act 2004, Sched.6A, and have been amended by the CPA 2004 to include the disposal to a civil partner or a disposal in pursuance of a property adjustment order under the CPA 2004.

If there is a disposal of a property acquired under the right to buy within the prescribed period there will be a clawback of some or the entire discount. A number of disposals are exempt from this, and a disposal to a civil partner or former civil partner and a disposal pursuant to a property adjustment order in connection with civil partnership proceedings is an exempt disposal (Housing Act 1985, s.160).

In certain circumstances, where someone ceases to be a secure tenant because the landlord has sold the property, the right to buy is preserved for as long as they live in the accommodation (Housing Act 1985, s.171B). Additionally, certain other people who have succeeded to the tenancy or have had the tenancy assigned to them benefit from the preserved right to buy. These categories have been amended by the CPA 2004 so that the right now applies equally to civil partners and the family members of civil partners.

12.4.2   Disposal of land

Part 2 of the Housing Act 1985 provides that councils can obtain ministerial consent for disposals of land held for housing purposes and can give the purchaser a discount on the purchase, as long as there is a covenant binding the purchaser and his successors in title to pay back the discount or a percentage of the discount if the property is disposed of within a prescribed period. A similar scheme exists to allow registered social landlords and Housing Action Trusts to dispose of land in the same way. Each scheme provides that certain disposals are exempt from the duty to repay the discount. A disposal to a civil partner or former civil partner, or a disposal pursuant to a property adjustment order in connection with civil partnership proceedings is now an exempt disposal.

12.4.3   Enfranchisement and long lease extension

The Landlord and Tenant Act 1987 confers on certain long leaseholders the right to acquire the landlord's interest by giving qualifying leaseholders the right of first refusal on certain disposals. Some disposals by the landlord are exempt from the right to acquire (Landlord and Tenant Act 1987, s.4). This includes some disposals to family members and those made pursuant to a property adjustment order within family proceedings. These provisions have been amended by the CPA 2004 so that disposals to a civil partner or someone with whom the owner is living as if they were civil partners are treated in the same way as disposals to a spouse or someone with whom the owner is living as husband and wife. The definition of family member is amended to include family members of a civil partner, and disposal made pursuant to a property adjustment order under the CPA 2004 are exempt.

The Leasehold Reform, Housing and Urban Development Act 1993 gives long leaseholders the right to collective enfranchisement, and also gives individual leaseholders the right to acquire a new lease. The definition of long lease (Leasehold Reform, Housing and Urban Development Act 1993, s.7) is amended. Where the definition is referable to a lease terminable by notice after death or marriage (s.7(1)(b) and (2)) this is amended by the CPA 2004 to include leases terminable on the formation of a civil partnership.

Where there is a resident landlord in the premises and the premises do not contain more than four units the right to enfranchisement does not apply. The Leasehold Reform, Housing and Urban Development Act 1993, s.10 defines resident landlord referable to the residence of the landlord or an adult member of the landlord's family. The definition of an adult member of his family is amended by the CPA 2004 to include a civil partner and family members of the civil partner.

The Commonhold and Leasehold Reform Act 2002 extends the entitlement to enfranchisement for long leaseholders. The Civil Partnership Act 2004 brings in amendments along the same lines as those made to the 1993 Act. So the definition of a long lease (ss.76 and 77 of the 2002 Act) is amended where it refers to a lease terminable by notice after death or marriage to include leases terminable on the formation of a civil partnership. Where there is an exclusion from the rights conferred by the Commonhold and Leasehold Reform Act 2002 where there is a resident landlord, the definition in Sched.6 to the 2002 Act is amended so that the reference to family members includes civil partner and family members of a civil partner.

The Leasehold Reform Act 1967 gives rights of enfranchisement or lease extensions to long leases of houses if certain criteria are met. Again, where the definition of long tenancy refers a tenancy terminable by notice after death or marriage (ss.1 and 1B) this is now amended by the CPA 2004 to include long tenancies terminable on the formation of a civil partnership. The Leasehold Reform Act 1967, s.7 sets out the rights of family members who succeed to a long tenancy on death of the tenant. This is now amended by the CPA 2004 to provide that civil partners are treated in the same way as spouses and family members of civil partners have the same rights as family members of spouses.

12.5 OTHER AMENDMENTS

12.5.1 Housing grants

The Housing Grants, Construction and Regeneration Act 1996 sets out the framework of entitlement to grants for housing renovation, Disabled Facilities Grants, Houses in Multiple Occupation grants and Common Parts Grants. An amendment to s.30 of the 1996 Act provides that the income and assets, needs and outgoings of a civil partner can be taken into account in assessing financial eligibility of an applicant for such grants. This is in line with other means-tested benefits (see **Chapter 10**).

12.5.2 Secure tenant's compensation for improvements

Section 99B of the Housing Act 1985 gives a secure tenant the right to be compensated for improvements carried out with the landlord's consent. This payment is made at the end of the tenancy and will be paid either to the original tenant, or to a person who has succeeded to the tenancy or to whom the tenancy was assigned. Section 101 of the Housing Act 1985 provides that the tenant's rent will not be increased on account of improvements carried out by the tenant. These provisions have been amended to provide that someone who is assigned the tenancy under a property adjustment order under the CPA 2004 will qualify to receive the compensation.

12.5.3 Assistance for owners of defective housing

Part 16 of the Housing Act 1996 establishes a scheme to compensate certain individuals who purchased from public sector authorities system-built housing which is defective and as a result is substantially reduced in value. Where under the scheme the property is purchased by a registered social landlord, a secure tenancy must be granted to the person who used to be the secure tenant, or to that person's spouse. This entitlement is now extended to civil partners, former or surviving civil partners.

12.5.4   Allocations of housing by local authorities

Part 6 of the Housing Act 1996 sets out the requirements that a local authority must meet when allocating housing. The Housing Act 1996, s.160 provides the definition for an 'allocation'. Where a secure or introductory tenancy passes to someone in pursuance of a property adjustment order under the CPA 2004 this is not an allocation and therefore is not governed by Part 6 of the Housing Act 1996.

12.5.5   Homelessness

Part 7 of the Housing Act 1996 sets out the duties of local housing authorities to the homeless. A person counts as homeless if that person has accommodation, but it is not reasonable for him or her to continue to occupy that accommodation. The Housing Act 1996, s.177 provides that it will not be reasonable for someone to continue to occupy accommodation if it is probable that occupation will lead to domestic violence. The definition of domestic violence means violence from an associated person, and this definition in the Housing Act 1996, s.178 has been amended by the CPA 2004 to include violence from a civil partner or former civil partner, and someone the person is or was living with as if they were civil partners. The definition of 'relatives' who are associated persons has also been amended to include family members of the civil partner.

CHAPTER 13

Wills, intestacy and tax planning

Julian Washington

13.1 INTRODUCTION

With the advent of civil partnership, advisers need to revisit financial and estate planning with their clients. The law of succession (notably wills and intestacy) is revised along with the whole of the tax code.

Advisers need to carry out a thorough review of the wills of clients who have decided to register as civil partners and to consider tax and financial planning with them. The key points to remember are that:

- existing wills are revoked automatically upon registration (**13.2.1**);
- on drafting trusts for any client, practitioners should consider the inclusion of civil partners as beneficiaries since they are not automatically included within the term 'spouse' (see **13.2.6**);
- the intestacy rules now apply to civil partners in the same way as they do to spouses (**13.3**);
- registration as civil partners means that an entirely different tax regime applies (**13.4**);
- most of the tax consequences of registration are beneficial to civil partners (especially in the realm of inheritance tax) but some of the tax consequences are detrimental to civil partners (such as the limit on principal private residence exemption for capital gains tax) (see **13.4.2**);
- civil partners who have been receiving benefits or tax credits are likely to be financially worse off after 5 December 2005 (see **Chapter 10**).

Before civil partnership, the law was largely blind to same-sex relationships. Among the most difficult problems which resulted from this were the inheritance tax charge on the death of a partner and the failure of the intestacy rules to recognise the survivor. These problems can now be consigned to history for those couples who choose to register under the new law.

In the writer's experience as a practitioner, same-sex couples often seem to be better informed about financial and estate planning than opposite-sex cohabitants. Many unmarried opposite-sex partners make the mistake of believing that they acquire the status of 'common law spouses'. Because of this too many of them assume that they will be protected by the law if they separate or when one partner dies. Same-sex couples have tended not to fall into this trap; they are more likely to have realised the need to seek advice in connection with making a will and to realise that the impact of tax (especially inheritance tax) should be taken into account. As a result, it is to be expected that this is the area of law where civil partners and those who are planning to register are most likely to seek advice, at least in the early years of the CPA 2004.

13.2 WILLS

Practitioners will be aware of the general rule that marriage revokes a will. That is to say, a will in existence when the testator marries will be revoked by that marriage unless it has been specifically drafted to achieve a different result. These rules are found in the Wills Act 1837 and the same treatment is extended to civil partnership (CPA 2004, Sched.4, Part 1).

13.2.1 Wills revoked by registration

The new s.18B(1) inserted into the Wills Act 1837 by the CPA 2004 makes it clear that the same general rule applies:

> . . . a will is revoked by the formation of a civil partnership between the testator and another person.

The exceptions to this rule are:

- where a will is expressly made in expectation of future registration;
- where particular clauses in a will are included in expectation of future registration; and
- in the case of certain powers of appointment exercised by will.

Before examining these exceptions, note that, if the civil partnership is a recognised overseas relationship under Chapter 2 of Part 5 of the CPA 2004, it is deemed to start on 5 December 2005 (s.215(2) and (3)). However, this does not have the effect of revoking any existing will (see the Civil Partnership (Treatment of Overseas Relationships (No.2) Order 2005, SI 2005/3284, para.2; see **8.4.3** for more details and an example).

Wills in expectation of registration

Where certain conditions are satisfied, a will which on its face contemplates the future formation of a civil partnership by the testator is not revoked by the subsequent registration of that partnership. The conditions (set out in the Wills Act 1837, s.18B(3)) are that it must be apparent from the will that:

- at the date of execution the testator was expecting to form a civil partnership with a particular person; and
- the testator intended that the will would not be revoked by the formation of that partnership.

An example of a suitable provision in a will would be:

> THIS is the last will of me ADAM BROWN of 1 Blackacre Lane London by which I REVOKE all previous wills and testamentary dispositions and I DECLARE that at the date of this will I am expecting to form a civil partnership with COLIN DAVIES of 2 Greenacre Road London and I intend that this will shall not be revoked by the registration of the said civil partnership

Gifts in expectation of registration

The new s.18B(4)–(6) of the Wills Act 1837 approaches this issue more narrowly. Rather than dealing with the will in its entirety, these provisions focus on a particular gift or 'disposition' in a will and prevent its revocation by a subsequent civil partnership registration. Again the conditions are that:

- at the date of execution the testator was expecting to form a civil partnership with a particular person; and
- the testator intended that that disposition would not be revoked by the formation of that partnership.

Other dispositions in such a will also take effect unless it appears from the will that the intention was to revoke them.

This approach (which is, once again, copied from the rules as they apply to marriage) has never found favour amongst draftsmen. The reason for this may be that getting married is likely to lead a testator to want to change the whole basis of a will rather than particular gifts. No doubt the same is true of wills in the context of civil partnership. In any event, it is tidier to draft the will so that the whole of it is preserved from revocation under s.18B(3) rather than to proceed on this piecemeal basis. Within the whole-will approach, there is nothing to prevent the testator also including particular dispositions which are only to have effect (or cease to have effect) if the civil partnership is registered.

Powers of appointment

Section 18B(2) of the Wills Act 1837 (as amended) preserves from revocation the exercise by will of certain powers of appointment. Of course, this is a reference to dispositive powers of appointment (where a testator has the right to dispose of trust property among a class of potential beneficiaries). Where a testator has such a power and exercises it by will, that disposition is not revoked by his subsequent registration of a civil partnership, except in one case. That is where, in default of appointment, the property subject to the power would pass to his personal representatives and form part of the testator's estate.

Other issues

As with future spouses, advisers should consider whether it is sufficient to draft wills for intending civil partners which simply come into force immediately and are then preserved from revocation. If, for whatever reason, the anticipated civil partnership registration does not take place (for example, because the couple split up) the wills would remain in force. Some clients may prefer wills which have effect only upon registration (i.e. which are conditional upon civil partnership). On the other hand, a conditional will produces an unfortunate result if the relationship ends, not because of a separation, but because of the untimely death of one of the partners before they have registered. The survivor in such a case would be disinherited.

For those couples who have already made wills in each other's favour in the past, the practical solution may be to dispense with the Wills Act protections described above and to leave the old wills in place until the civil partnership is registered. The partners should have their new wills ready to sign immediately afterwards. Before legally recognised civil partnerships, one of the ways in which some couples added a degree of legal weight to their otherwise symbolic commitment ceremonies was by the signing of wills, sometimes as part of the ceremony itself. This approach also has something to commend it under the new regime.

13.2.2 Effect of dissolution or annulment

The effect of the dissolution or annulment of a civil partnership on a will mirrors the effect of divorce or annulment in the context of marriage. The Civil Partnership Act 2004 has added a new s.18C to the Wills Act 1837 which makes it clear that, unless a will is drafted to the contrary, the former civil partner is to be treated as if he or she had predeceased. Specifically:

- any appointment of executors or trustees,
- any conferring of a power of appointment, and
- any testamentary gift to the former civil partner

are construed as if the former civil partner had died on the date of the dissolution or annulment (Wills Act 1837, s.18C(2)). These rules apply to any decree of dissolution or nullity whether made by a court in England and Wales or by a foreign court if it is recognised here under the provisions of Part 5, Chapter 3 of the CPA 2004 (see **8.6**). As one would expect, nothing in s.18C of the Wills Act 1837 prevents a disinherited former civil partner from bringing a claim under the Inheritance (Provision for Family and Dependants) Act 1975 (Wills Act 1837, s.18C(3), see **6.5**).

13.2.3 Witnesses

Practitioners will be familiar with the rule that a beneficiary's gift does not take effect if the beneficiary or his or her spouse acts as a witness to the testator's signature. The same applies if it is the beneficiary's civil partner who witnesses a will (Wills Act 1837, s.15 is now to be so construed).

The only exception to this is in the rare case where the execution of the will would still have been valid without the offending witness. Consider the following example.

Example 13.1

Jack's will includes a pecuniary legacy of £10,000 to Angela. He signs the will in the presence of John, Andrew and Rachel. All three sign as attesting witnesses but Rachel is Angela's civil partner. In this case Angela's legacy is not forfeited because Rachel's signature as a witness was not required for the will to be executed validly.

The decision in *Thorpe* v. *Bestwick* (1881) 6 QBD 311 made it clear that the restrictions upon beneficiary-witnesses do not apply retrospectively. That case decided that if, at the date of execution, the witness in question was not the spouse of a beneficiary then all was well. It did not matter that the witness subsequently married a beneficiary. The rationale here was that the rule that a will 'speaks from (the date of) death' applies to that property which is subject to the will (Wills Act 1837, s. 24) but not to the persons entitled to it. In other words, the moment at which the beneficiary-witness restriction is relevant is not the date of death but the time that the signing and witnessing takes place.

This principle applies equally to civil partnership. Thus if X has acted as witness to the will of Y, a gift to Z will not be forfeited on Y's death if X and Z have registered as civil partners at some point after the date on which the will was executed. Note also that if the civil partnership is an overseas relationship recognised under Chapter 2 of Part 5 of the CPA 2004 (see **8.4.4**), the deeming provisions of s.215(2) mean that the civil partnership starts on 5 December 2005. As a result any witnessing before that date by the same-sex spouse or registered partner in an overseas relationship is thought not to make a gift to their civil partner ineffective. However, for certainty's sake it is preferable to recommend completely independent witnesses and avoid any potential problem.

13.2.4   Other Wills Act provisions

Unlike in the case of a civil partner of a beneficiary, the witnessing of a will by the civil partner of a creditor of the testator has no effect on the creditor's position (see Wills Act 1837, s.16 as amended by CPA 2004, Sched.4, para.4).

If a will includes conflicting provisions such that the same property is the subject of a gift giving an absolute interest to the surviving civil partner and another gift to the testator's issue, the effect of CPA 2004, Sched.4, para.5 is that the absolute gift to the civil partner prevails.

13.2.5   Wills and tax planning

Civil partners are to be taxed in the same way as spouses (see **13.4** below). Therefore, practitioners should consider the same tax planning techniques when advising civil partners on their wills and on estate planning as they employ with married couples.

13.2.6   General points regarding wills and trusts

Although many of the issues when drafting wills or settlements are the same as for spouses, some different considerations are likely to apply to civil partners. One example is the subject of children. Although many civil partners have children, whether as a result of a previous opposite-sex relationship, by adoption or by other means (see **7.1.2**), a large number – probably the majority – do not. Where there are no children who inherit, the question arises of how to deal with the estate when both partners have died. Many may ultimately want to benefit their birth families and this means that, after the second death, the combined estate will need to be gifted to the families of both partners. That could be an equal division between the two families or it could be unequal, to reflect the value of the assets which each partner has contributed to their combined wealth.

A similar issue arises where one or both partners have children from a previous (opposite-sex) relationship or marriage who were never brought up by the other partner but whom the parent wants ultimately to benefit. Whatever is decided, it is essential that the division is agreed and that the same gifts are included in each will. This will ensure that, regardless of the order in which the partners die, their wishes for each family are honoured. Wills such as these are likely to be drafted so that each is the mirror image of the other, but they will not be mutual wills in the strict sense. Strictly mutual wills are those made pursuant to an explicit agreement to make wills in terms that one party will not revoke his or her will without the other's consent. In the absence of such an agreement it will always open to the surviving partner to make a new will after the first death. If this is a concern, practitioners should consider with their clients whether to give the surviving partner, not an outright gift of the residue, but a life interest (which is a better solution than to rely on the mutual wills doctrine). Since the 2006 budget, such life interest would need to comply with the conditions for an 'immediate post-death interest' in order to avoid inheritance tax.

Practitioners should also remember that the general approach of the civil partnership legislation is to make specific amendments to specific rules so as to apply them to civil partners, usually on the same footing as spouses. There is no general provision that all references to marriage must also be deemed to include civil partnership. One consequence of this is that the term 'spouse' in any will or trust will not include civil partners (unless it is stated to do so). Advisers should keep this in mind when advising all clients and not just those for whom civil partnership is directly relevant. Consider an example.

Example 13.2

Jessica and Christopher are recently married. They have two children aged three years and 18 months respectively and they want to make new wills. Their combined assets are worth £1m and they are keen to minimise the inheritance tax on their deaths. Their solicitor advises them to include a discretionary trust in each will up to the value of the nil rate band.

When drafting the trust provisions for clients such as these, the class of discretionary beneficiaries would often extend to the surviving husband or wife, their issue and any 'spouse or former spouse widow or widower' of the issue. These words do not include civil partners. The question arises as to whether clients like Jessica and Christopher will wish to allow for the possibility of their minor children growing up and forming civil partnerships. Assuming that they do, the wording needs to be amended. Even including civil partners in the class of beneficiaries will not necessarily include the children of that family because children of same-sex relationships are often still not legally the children of both partners. One approach would be to give the trustees or executors a power to add beneficiaries. This would give the necessary flexibility to take account of future relationships arising from civil partnership but would avoid the need to address the point more thoroughly at the drafting stage. This could be particularly useful with young beneficiaries, such as Jessica's and Christopher's children in the example, where it is impossible to know whether civil partnership might be relevant for them in the future.

Another approach when drafting trusts or settlements for any client would be to include within the definitions a statement such as:

any reference to marriage (and to any status derived from marriage) is to be deemed to include civil partnership in accordance with the Civil Partnership Act 2004 (and the equivalent status derived from civil partnership).

Alternatively one might prefer to set out in full the fact that spouses and civil partners, widows/widowers and surviving civil partners, etc. are included within a class of beneficiaries.

Practitioners should note the minor amendments to the Trustee Act 1925 made by CPA 2004, Sched.27, para.5. In the Trustee Act 1925, s.31(2)(i) (setting out the statutory trusts upon reaching 18, or upon earlier marriage, for income accumulated during minority) references to 'marrying under that age' are amended to include civil partnership registration. This is not likely to be of great importance: the registration of civil partnerships by 16- and 17-year-olds will probably be as uncommon as the marriage of minors.

Finally, the Trustee Act 1925, s.33 (which creates the protective trust regime, designed to protect beneficiaries from the effects of bankruptcy) is also amended. After the principal beneficiary's life interest has come to an end, the discretionary trusts which then apply now allow for the maintenance of the principal beneficiary's civil partner on the same basis as a spouse.

13.3 INTESTACY

Historically, intestacy is one of the areas which has caused the most acute problems for cohabiting couples. The intestacy rules of course recognise marriage and blood relationships but not cohabitation, whatever its duration. Bereaved cohabitants in this situation have often had to consider making a claim under the Inheritance (Provision for Family and Dependants) Act 1975. For those same-sex couples who register as civil partners the position under the new law has improved. It goes without saying that it is always better for clients to apply their minds to the issue of succession and to execute a valid will. However, for those who fail to do so, the intestacy rules will at least make basic provision for those they leave behind. The treatment of a bereaved civil partner on intestacy exactly mirrors the treatment of a bereaved spouse. This is true not only of the right to apply for a grant of letters of administration but also, more importantly, to the entitlement to share in the intestate's estate. The amendments to the Administration of Estates Act 1925 and the other relevant statutes are set out in CPA 2004, Sched.4, Part 2 and the combined effect of these changes when a civil partner dies intestate is summarised below.

1. If the deceased did not leave issue, the surviving partner's entitlement extends to the personal chattels, a statutory legacy of £200,000 and half the residue. The rest of the estate passes to other relatives according to the usual order of priority.
2. If the deceased leaves issue, the surviving partner's entitlement is limited to the personal chattels, a legacy of £125,000 and a life interest in half the residue. The issue take the rest of the estate on the statutory trusts.

3. A surviving partner who becomes entitled to a life interest upon intestacy has the same right as a surviving spouse to convert that life interest into a capital sum (see Administration of Estates Act 1925, s.47A).

4. The surviving partner also has the same rights as a spouse to acquire the deceased's interest in their home as part of the entitlement on intestacy (see Intestate Estates Act 1952, Sched.2).

Practitioners should refer to any of the standard works on the administration of estates for more detailed treatment of these rules.

One point to bear in mind in the context of intestate civil partners is that, when it comes to children, it is only the deceased's own children (if any) who benefit from the statutory provision on intestacy. Stepchildren do not inherit unless they have been adopted. This serves as another reminder that the making of wills is absolutely essential for same-sex couples, especially where a bespoke division between the surviving partner, children and/or different sides of the family is what the circumstances demand. Of course it may be possible to use a deed of variation to re-order the statutory division of an estate after the event. Where this is not possible or practical (for example because minor children are involved), as a last resort it may still be appropriate to consider a claim under the Inheritance (Provision for Family and Dependants) Act 1975 (see **6.5**).

13.4   TAX

Civil partners are taxed in the same way as spouses. Section 103 of the Finance Act 2005 gave the Treasury power to make changes to existing tax legislation to put this into effect. The amendments were then set out in the Tax and Civil Partnership Regulations 2005, SI 2005/3229 (and the Tax and Civil Partnership (No.2) Regulations 2005, SI 2005/3230 which dealt with changes to secondary legislation). The change in tax status for those couples who register as civil partners is highly significant. Before registration, cohabiting couples are taxed as two single people; none of the fiscal consequences of marriage apply to unregistered cohabitants. This has caused a good deal of hardship, especially in the context of the inheritance tax charge on the death of a partner (which often leaves the survivor with a burdensome tax bill). The new inheritance tax treatment of civil partners provides an answer to that problem for those couples who register. However, not all of the fiscal consequences of civil partnership registration are advantageous: consider the principal private residence exemption for capital gains tax which is examined below. An overview of the major taxes as they apply to civil partners follows.

13.4.1 Inheritance tax

Exemption for civil partners

Transfers between civil partners, whether on death or during lifetime, are generally exempt from inheritance tax (IHT) in the same way as transfers between spouses (Inheritance Tax Act 1984, s.18 as amended). Thus, for example, relief is unrestricted between couples who share the same domicile, but restricted to £55,000 where the transferor-partner is UK domiciled but the transferee-partner is not.

Other exemptions

There is an exemption for gifts in consideration of the registration of a civil partnership (up to a limit of £5,000 for a parent, £2,500 for a grandparent and £1,000 for others) under the Inheritance Tax Act 1984, s. 22 as amended.

Inheritance tax planning

For many same-sex couples, especially older couples, the absence of IHT relief on transfers between them may be a significant factor influencing their decision as to whether or not to form a civil partnership. Just as one would never advise a heterosexual couple to get married solely for tax reasons, so civil partnership should not be seen in isolation as an IHT-saving device. However, other things being equal, where IHT is a concern, the tax exemption (especially on the death of a partner) is compelling.

In terms of testamentary IHT planning, advisers need to consider exactly the same techniques that they employ for spouses. For example:

1. Advisers should ensure, so far as possible, that each estate has sufficient assets (perhaps by severing the joint tenancies of assets so held) to use up both nil rate bands.
2. Wills should be drafted to exploit the nil rate band by including a gift up to the value of the nil rate band (£275,000 for 2005/06; £285,000 for 2006/07 and £300,000 for 2007/08) to chargeable beneficiaries.
3. The nil rate band provision can take the form of an outright gift, e.g. to any children of the couple, provided that each partner is sufficiently affluent to forgo that sum when the other dies. In other cases, advisers should consider a nil rate band trust. Prior to the 2006 budget it was standard practice to use a discretionary trust. The class of discretionary beneficiaries was drafted to include the surviving partner as well as other beneficiaries to give maximum flexibility. This allowed the executors to consider all the circumstances after the death so as to determine how best to exploit the nil rate band. It will now be possible to use other structures such as a flexible life interest trust for the survivor (subject to an over-

riding power of appointment) which would not qualify as an 'immediate post-death interest'. Practitioners will need to review this in light of the Finance (No.2) Act 2006 when it is passed.

13.4.2   Capital gains tax

Transfers between civil partners

Just as husbands and wives have the advantage that they can generally transfer assets between them without triggering a capital gains tax (CGT) charge, so civil partners enjoy the same tax treatment (Taxation of Chargeable Gains Act 1992, s.58 as amended). Such transfers are on a no-gain-no-loss basis, which means that the donee acquires the asset at the donor's base cost and inherits his period of ownership. In other words, when the donee ultimately disposes of the asset, the donee is treated as if he or she had acquired it for the cost and at the time that the donee's civil partner originally acquired it; the donee then pays CGT accordingly.

The position is different where civil partners no longer cohabit. Where they are formally separated (by a court or by deed) or where they are in fact separated and the separation is likely to be permanent, the no-gain-no-loss rule does not apply. Any transfer between them is treated as if it were a disposal at the then market value at that time and a chargeable gain (or a loss) may be the result.

Other exemptions

Principal private residence exemption is an area which needs to be considered carefully by those who are advising couples who plan to register a civil partnership. At present, couples who cohabit without being registered are taxed as two single people. There is one significant advantage of this, namely, that if both partners own a property, they may each be able to claim exemption so that both properties are covered. Upon registering a civil partnership this advantage is lost because like spouses civil partners can for these purposes have only a single residence between them whilst they remain civil partners and cohabit (Taxation of Chargeable Gains Act 1992, s.222(6) as amended).

Capital gains tax planning

Partners should consider CGT planning even before civil partnership registration. For example, if the couple between them own more than one property and face the loss of one of their principal private residence exemption claims (as above) they should consider making a CGT disposal whilst they both still have the relief. The simplest option is, of course, to sell one of the properties, realise the gain and be protected by the exemption. Prior to the

2006 budget, an alternative, if they did not want to sell the property, was for it to be transferred by the owner into an interest-in-possession settlement for himself. The gift to the settlement was to be a disposal and, again, assuming exemption was available, there would be no charge to tax. In other words, the historic gain between the base cost and the deemed market value at the disposal was covered by the exemption. This did not avoid a tax charge in the future, but it did mean that any future tax liability was based only on the gain since the gift to the settlement. Unfortunately, since the 2006 budget, the creation of such a trust is likely to lead to an immediate IHT charge (unless the value of the property is within the nil rate band). There will also be further charges every 10 years.

In some circumstances, partners may wish to consider selling the property and buying a replacement in the same area (for example, if they have a second home in a favoured location which they want to continue to use for a period of time). Of course, they would have to take into account the costs of sale but, because of the way in which CGT is calculated, a sale and replacement purchase may be less expensive than simply delaying the sale until they are finally ready to leave the area. The graph below gives an example of a property that has risen in value significantly in the five years since it was bought in 2000. After five years (in 2005) the couple register as civil partners. For the subsequent period of their ownership they have no claim for principal private residence exemption for this property. The couple would like to retain the property for a further five years but think that the housing market is going to be flat. In such circumstances, the later the sale, the more tax they would have to pay because the increase in value from the date of acquisition to the date of disposal is averaged out across the whole of the period of ownership (see **figure 13.1**).

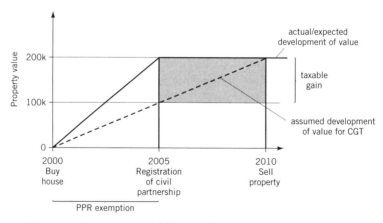

Figure 13.1 Property values and CGT planning

Other tax planning, for example, taking advantage of the no-gain-no-loss rule can only be done after the creation of the civil partnership. Consider these possibilities:

1. CGT is charged at the taxpayer's marginal income tax rate. Where one partner is a higher rate tax payer but the other is a basic rate tax payer it may be advantageous to transfer assets from the former to the latter so that, when a disposal is made, the applicable rate of CGT is lower.
2. If one partner has already used (or is likely to use) his or her annual CGT allowance, but the other partner's allowance is still available, consider a transfer of assets between them to utilise both annual allowances fully.
3. If one partner has unused losses, but the other is set to make chargeable gains, a transfer of assets from the partner who is set to make gains to the one with unused losses will reduce the possibility of a charge.

However, when transferring assets with a view to a subsequent disposal (to take advantage of a partner's lower tax rates), practitioners should consider the application of the anti-avoidance rule articulated in *Furniss* v. *Dawson* [1984] STC 153: if what is undertaken is a pre-ordained series of steps with no purpose other than the avoidance of tax, HMRC is likely to disregard it. The ultimate disposal would then be taxed as if it had been a disposal by the original owner, rather than by the recipient civil partner with the lower tax rate. Having this in mind, it is sensible to ensure that the subsequent disposal does not follow too quickly on from the transfer between the partners (and that there is no identifiable purchaser at the time of the original transfer).

Civil partners, like spouses, are 'connected persons'. They are also 'connected' for these purposes to their siblings, ancestors and descendants (and to each other's). Transactions between connected persons are treated for CGT as if they had not been at arm's length so that the acquisition and disposal are deemed to be at market value; the tax is calculated accordingly. Therefore, where such a transfer is contemplated it would be wise to organise it prior to civil partnership registration if this is possible (see Taxation of Chargeable Gains Act 1992, s.18).

13.4.3 Income tax

Civil partners are assessed independently for income tax and there is no major advantage upon registering. Advisers should note, however, that the remnant of the married couple's allowance (which is only available to married couples where one of the spouses was born before 6 April 1935) has also been made available to civil partners who meet the same criterion (Income and Corporation Taxes Act 1988, s.257A). This benefits a small number of elderly couples. The allowance stands at £6,065 for 2006/07 and is limited to 10 per cent, thus worth a maximum of £606.50.

This retention of a relic of past income tax relief in the civil partnership regime nicely illustrates the point that although civil partnership is, legally, a quite distinct entity from marriage, it has been designed to be as close to marriage as possible.

Income tax planning

Where one partner is a higher rate tax payer and the other is not, the partners may be able to take advantage of the CGT rules discussed above to transfer income-producing assets between them. The future income from the asset will then be taxable at the recipient-partner's lower income tax rate (if it is not covered by the personal allowance). See also **13.4.5** for the anti-avoidance rules for settlor-interested trusts.

13.4.4 Stamp duty land tax

There is no exemption from stamp duty land tax (SDLT) for transfers between civil partners (although no SDLT is payable on gifts (Finance Act 2003, Sched.3, para.1). There are however exemptions for transactions made in pursuance of court orders made on the granting of (or at any time after the granting of) a decree of dissolution, annulment or separation orders (Finance Act 2003, Sched.3, para.3A). The para.3A exemption also extends to any agreement made in contemplation of or in connection with a dissolution, annulment or the making of a separation order (Sched.3, para.3A(d)).

13.4.5 Settlor-interested trusts

In the case of trusts where the intention is not to benefit the settlor (nor the settlor's spouse or civil partner) it is important to exclude these people from benefit altogether. A trust which does not do this is described as 'settlor-interested' and a UK resident, settlor-interested trust is subject to the CGT anti-avoidance rules in the Taxation of Chargeable Gains Act 1992, s.77 (as to be amended by Finance (No.2) Act 2006) and the equivalent income tax rules (in particular, the Income Tax (Trading and other Income) Act 2005, s.619).

Broadly, the effect of these provisions is that income and gains arising in such a trust are assessed, not on the trustees, but on the settlor personally. There had been a concern that pre-existing trusts might automatically become settlor-interested when the CPA 2004 came into force on 5 December 2004. The thinking was that such trusts could be caught by the rules because they would not have excluded civil partners from benefit and they may, for example, give the trustees power to add beneficiaries.

However, as is the case with spouses, the rules have not been extended to 'a person of whom the settlor is not for the time being as civil partner but of whom he may later be a civil partner' (Taxation of Chargeable Gains Act 1992, s.77(3)(ab); and see the Income Tax (Trading and other Income) Act 2005, s.625(4)(d) for the equivalent income tax rules). This means that trusts that existed before 5 December 2005 are not caught for either CGT or income tax purposes unless and until the settlor registers a civil partnership.

For trusts created after 5 December 2005, civil partners should routinely be excluded from benefit in the same way as spouses. This applies whether the settlor is married or single; homosexual or heterosexual. Naturally, these beneficiaries should not be excluded if the intention is indeed to create a trust for their benefit, notwithstanding the tax consequences.

13.4.6 Close companies

A 'close' company, broadly speaking, is one which is controlled either by:

- five or fewer 'participators' (including 'associates' of participators) or by
- any number of participators who are directors (see Income and Corporation Taxes Act 1988, s.417).

Special tax rules apply to close companies. Those advising in this area must be aware of the consequences of the introduction of civil partnership and of the amendments to the relevant tax legislation. For example, the definition of an 'associate' in s.417 of the Income and Corporation Taxes Act 1988 includes a 'relative' and this term has been redefined to include a civil partner. As a result, it might be the case that where two shareholders of a company register a civil partnership (thereby becoming 'associates') they might cause the company to become close with unintended consequences for all the shareholders.

Another problem might arise where a couple have interests in two different private companies which are commercially associated businesses. The registration of a civil partnership by the couple may mean that the two companies have to be assessed together for corporation tax purposes. This could mean that companies which, prior to the creation of the civil partnership, had qualified for the lower, small companies' rate of tax in the Income and Corporation Taxes Act 1988, s.13, cease to do so.

13.5 CONCLUSION

Advisers will need to review thoroughly the wills of those clients who have decided to register as civil partners and should consider tax and financial planning with them. To recap, the key points to remember are that:

- existing wills (made prior to the advent of civil partnership) are revoked automatically upon registration;

- the intestacy rules now apply to civil partners in the same way as they do to spouses;
- registration as civil partners means that an entirely different tax regime applies;
- most of the tax consequences of registration are beneficial to civil partners (especially in the realm of inheritance tax); but
- some of the tax consequences are detrimental to civil partners (such as the limit on principal private residence exemption for capital gains tax).

The problems which same sex-couples have traditionally faced in these areas are now a thing of the past for registered civil partners. Of course, advisers should not forget that unregistered couples (and unmarried, opposite-sex cohabitants) continue to face the same difficulties, in particular in the area of tax and intestate estates.

CHAPTER 14

Other issues

There are of course a host of other issues that could be mentioned in this book and a long list of amended legislation and common law rules. Some have been amended by the CPA 2004 itself and others by subsequent statutory instruments. It would be dreary to list them all and probably of little use to the practitioner because any standard update to legislation in a particular field will merely find the words 'or civil partner' added after 'spouse' in the relevant place (or a similar amendment). If in doubt, a thorough search of the material in the CD-ROM accompanying this book or the Government's legislation website (**www.opsi.gov.uk**) should provide the answer. It is of course possible that some statute, statutory instrument or common law rule has been overlooked, in which case the relevant Government department should be alerted and may provide the answer or remedy the oversight.

This chapter will look briefly at three areas:

- mental capacity and 'next-of-kin' status;
- domestic violence; and
- employment.

14.1 MENTAL CAPACITY AND 'NEXT-OF-KIN' STATUS

The current law will change when the Mental Capacity Act 2005 (MCA 2005) comes into force. This section is therefore confined to a brief overview of the current and the new law. Detailed information about the new law can be found in Greaney, Morris and Taylor *Mental Capacity Act 2005 – A Guide to the New Law* (Law Society Publishing, 2005).

Neither the existing nor the new law will give civil partners any automatic rights in this area and therefore anyone who wishes their civil partner to make decisions in case of mental incapacity should make the necessary formal appointments and decisions.

14.1.1 The existing law

Mental capacity

At the moment anyone can make an enduring power of attorney under the Enduring Powers of Attorney Act 1985 to appoint someone else to look after their finances in case of mental incapacity. Civil partnership is treated in the same way as marriage for the Enduring Powers of Attorney Act 1985 (CPA 2004, Sched.27, paras.106–108). If an individual has not made an enduring power of attorney, the Court of Protection can appoint someone to manage their finances. There is no precedence between spouses or cohabitants here and same-sex cohabitants and civil partners should be treated by the court in the same way as spouses and opposite-sex cohabitants.

Medical treatment and the next of kin

There is no legal foundation to the 'next-of-kin' status and this is effectively a matter for each hospital. This is of course deeply unsatisfactory as it can play to common prejudices or downright hostility against lesbians and gay men. The person who is regarded as the next of kin may ultimately depend on what the patient filled in when he or she completed the hospital admission form. However, there should be no discrimination on grounds of sexual orientation and hospitals should therefore regard a civil partner as the next of kin rather than a parent or relative. Whether this is going to happen in practice is a different question, at least until the Equality Act 2006 comes into force for sexual orientation.

People have made advance decisions about medical treatment by way of a 'living will' in written form. There is no statutory footing for this, but living wills have been endorsed by the courts (*HE* v. *A Hospital NHS Trust* [2003] 2 FLR 408). Such advance directives do not, however, need to be in written form and can be revoked orally even if made in writing.

14.1.2 The new law

Mental capacity

Under the MCA 2005 any person can make a new form of power of attorney, a 'lasting power of attorney', to appoint someone to look after their finances and/or their welfare. Different people can be appointed for each aspect. All lasting powers of attorney need to be registered with the Court of Protection. If no lasting power of attorney has been made and registered, the Court of Protection may appoint a 'deputy' to look after the person's finances and/or welfare and there is no prescribed group of people to choose from (MCA 2005, ss.15–21). The main novelty in the new law is that the question of whether someone has capacity is looked at in relation to the specific decision in question, and so people can have capacity in one area but not in another (MCA 2005, s.2(1)).

Medical treatment

Under the MCA 2005 a lasting power of attorney may confer on the attorney the power to make decisions about medical treatment. If this is to include decisions about life-saving treatment, it must be expressly stated. Apart from the power of attorney, people can make advance decisions about medical including life-saving treatment (MCA 2005, ss.24–26), giving 'living wills' a statutory footing. There are requirements about the formality of the decision, but it can be revoked informally.

The position on next-of-kin status as such has not changed, but if a same-sex partner or civil partner has been appointed to make welfare decisions under a lasting power of attorney, this will be binding on the hospital.

14.2 PROTECTION FROM HARASSMENT AND VIOLENCE AND THE HOME

Protection from harassment and violence and the occupation of the family home are mainly regulated by Part 4 of the Family Law Act 1996 (FLA 1996). In the past, same-sex couples did not have the same protection as opposite-sex couples, and the definition of cohabitant excluded them. As a result, a member of a same-sex couple could only apply for an order that the violent partner must leave the home if the victim was a joint owner or joint rental tenant of the home. All this has now changed by amendments made by the Domestic Violence, Crime and Victims Act 2004 and:

- cohabitants include same-sex partners, who now have the same rights to protection from harassment and to apply for occupation orders as spouses and civil partners;
- civil partners have the same rights as spouses to occupy the family home.

The Domestic Violence, Crime and Victims Act 2004 made other changes to the law in this area including making a breach of a non-molestation order a criminal offence. A detailed analysis of the provisions goes beyond the scope of this book and readers are referred to Claire Bessant *Domestic Violence, Crime and Victims Act 2004 – A Guide to the New Law* (Law Society Publishing, 2005).

The main changes for people in same-sex couples are set out below.

14.2.1 Definition of cohabitant

The Domestic Violence, Crime and Victims Act 2004, s.58(1) and Sched.10, para.40 amended the definition in FLA 1996, s.62 as follows:

> two persons who, although not married to each other, are living together as husband and wife or (if of the same sex) in an equivalent relationship.

This change did not come into force until 5 December 2005. There was really no reason for the delay and one can only hope that no hardship was suffered as a result. The Civil Partnership Act 2004, Sched.9, para.13 was supposed to amend this further to read:

> two persons who are neither married to each other nor civil partners of each other but are living together as husband or wife or as if they were civil partners.

This Part of the CPA 2004 has not come into force. The reason may be that the Government discovered the hollowness of the term 'living as if they were civil partners' (see **1.4.8**).

The consequence of the inclusion of same-sex couples within the definition of cohabitants means that they can now apply for:

- occupation orders under FLA 1996, ss.33, 36 or 38; and
- transfers of tenancies under FLA 1996, Sched.7.

Occupation orders can regulate who lives in the home or who lives in which part of the home, they can order one cohabitant to let the other into the home and they can exclude a cohabitant from the home. Under FLA 1996, s.40 the court can also order who is to pay the rent or mortgage and the bills, and order one party to make periodical payments to the other for such outgoings. However, there seems no procedure to enforce such orders under s.40. The power to transfer tenancies under Sched.7 may not, on the face of it, seem very valuable especially if a private landlord could terminate the tenancy after a short time or a social landlord would grant a new tenancy to either partner. However, with the growing shortage of social housing in this country, a housing association or public sector tenancy is hard to come by and a transfer is therefore extremely valuable as these rents are lower than market rents in the private sector. In addition, certain tenants in the public sector have the right to buy their homes at a discount and this way a transferred tenancy can be financially advantageous if the right to buy is exercised and the property sold subsequently (see also **Chapter 12**). The danger is, however, that a spiteful former spouse or cohabitant who has moved out simply serves notice to quit and ends the tenancy so that there is nothing to transfer, as in the case of *Wandsworth London Borough Council* v. *Osei-Bonsu* [1999] 1 FLR 276, CA.

14.2.2   Home rights

Part 1 of Sched.9 to the CPA 2004 amends FLA 1996 to make what were previously 'matrimonial home rights' available to civil partners. They are now called 'home rights' for spouses and civil partners. These rights mean that a spouse or civil partner who is not the owner or tenant of his or her home cannot be evicted or excluded from the home except by order of the court under FLA 1996, s.33 (FLA 1996, s.30(2)(a)). If a property that one spouse or civil partner owns or rents is not the home of the other, the other can with the permission of the court move in and live there (FLA 1996, s.30(2)(b)). If the property is registered land, the rights can be registered at the Land Registry without a fee on form HR1, which is available to download from the Land Registry website (**www.landregistry.gov.uk**). The other civil partner will be notified by the Land Registry in the post. Similar provision exists for unregistered land. The registration will warn any purchaser or lender that the civil partner has a charge on the property that takes priority over a sale or a subsequent charge. In practice this means that the property cannot be sold or mortgaged, at least not on the open market. Home rights end on the final order of dissolution or nullity unless an application to the court extends them under FLA 1996, s.33(5).

14.2.3   Non-molestation orders – protection from harassment

Protection from harassment is referred to as 'non-molestation' although many clients assume that 'molestation' only includes sexual harassment when in fact it includes all forms of harassment. The Domestic Violence, Crime and Victims Act 2004 has now made a breach of a non-molestation order under FLA 1986, s.42 a criminal offence (new s.42A). The maximum penalty is five years' imprisonment or a fine or both. The offence is an 'arrestable' offence and no separate power of arrest is required. As a result the police can and should deal with breaches of non-molestation orders by arresting and charging the offender. If in a particular case the police refuse to do so (for example as a result of discrimination on the ground of the victim's sexual orientation), the victim can still bring his or her own proceedings for contempt of court.

14.3   EMPLOYMENT

Discrimination on the grounds of sexual orientation was made unlawful as a result of the implementation of an EU Directive by the Employment Equality (Sexual Orientation) Regulations 2003, SI 2003/1661. These have now been amended by the Civil Partnership Act 2004 (Amendments to Subordinate Legislation) Order 2005, SI 2005/2114 to make it unlawful to discriminate between a married employee and one who is in a civil partnership (SI 2005/ 2114, Sched.17, para.7 inserting reg.3(3)):

> For the purposes of paragraph (2), in a comparison of B's case with that of another person the fact that one of the persons (whether or not B) is a civil partner while the other is married shall not be treated as a material difference between their respective circumstances.

However, this does not apply to pension rights for years of service before the CPA 2004 came into force (amended reg.25, see **9.5**).

The Sex Discrimination Act 1975 is amended by the CPA 2005, s.251 to include civil partners in the provision against discrimination on marital status.

Bibliography

BOOKS

Bessant, Claire *Domestic Violence, Crime and Victims Act 2004 – A Guide to the New Law* (Law Society Publishing, 2005)

Boele-Woelki, Katharina and Fuchs, Angelika (eds.) *Legal Recognition of Same-Sex Couples in Europe* (Intersentia, 2003)

Burns, C, Marshall, S, McNab, C, Whinnom, A, Whittle, S *Recognising the Identity and Rights of Transsexual and Transgender People in the United Kingdom: A Report for the UK Government Interdepartmental Working Group On Transsexual Issues* (Press For Change, 1999)

Davison, David *Pensions and Marriage Breakdown* (Law Society Publishing, 2005)

Dicey and Morris on the Conflict of Laws, 13th Edn (Sweet & Maxwell, 2000)

Greaney, Nicola, Morris, Fenella and Taylor, Beverley *Mental Capacity Act 2005 – A Guide to the New Law* (Law Society Publishing, 2005)

Hammonds *Pensions Act 2004* (Law Society Publishing, 2005)

Harper, Mark, Downs, Martin, Wilson, Gerald and Landells, Katharine, *Civil Partnerships: The New Law* (Jordan Publishing, 2005)

Puttick, Keith *Child Support Law: Parents, the CSA and the Courts* (EMIS 2003)

Puttick, Keith *Welfare Benefits Law and Practice* 9th Edn (EMIS, 2006)

Rayden and Jackson on Divorce and Family Matters, 17th Edn (Butterworths, 1997)

Whittle, S *Respect and Equality: Transsexual and Transgender Rights* (Cavendish Publishing, 2002)

Whittle, S *The Transgender Debate: The Crisis Surrounding Gender Identity* (South Street Press, 2000)

OTHER DOCUMENTS AND ARTICLES

Content of Civil Marriage Ceremonies – A consultation document on proposed changes to regulation and guidance to registration officers, General Register Office, June 2005

CPAG *Welfare Benefits and Tax Credits Handbook*

Doerfel, J, Marshall, S, Playdon, Z-J, Whinnom, A, Whittle, S *Transsexual People in the Workplace: A Code of Practice* (Press For Change, 1998)

DWP Consultation Document, *Occupational and Personal Pensions: the Civil Partnership (Amendment of Provisions Relating to Contracted-Out Occupational and Appropriate Personal Pension Schemes) (Surviving Civil Partners) Order 2005* (March 2005)

Gender Recognition Panel *Guidance for Married People or those in Civil Partnerships* (updated May 2005)

Guide NP46, Pension Service (available at **www.dwp.gov.uk**)

Judicial Studies Board Equal Treatment Bench Book (esp. chapter 7) (available at **www.jsboard.co.uk**)

Precedents for Consent Orders, 7th Edn (Resolution, 2005)

Review of the Human Fertilisation and Embryology Act, Government Consultation which closed on 25 November 2005

Whittle, S 'New confidentiality responsibilities to transsexual people', *Community Care* (forthcoming)

Whittle, S 'New HR obligations for transsexual people', *Personnel Today*, 6 April 2005

Whittle, S 'New occupational health responsibilities to transsexual people', *Occupational Health*, 1 August 2005

Whittle, S 'The Gender Recognition Act 2004', *Diversity Exchange* (forthcoming)

Whittle, S 'The Gender Recognition Act 2004', *Childright: Journal of Law and Policy affecting Children and Young People* (October 2004), cr210, pp.10–11

Whittle, S 'The Gender Recognition Act 2004: technical update', *Workplace Law* (forthcoming)

Women and Equality Unit (WEU) *Civil Partnership: A framework for the legal recognition of same-sex couples* (June 2003)

Women and Equality Unit (WEU) *Responses to Civil Partnership: A Framework for the Legal Recognition of Same-Sex Couples* (November 2003)

Useful websites

Criminal Injuries Compensation Scheme	www.cica.gov.uk
Department for Work and Pensions	www.dwp.gov.uk
European Court of Human Rights	www.echr.coe.int
Foreign and Commonwealth Office	www.fco.gov.uk
FTM Network	www.ftm.org.uk
Gender Recognition Act Information	www.gra-info.org.uk
Gender Recognition Panel	www.grp.gov.uk
The Gender Trust	www.gendertrust.org.uk
HM Revenue & Customs	www.hmrc.gov.uk
HMRC tax manuals	www.hmrc.gov.uk/manuals/index.htm
Immigration and Nationality Directorate	www.ind.homeoffice.gov.uk
International Lesbian and Gay Association	www.ilga-europe.org
Land Registry	www.landregistry.gov.uk
Medical Research Council	www.mrc.ac.uk
Ministry of Defence	www.mod.uk
National Statistics	www.statistics.gov.uk
Office of Public Sector Information	www.opsi.gov.uk
Press for Change (Campaign Group)	www.pfc.org.uk
Resolution	www.resolution.org.uk
Social Security and Child Support Commissioners	www.osscsc.gov.uk
Terrence Higgins Trust	www.tht.org.uk

Index